PREDATORY MAR

PREDATORY MARKETING

**What Everyone in Business
Needs to Know to
Win Today's Consumer**

C. BRITT BEEMER with Robert L. Shook

WILLIAM MORROW AND COMPANY, INC.
NEW YORK

Library of Congress Cataloging-in-Publication Data

Beemer, C. Britt.
    Predatory marketing : what everyone in business needs to know to
win today's consumer / by C. Britt Beemer & Robert L.
Shook.
        p.   cm.
    Includes index.
    ISBN 0–688–14836–0
    1. Marketing—United States.   2. Consumer behavior—United States.
I. Shook, Robert L., 1938–   .   II. Title.
HF5415.1.B44   1997
658.8'00973—dc20   96–9732
                                                                                 CIP

Printed in the United States of America

First Edition

1   2   3   4   5   6   7   8   9   10

BOOK DESIGN BY LEAH S. CARLSON

This book is dedicated to my very beautiful wife,
Jan Beemer, who, with the patience of Job, picked me up
on all those delayed Friday-night flights.

ACKNOWLEDGMENTS

When I think about all the people in my life who contributed to this book, I'm overwhelmed.

First of all, I thank Bob Shook for his patience, his creative writing, and his professionalism. I am grateful to Norman Weissman, my public relations consultant, who introduced me to Bob. Then there's Al Zuckerman, our literary agent, who is a star in his field. I also thank Will Schwalbe of William Morrow and Company, who assisted in putting greater meaning into each chapter.

There were many who encouraged me—like my teacher, Mrs. Gladys King, who had a sign in her room with a message I have never forgotten:

Little minds talk about people.
Average minds talk about events.
Great minds talk about ideas.

During my college days, professors like Gerald Hickman, William Gerdes, William Maxam, and Jack Johnson challenged my ideas. My ideology was shaped by Congressman Bill Scherle, who made me look at the big picture.

However, this book would not be possible without my staff—in particular, Kathy Hilleshiem, who worked very hard to collect my client interviews, as well as to coordinate my schedule, which may change multiple times in a single day. Also, there's Maggie Abel, who transcribed hundreds of hours of taped interviews, which I very much appreciate.

And one client in particular reminds me that the customer is always right. Art Van Elslander constantly changes to run the best-marketed retail operation in America.

But family is always the place I go to seek guidance. It took me many years to understand my father's advice: "Never mistake knowledge for wisdom. One helps you make a living and the other helps you make a life." I am grateful to my mother and father, Elvin and Margaret Beemer, for their guidance and encouragement.

My clients give me challenges, the consumers give me answers, and my family gives me confidence. These three groups, working in harmony with God's love, allow me to create new marketing strategies.

CONTENTS

INTRODUCTION

As founder and CEO of America's Research Group, I conduct surveys on consumer and corporate behavior. Once you've studied the needs—and whims—of Americans, trends in the marketplace become solidly predictable. Knowing your customer's wants in advance gives you an incredible edge over your competition. It's akin to placing an order with your stockbroker based on next week's stock quotations!

For the record, research and marketing strategies are not exclusively for the use of big corporations. After all, the objective of research is merely to get a clear understanding about customers. And a marketing strategy simply enables management to plan for the future—something every businessperson should do. Without a long-term plan, a business has no direction and operates in the dark. And no business—big or small—wants to do that.

Survival in today's business environment depends on constant change. No one can stand still; those who don't change go backward. As the Red Queen advises Alice in *Alice's Adventures in Wonderland*, "Now, here, you see, it takes all the running you can do to keep in the same place. If you want to get somewhere else, you must run twice as fast!" The Red Queen might very well have been referring to today's marketplace.

In our hectic, technology-driven world, we are inundated by a superabundance of information. In an age of computers and the Internet, literally billions of bits of knowledge can be at our fingertips in micro-seconds. The access to what appears to be unlimited information is sup-posed to make our lives run more smoothly. But in truth, it presents its own set of problems because of the sifting process required to separate the essential from the nonessential. To complicate matters further, there is the problem of analyzing what it tells us.

There's a story about an incident aboard a train en route from Paris to Barcelona. In a compartment are four people: a beautiful young girl traveling with her elderly grandmother, and a stately general, who is accompanied by his young, handsome second lieutenant. The foursome are sitting in silence as the train enters a tunnel in the Pyrenees, the mountain range on the border between France and Spain.

It is pitch-dark in the tunnel. Suddenly the sound of a loud kiss is heard. It is followed by a second sound, that of a loud, hard smack. Upon exiting from the tunnel, the four people remain silent, with no one ac-knowledging the incident.

The young girl thinks to herself, "Boy, that was a swell kiss that good-looking lieutenant gave me. It's a shame that my grandmother slapped him, because he must have thought it was I who slapped him. That's too bad, because when we get to the next tunnel, he won't kiss me again."

The grandmother thinks to herself, "That fresh young man kissed my granddaughter. But fortunately, I brought her up to be a lady, so she slapped him real good. That's good, because now he'll stay away from her when we get to the next tunnel."

The general thinks to himself, "I can't believe what just happened! I personally handpicked him to be my aide, and I thought he was a gen-tleman. But in the dark, he took advantage of that young girl and kissed her. But she must have thought it was I who kissed her, since she slapped me instead of him."

The young lieutenant thinks to himself, "Boy, that was wonderful! How often do you get to kiss a beautiful girl and slug your boss at the same time?"

This story illustrates that while people can receive the same information, they may arrive at entirely different conclusions. The purpose of this book is to tell you how to get information, and most important, analyze it so you can make the right decisions. After all, failure to analyze information properly can hurt you as much as or more than if you never had it.

This is illustrated by what happened in February 1995. That's when the American consumer was rocked by announcements of more midlevel management cuts to add to downsizing woes in the United States. Our research revealed interesting information about the far-reaching effect of this news on the nation. We determined that in at least 38 percent of all American households, either the man or the woman or both were so concerned about keeping their jobs that they increased the number of hours they worked by 10 to 20 percent. They figured that those additional hours would cause their boss to consider them more valuable employees and make their jobs more secure.

This change dramatically impacted consumer spending in 1995 and into 1996. American workers said, "If I'm going to work 10 to 20 percent more at my job with no increase in pay, I want to get an equivalent return when I spend my money." One of our studies, for example, showed that Southwest Airlines, a low-fare carrier, had a marked increase in business as travelers became more concerned about the price of their airline tickets. In February 1996, Southwest Airlines expanded its operations to the Northeast, an area of the country that was especially suffering from downsizing.

Also, with Americans working four to eight hours more each week, there was less disposable time, and therefore fewer stores were shopped. This translates into more people who demand better service and larger selection and who want to get out of the store in less time. With a little thought, you can imagine the many ramifications of this change on the nation's retailers.

The downsizing has also caused consumers to think more about their future—as well as their parents' and children's future. This resulted in as many as 29 percent of all Americans spending less on retail items, so that those same dollars could be saved for their retirement, their children's educations, and their parents' and their own medical costs. As a consequence, the sale of mutual funds has been booming. And millions of parents are even opening trust accounts for college funds for children aged five and under and IRA accounts for teenagers.

Downsizing is only one of many changes occurring in America. In order to survive in our highly competitive business environment, you must be privy to the right information—and interpret it to anticipate the changes that will affect your customers and, consequently, your company.

When we speak of customers, it is not only your customers who change, but your competitor's customers as well. In this regard, as I will explain in detail, you must have a clear understanding not only of your customers, but also of the customers who *don't* buy from your business or shop your store—in order to get them in your front door. When you do this right, you'll discover you know more about your competition's customers than your competition does.

Just how fast is today's marketplace changing? Consider that from 1980 to 1985, a company in some industries could run a marketing strategy for three years straight without alteration. Now, in 1995, that strategy must change within a six-to-eight-month window. Another way of looking at the changing marketplace is to say that a strategy that was 100 percent effective in the 1970s would have lost only 40 to 50 percent of its effectiveness by the 1980s. But in comparison, a marketing strategy that was 100 percent effective in the 1980s would have lost 84 to 96 percent of its effectiveness by today.

The theme that every marketing strategy ultimately fails recurs throughout this book. An explanation of why mediocre marketing strategies fail is, I believe, unnecessary. But why is *even the best* marketing strategy doomed to fail? Because, if it is good, competitors won't stand idly by; they will copy the strategy and, in time, improve it, rendering the original version obsolete. For this reason, a market leader must be continually tweaking his winning strategy—ideally at the peak of the trend when profit margins are at a high.

As a way of introduction, allow me to highlight my background prior to founding ARG in 1979. For nine years, I managed or consulted political campaigns; in sixteen U.S. Senate and U.S. House campaigns, fourteen of my clients won their elections. Talk about fierce competition! In a winner-take-all contest, only one person is elected to office; the losers pack their bags and head home.

My forte was providing my clients with strategic planning based upon voter behavior and attitudes. In short, I told politicians what issues their constituents wanted them to address and what they expected in the future. I was just under thirty years old when I moved into the private sector. Today, I provide a similar service outside the political arena; based on what consumers say in surveys my firm conducts, I make recommendations to CEOs who operate retailing and manufacturing companies. As a whole, my clients who abide by some, but not all, of my recommendations typically grow at three times their industry growth rate. Those clients who follow *every* recommendation enjoy an average growth rate five to ten times their industry growth rate. My long list of clients consists of leading corporations in a variety of industries—home furnishings, appliances and electronics, banking and finance, chain stores, medical specialists, and real estate.

Throughout this book, I'll tell you dozens and dozens of anecdotes, and I'll roll up a wheelbarrow full of statistics about the American consumer that you can put to use right now. Much of this information is based on research studies my firm conducted for specific clients. My examples will come from a variety of fields, but the lessons to be learned from these stories are transferrable to what you do. So remember, it's the concept, not a bunch of numbers, that matters. And while I head a marketing research company, I am aware that the vast majority of my readers will never use the services of such a firm. So the main theme of this book is not to promote research—it's to inform you of ways to find out more about your customer, your competition's customers, and trends in the marketplace. This book also acquaints you with how marketing strategies are put together. In particular, I'll stress predatory marketing strategies.

As you'll learn, I'm a firm believer in taking an offensive—rather than a defensive—position; marketing is always an offensive weapon.

A common theme that appears throughout this book is *increasing market share*—another way of saying getting more customers. It's not a term expressly reserved for Fortune 500 companies. Everyone out there is in the business of trying to get more customers. That's the name of the game. The only difference between the giant corporation and the small entrepreneur is that in order to survive, the big companies have to get bigger chunks of market share.

NOTE: After each chapter comes something I call a "consumer mind reader." These are the results of special surveys I conducted right before this book went to press in order to give the reader of *Predatory Marketing* specific information on consumer behavior which could be put to use right away for a variety of different business purposes. This research was conducted by my company, America's Research Group, especially for publication in this book. The results of these special surveys have never before been published or made available.

CHAPTER ONE

WHAT THE NUMBERS TELL

Some businesspeople think the most important numbers to a business are those that appear in its financial statement. Often the bean counters think these are the only numbers that matter. So it's no wonder that when I meet with new clients, the first thing many of them do is hand me their financial reports.

While I don't want to minimize the significance of a P&L, I believe a weak financial statement is a symptom, not the cause, of a company in trouble. It bothers me to see investment analysts forecasting a company's future based simply on what's reported in its financial statements. Those numbers are a faint reflection in the mirror but don't adequately project a company's image.

Some other important numbers that financial wizards frequently overlook aren't found in a financial statement and don't even get mentioned in the annual report. These include the number of people who shop your competitor's store before they shop your store, how frequently consumers shop, how much time they expect to spend making their buying decisions—the list goes on and on. Very few businesspeople are aware that these numbers exist; those who are often make the mistake of ignoring them.

On the surface, these numbers appear insignificant, but in my opinion, they are the heart and soul of a company. I place a high value on them because when you carefully analyze them, they reveal a company's past, its present, and most important, its future.

Certain numbers in particular have a lot to do with customers. America's Research Group, my company, conducts extensive surveys, which reveal valuable information about consumers. Instead of focusing on individuals, we develop a profile of a customer. It is only in this sense— for analytical purposes—that we think of people in terms of numbers. However, we do not condone treating anybody like a number. *Never!*

For the record, it is imperative that every business manager and entrepreneur understand what the numbers tell about the consumer. Our clients who use this information as instructed enjoy a 95 percent probability of making the most profitable decisions.

In my field, for the numbers to get these results, the following conditions are required: (1) A survey must be conducted of the right people. (2) The right questions must be asked. And (3) The responses must be accurately analyzed. For the past eighteen years, I have conducted market research for a living. Over the years, through trial and error, I've ironed out all the kinks. More than three million people have been interviewed by my firm, and with this much experience, I've now got it down pat. By conducting a seventeen-to-thirty-minute interview with the right number of interviewees and encouraging more than just yes-or-no answers, we determine what motivates consumers to behave the way they do.

It's not an exact science. Still, our high rate of accuracy makes it foolish for anyone not to follow our recommendations. What the numbers tell us, or more specifically, what the answers reveal about my clients' customers as well as their competitors' customers, is vital information in today's highly competitive marketplace. Without this essential knowledge, the future of a business is in jeopardy.

Early in my career, I had the good fortune to meet George Gallup, Sr., undoubtedly one of the world's most renowned pollsters. His advice has since significantly influenced my career. During one meeting, Gallup stressed: "Be sure your research reveals answers that are *actionable*." He emphasized, "If you can't tell your client what to do with your research, Britt, you've failed." So you see, numbers alone don't amount to a hill of beans. It's knowing how to follow up on what they tell you that counts.

As Gallup instructed me, my job is to make people aware of what their customers really think and have them act on that knowledge quickly. To react scientifically, a client must adopt a plan that is uncontaminated by personal opinion. When a client understands that research is not an enemy but, instead, a framework on which successful daily decisions can be based, then I know I'm doing my job properly.

HOW SURVEY RESEARCH WORKS

While most people refer to what ARG does as market research, it is really survey research. We must start out knowing our client's problems and concerns right at the beginning. From there, we customize a questionnaire that we use to talk to consumers and decision-makers.

For example, a client might say, "Here are twelve things I have always wanted to know." We know that if we can get the person who buys the product to discuss these concerns, then, following our survey, we can answer the client's questions. Of course, there are some things we can't find out from the customer. Let's say a client wants to know how to improve inventory controls or solve a warehouse problem. These are areas in which customer knowledge can't help. On the other hand, when somebody is seeking information such as how a particular brand product is perceived by a customer, we can provide the right answers.

We conduct surveys for two basic groups: first, the client who wants to know what the consumer is thinking, and second, the client whose product or service is sold to another company (i.e., a manufacturer that wholesales its product to a retailer) and who wants to know what its buyers or retailers are thinking. For instance, we have conducted surveys for Sealy Mattress. In one study, we did a Sealy survey that focused on consumers, to determine how they viewed mattress brands in general— Sealy as well as its competitors. In another study, we interviewed buyers who worked for furniture, bedding specialty, and department stores. With our research, Sealy was able to get a better handle on how to service the retailers, who, in turn, sell mattresses to the consumer.

A survey must be designed to answer specific questions. Ours differ from those of other survey research firms because our competitors typically pre-program the interviewee by asking a question such as "Which one of the following do you like?" Then five or six choices are given that require the interviewee to select an answer. In our research, we ask questions such as "What do you like?" and "What's most important to you?" Then we let the consumer tell us.

We also ask questions that require follow-up questions. For example, we might ask, "Why didn't you buy in this particular store?"

"Well, the prices were too high," someone replies.

Our interviewer follows up, asking, "In what product area did you think the prices were too high?"

Armed with this ammunition, we report to our client, "In this product category, you are not merchandised properly. Consumers who didn't want to buy in your store said your prices were more than they wanted to spend in that area."

Although many surveys are twenty-three to twenty-seven minutes long, we get the interviewee involved by asking several interesting, open-ended questions. This technique elicits more information from an interviewee than a multiple-choice question can yield. When an interviewee answers a question, our people are trained to say, "Tell me more about that," and to ask, "Is there another reason you feel this way?" By probing, we are able to get an interviewee to elaborate, which produces detailed feedback.

A client typically will want answers to a question such as "How are we perceived in the marketplace?" A year or two later, a follow-up study might focus on "How are we doing?" An early study may be conducted to design a marketing strategy to influence people to buy something. A follow-up study might not require us to go back to interview people in the entire marketplace, but perhaps only buyers of that product, in order to find out how our client did. Were the customer's expectations fulfilled?

Today, with the millions of interviews we have conducted, I believe our experience gives us an edge over our competition, because we have the perspective to determine what's normal and abnormal. So today, our real value to a client isn't only what we observe from a single study about his business, but rather that we can compare those findings to results from previous studies.

When you're through reading this book, your perspective on the marketplace will have changed dramatically. Not only will you view customers and your competitor's customers differently, even your own company won't seem the same. Most important, *Predatory Marketing* will serve as a road map to guide you into the future.

KNOWING THE NOT-SO-OBVIOUS

A survey research study can reveal some important surprises, and that's why it plays such an important role in running a successful business. I'll cite many studies in this book, and from the lessons they have taught others, you'll learn a lot about marketing that's applicable to your own business.

For as long as anyone can remember, the upper-end furniture industry assumed that people with bigger incomes are the high-end furniture buyers. Who doesn't know that? Common sense supports it. However, at the end of 1994, a two-year ARG study revealed there is only a 65 percent correlation between high earnings and money spent on big-ticket furniture. After this revelation, we delved deeper and looked at the value of a person's home. We found that only a 53 percent correlation exists between home value and furniture purchases. Next, our study focused on people with better educations (college and graduate-school levels), and we learned there was only a 38 percent correlation between education level and high-end furniture purchases.

Imagine our surprise when we discovered that an issue that furniture people never paid much attention to was the single overriding factor. *In over 95 percent of the high-end furniture purchases, the single factor that influences Americans most is how often they entertain guests in their home.*

Before I continue, let me explain how entertainment was defined for this study. It does not mean sending out for pizza when a friend stops over unexpectedly; for the purposes of our study, entertainment is defined as an occasion when a prepared meal is served to invited guests. For many Americans, this encompasses only Thanksgiving and Christmas dinner and perhaps two or three other times during the year. Actually, 29 percent of all Americans entertain only four to five times a year. Our study showed that just 20 percent of people entertain a full six to nine times a year. Finally, the people who entertain a whopping ten or more times a year make up only 6 percent of the total population. This small, select group of people was identified by our study as the most desirable prospects for high-end furniture.

With this information, many new avenues are opened to high-end furniture manufacturers and retailers. Note, for instance, *Architectural Digest*, a magazine filled with ads that cater to this furniture-affluent shopper. But a far better place to reach these consumers would be magazines such as *Gourmet* and *Bon Appétit*. This is where the upper-end furniture company is likely to get more bang for its advertising buck.

Another study of consumers told us that in 1980, Americans expected to shop 3.5 stores to purchase an appliance or electronics item. Ten years later, in 1990, they visited 2.8 stores, and only five years later, the number dropped to 2.1 stores. I anticipate the number will drop to 1.3 stores by the year 2000. This information is vital for appliance and electronics retailers, because it means that by the turn of the century only 30 percent of the people in the United States will buy merchandise at a second store. Knowing this, a merchant must make sure his store is the first shopped. If it's in third, fourth, or fifth place on the shopper's list, the store is in serious trouble.

Likewise, a 1990 study showed consumers throughout the 1980s were willing to wait five to seven minutes for service when walking into an appliance store. After waiting for this period, they were ready to leave, concluding that the store was not responsive to their needs. Five years later, in 1995, the average American shopper's patience lasted only three minutes before he was ready to walk.

We did another study which compared the reactions of the people who walked into an electronics and appliance store in 1985 to those in 1995. In 1985, the former so-called "big box" stores typically had twenty-five to forty refrigerators displayed on the floor. If five were missing, consumers noted the gaps and said to themselves, "Oh, a customer must have had an emergency and needed a refrigerator off the floor immediately," or "It must have been the last one the store had, so it was sold to a customer as a service." Ten years later, the big box stores spread across the country like wildfire and their floor space doubled. Now these stores have to have over fifty refrigerators on display to remain competitive. Interestingly, our survey reveals that when only five gaps appear on the floor, this is interpreted in a strikingly different way. Today's consumer says, "This store must be going out of business." Even though the retailer still has a large selection, the customer's perception is that the retailer has financial troubles. And if the same customer walks over to the store's TV wall and sees exposed cables because a few sets have been sold off the floor, his suspicions about the retailer's financial woes have been verified! In today's marketplace, a customer's perception of a store's survivability is a determining factor in deciding where to shop, particularly when purchasing a product that requires servicing after the sale.

Then, too, American consumers today are so pressed for time that they become upset when they walk into a store and the advertised merchandise has been sold. A recent study showed that the average American who previously was working a forty-hour week is putting in 10 to 20 percent more time—four to eight hours more—to maintain the same standard of living. The consumer who has less time to shop and can't find what he or she came in for because the shelves are bare feels, "You've wasted my time!"

People who entertain more buy more expensive furniture. Customers shop at fewer stores. Gaps in between refrigerators are a no-no. Customers are upset because their time has been wasted. What does all of this mean? If you expect to survive in today's highly competitive marketplace, you must understand what drives your customer.

A PROFILE OF CUSTOMERS

Art Van Elslander, founder and CEO of Art Van Furniture Company, is one of the nation's most successful retailers. His twenty-plus stores have a dominant market share of the state of Michigan, with sales in the $400 million range.

Over the years, we have developed a mutual respect for each other. I know Art has a clear understanding of my field, because he often says to me, "Britt, is this your opinion, or something you've researched?" As I've heard Art explain to other Art Van executives, "If it's something that's been researched, then we're dealing with facts—and Britt can substantiate it." I love to hear my clients make a remark like this, because it means we're on the same wavelength.

Art has the right idea. Far more important than my opinion or anyone else's is what a study reveals. Likewise, while the sum of the opinions of the people we interview is valuable, any one person's opinion is not significant. Such an opinion may, in fact, be dangerous, because how a single individual feels may not reflect the sentiments of large numbers of customers. With this in mind, note that our survey research provides a *profile of customers*. Somebody once referred to one of our reports as a composite of customers, and this is an accurate description.

As an example of how this works, let's say a lawn mower manufacturer wants to advertise on national television. Before this company takes such an expensive position, it had better obtain a profile of what television programs its lawn mower buyers watch, as well as what a competing company's customers watch. Obviously, with such a profile, a lawn mower manufacturer can focus to get maximum mileage out of an advertising budget.

Two years ago, we counseled a retailer in a medium-size community. The owner was concerned because a national competitor was coming to town to open a big box (in this case, a 60,000-square-foot store). Our survey indicated our client's store had a 60-percent-plus selection-driven customer. With that customer profile, this client had good reason to worry. The big box store's selection would be up to four times greater than his store's. Clearly and simply, his relatively small store would be unable to compete. The client had some choices to make. Fortunately, approximately eighteen months would pass before the big box opened, so, based on our findings, we helped our client devise a marketing strategy to put into place prior to the grand opening.

The decision was made to construct a large addition to the small store, and by the time the big box store opened, my client offered a comparable selection. Hence, while he lost less than 10 percent of his customer base, his business continued to generate a healthy bottom line. Had this retailer not been alerted to the profile of his customer, it is probable that the big box competition would have knocked him out of business.

If you are a business owner working on a tight budget, you might want to try conducting your own surveys. Before you telephone or make in-person calls to your customers, however, be sure to prepare some well-thought-out questions. Then call enough customers to have a cross-section of opinions. With too small a sampling, you could reach wrong conclusions.

Fred DeLuca, cofounder and CEO of Subway, likes to see firsthand what's happening in his stores. With more than ten thousand sites, he can't possibly visit them all, but he does "spot-check" several dozen at a time. Every few years, DeLuca conducts a personal four-or-five-state tour. In the summer of 1995, for instance, he flew to Cincinnati, rented a small car, and, dressed in a T-shirt and blue jeans, drove to Columbus, then Toledo, Detroit, and so on, ending up in Wisconsin—stopping at company sandwich shops along the way. Not a single employee recognized him as the company's owner! "This way," he explains, "I'm able to get a firsthand feel about what's going on. I travel with a tape recorder, and in between stops, I record my thoughts. I always come home with tapes filled with ideas on improvements we could make—from a customer's point of view."

There are also "secret shopper" or "silent shopper" companies that will visit your store and report their observations back to you. A service of this type sends anonymous shoppers to shop your company, so your employees will give them the same everyday treatment your real customers receive. Later, the shoppers fill out a questionnaire. This type of shopper program is relatively inexpensive.

Every business should have a profile of its competition's customers, as well as its own. If you operate a small business, this could be even more important than knowing who your existing customers are. After all, if you have only a 2 percent market share, it's vital to find out what motivates the other 98 percent, and with this knowledge, you can win their business.

One inexpensive way to find out about your competition's customers is to buy a list from a list broker. Obviously, any listed people that aren't your customers are giving their business to someone else! A manufacturer of golf equipment, for example, could obtain the names and addresses of all the country clubs and public golf course pro shops in the United States, and scan the list for potential accounts. With this information in hand, the golf equipment manufacturer can start a mailing program or a direct-sales telephone campaign, or provide incentives to its sales representatives in the form of higher commissions, recognition, or bonuses for each new opened account.

ONE OPINION VERSUS EIGHT HUNDRED OPINIONS

After each study is completed, I conduct a four-to-six-hour consultation with my client to review our findings about customers—both the client's and the competition's. At this meeting, I suggest specific marketing strategies for my client to implement.

As you can imagine, because the nature of my work involves counseling top corporate executives and entrepreneurs, I come face to face with some rather large egos. Nonetheless, my job is to tell them what the research reveals about their customers, whether or not they see things my way.

"I've been running this company for twenty years," a CEO might tell me in a raised voice. "I know this business like the back of my hand. I don't care what your survey says!"

When I hear this, my standard answer is "I've talked to three million consumers. How many have you talked to lately?"

A brief silence generally follows.

Then I explain, "What would you rather do, take one person's opinion to make a decision, or would you rather bet on eight hundred people's opinion to make a decision?"

Some people are bound to insist that no matter what our survey reveals, they're sure they're right and we're wrong. If I suspect they might take this approach, I tell them before we start, "If that's going to be your attitude, don't hire us to do your research, because you're not going to do what we tell you."

It's interesting what some clients had perceived about their companies. For example, an owner of an appliances and electronics chain store once told me, "In my marketplace, Sears isn't a factor. I never hear anyone in our stores even mention them. I don't consider Sears to be a strong competitor of ours."

But after we did our research, we reported that Sears had a 90 percent closing rate in this retailer's market. He had never heard about Sears because Sears customers never came into his stores; they were sold when they shopped Sears and so they never made it to his stores!

Did I have an opinion about Sears in this particular marketplace? Prior to doing my research, I had no opinion. As I tell my clients, I have no opinion. After our study is completed, I say, "The only opinion I have is the opinion of your customer, or the opinion of the people who live in your marketplace."

Another way I like to put it is to describe my view as a treetop perspective of the terrain. I can stay above the battle, and I can be non-emotional.

Even without conducting a marketing survey, there are many ways to get a profile of your customers. Many small business owners make it a point to take customers to lunch, and in a relaxed atmosphere ask pointed questions, settling only for honest answers. "Don't worry about hurting my feelings," you might tell a customer. "It's very important to me to know what you're thinking, and I truly value your opinion. You'll help me more if you give it to me straight. I have to know what you honestly think." After your customer confides in you, be sure to express your gratitude, even though you might not have heard the answer you wanted to hear. People want to avoid confrontation, so if you try to defend your company, your customer may clam up.

This one-on-one approach is particularly effective with businesses that sell to other businesses. As one businessperson to another, this person understands your need for bona fide feedback, because his business has the same need. Then too, his success is dependent upon how you serve his business—this gives him a vested interest in being upfront with you.

While big companies have elaborate customer conferences to zero in on customer problems, a small business owner can do the same thing on a smaller scale. The business can provide a catered lunch, or perhaps a series of lunches, to a handful of customers. To entice your customers to take time away from their businesses, you might consider having a speaker. Depending on your budget, this can range from a local politician or college professor to a nationally known figure.

AN AGE OF MISINFORMATION

Upon its publication in 1982, *In Search of Excellence,* written by Tom Peters and Robert Waterman, Jr., took the American business community by storm as one of the all-time-biggest-selling business books. By the mid-1980s, huge armies of managers had become advocates of MBWA ("Management by Wandering Around"), a concept introduced by the two authors, employees of the prestigious McKinsey & Co. consulting firm. Shortly before the book was published, Peters left the firm and went on to become one of the nation's most illustrious management gurus.

For those of you who have not already been enlightened, the purpose of MBWA is to listen to what customers and workers have to say, and, in consequence, manage a business more effectively. Naturally, I also endorse listening (who doesn't?); however, I don't think it is best executed by wandering around. Actually, I even object to the word "wandering," because people who wander are prone to get lost.

Frankly, I believe this is what happens when managers rely on the feedback received by walking factory floors and retail floors in order to get a "feel" for what motivates workers and customers. In reality, it's probable that these wandering managers will lose touch with what's really going on. The sort of information generated from these strolls tends to be misleading, causing managers to move in the wrong directions altogether.

What do you think results when the CEO of General Motors wanders through an assembly plant with an entourage of executives and strolls up to an hourly worker for a friendly chat? Do you truly believe he's getting the lowdown about how that factory employee feels about working for the company?

Picture this scenario: "How do you like working for GM?" a senior manager asks a worker working on the shop floor.

"And by the way, what do you think about the working conditions in this plant?"

"What can you tell me about how your foreman treats you?"

"And what are your thoughts about the Japanese making better cars than we do?"

Do you seriously believe this is an effective way for a top executive to receive honest answers from hourly, or for that matter middle-management, employees? I for one don't recommend relying on feedback of this nature. It doesn't matter that the CEO takes off his suit jacket and wears a hard hat and protective eyeglasses so he'll appear like "one of the guys on the line." In fact, I don't care how you cut it, very few subordinates are likely to feel comfortable elaborating on what it's really like working for the company.

Your worker is no more apt to level with you than were the troops General Patton chatted with during his tours of the front lines.

"Any complaints, soldier?" Patton would inquire. When a military general asks an enlisted man for his opinion, very few speak freely. Sure, they may say the food could be better or voice a complaint about the weather—but that's about all the information they'll divulge. Unquestionably, Patton's visits to his troops on the battlefield served as a tremendous morale booster, but I've never been convinced that the great World War II general received the valuable feedback he sought.

People simply don't like to be confrontational—especially with the CEO or one of the top executives of a company. Employees aren't likely to share how they truly feel about the company, and, for the same reason, neither are customers. When I was running political campaigns—and that's an arena where people are more prone to tell it as it is—only on rare occasions would somebody walk up to me and say, "I don't like your candidate and you're not going to get my vote, and here's why." In many elections, our candidate barely won by 50 percent, so obviously nearly half the people weren't in favor of our side. Still, only a handful of people ever confronted me about a candidate during all those years in politics.

The same thing is true when a store owner or a senior executive walks the sales floor in a retail outlet. Rarely will a customer approach to voice an opinion: "I don't like your store because . . ." I repeat: People don't like to be confrontational.

And if you do ask a customer for an opinion, chances are you still won't get an honest one. At a recent men's clothing store opening, for example, even the owner was upset that the color combination of the carpeting and wall coverings clashed. "Britt, I should never have let my interior decorator talk me into it," he confided.

Yet, when he approached customers to ask them what they thought about his store, not a single one voiced a negative comment.

"You know, Britt," he said, "could it be it's just me? Maybe the store doesn't look so bad after all."

"Believe me, it does," I told him. "What would you say if you were a guest in someone's home and he asked your opinion on a new living-room sofa?"

"I see your point," he concurred.

The truth is, customers rarely complain in person—they just take their business elsewhere!

There are other times when you might withhold expressing how you really feel for fear of personally offending somebody.

For instance, a client of mine, a retailer whose name I won't mention for obvious reasons, used his children in his TV commercials. Everyone— friends, customers, and employees—always told him the same thing: "I love your kids in those TV ads." In truth, they were really thinking, "Why did he put those children in that commercial? Those kids couldn't act to save their lives!"

His business had dropped significantly by the time my client asked me to do a research study to find out why his store was experiencing a down-turn. After all, the local economy was booming. Well, our survey showed that his store would have 20 percent more customers if those kids disappeared.

I tactfully recommended that he hire professional talent to use in his commercials, but his feelings must have been hurt, because my suggestion was vetoed. The following summer, I learned that his children had gone away to camp, so I hastily approached him again with a new commercial. He liked it, but since his kids weren't around, he had to hire professional actors. Without his kids, the commercial generated not a 20 percent but a 26 percent higher response. Apparently an additional 6 percent of consumers objected to the kids, over and above my projection! A happy compromise has been reached. He still uses his entire family for his TV commercials—at Christmas. Fortunately, Christmas comes only once a year.

On the occasions when customers do speak out, there is still another danger. They may give you wrong information, causing you to form an ill-advised marketing strategy. For instance, one of the simplest ways to brush off a salesperson is to say, "I can't afford it." Americans have become conditioned to use this excuse when somebody approaches them in a store, because this is an easy way to get an aggressive salesperson to quit following them around. It doesn't matter that the customer can actually afford to make the purchase; most salespeople will leave a poverty-pleading browser alone. In truth, the customer's real reason may be that he doesn't like the store's selection, the brands, or the styles in the inventory. Pity the poor store manager who accepts at face value that his customers want lower-priced merchandise, and consequently embarks on a merchandising strategy to restock his store with inferior-quality goods!

Misconceptions can be harmful, and so can an entrepreneur's preconceived opinion of his business. Often a businessperson's view of his company is different from a consumer's. A major appliance retailer in Virginia Beach once told me he was upset with his next-door neighbor. "I've known them for twenty years," he said. "My wife and I play cards at their home each week, but they bought a new refrigerator from our competitor!"

As a favor, I surveyed the neighbor by phone concerning his most recent appliance purchases. Among other things, I asked, "Did you know that [my client's store] sells side-by-side refrigerators in the $1,500 price range?" He was surprised to learn that his good friend and neighbor's store sold the exact refrigerator he bought. Because this retailer advertised only low-price points, the people in his marketplace—even his next-door neighbor—were unaware that the store also carried the better-featured, higher-priced models.

GUT FEELINGS AND BIG EGOS

I've lost count of how many times a founder or CEO of a successful company has told me, "I live, sleep, and breathe this business. I can *sense* what my customers want."

I don't deny that there is some truth to that. An entrepreneur or highly focused executive can seem to have an instinct for making the right business decisions. But *watch out!* The bankruptcy courts are filled with men and women who bet the future of their company on a gut feeling!

You take a tremendous risk when you let your guts dictate the future course of your business. This is especially true when you've built a successful enterprise and are no longer down in the trenches working on a daily basis with your customers. And even if you are, as I mentioned earlier, most people want to avoid conflicts. So don't expect customers to level with you when they have negative feelings about your product or your employees' attitudes.

Closely related to those who rely on their gut feelings to make important business decisions are successful businesspeople who possess enormous egos—ones that frequently get in their way. No wonder they have a high opinion of themselves—because everybody else does, too! High-profile business leaders are constantly being praised, asked to serve on community boards and bank boards, and beseeched for their advice. Of course, it's understandable that with everyone coming to them for the answers, they begin to think they know all the answers.

This often happens with entrepreneurs who have no board of directors to hold them accountable. With 100 percent ownership or even just controlling interest, they rule their own fiefdoms as if they were royalty. Many of these individuals with strong personalities unwittingly surround themselves with people who tell them only what they want to hear. Consequently, they never hear the word no. All too often, their subordinates avoid conflict by withholding negative information. Sometimes this is a result of fear—perhaps the boss is an intimidator. In other cases, staff members simply don't want to reveal their true thoughts—they shudder at the thought of being the bearer of bad news. With no one to challenge the boss's decisions, what the head honcho views as consensus is, in truth, the consensus of a single person—himself. Subconsciously discouraging feedback, he denies himself the advantage of a second opinion.

Senior managers sometimes earn a reputation among their employees for not welcoming bad news. One particular Napa Valley winemaker, who ranted and raved when subordinates relayed customer problems, had them so intimidated that nobody brought him complaints voiced by the company's major distributors. When several major accounts were lost to its competition, the winery nearly went under.

A lot of CEOs I've known claim to have an open-door policy when what they really have is a closed mind. Not only do they not listen, they browbeat their employees for occupying their time with incidental matters. In such cases, it's only a matter of time before their employees no longer share their ideas.

Another often overlooked source of valuable feedback is that pain-in-the-neck customer who gives you more grief than your next ten "worst" customers. While a lot of managers tend to view this guy as a trouble-maker and not worth the aggravation for the relatively small amount of business his company gives them, I recommend listening very carefully to him. Often these customers are valuable sources of feedback that nobody else is giving you. So rather than resisting this customer, embrace him!

THE FIVE SETS OF NUMBERS EVERY BUSINESS OWNER MUST UNDERSTAND

When I take a good, hard look at a client's company, there are certain numbers I must know. Following are the sets of numbers about your business that you should make it your business to know:

1. HOW MUCH VOLUME DOES THE COMPANY DO ON A DAILY BASIS? Too many people fail to realize that their businesses experience dramatic peaks during certain times of the day, week, and year. Some retail stores, for example, generate as much as 70 percent of their sales between 6:00 p.m. on Friday and 6:00 p.m. on Sunday. In other industries it may be 50 percent during these same hours.

2. WHAT PERCENTAGE OF A COMPANY'S TOTAL REVENUE IS ITS ADVERTISING COST? You must know the average cost for advertising and marketing in your industry. If yours is two points higher than the norm, you have virtually no customer loyalty. Conversely, if it's two points lower than the norm, you have high customer loyalty. Furthermore, too many companies make an arbitrary decision to set next year's advertising expense ratio at a certain percentage. For instance, a $10-million-a-year retailer might set his advertising budget at 6 percent, or $600,000. Then, at the end of the year, the merchant says, "I don't understand why we didn't do more business this year." What he failed to realize is that if his advertising budget was increased by 20 percent and he spent $720,000, his sales volume might have increased to $12 million. In other words, if this retailer wants to be a $12 million company, he can't operate on the advertising budget of a $10 million company.

3. HOW MUCH IS A COMPANY SPENDING ON TRAINING ITS PEOPLE? This is somewhat related to the advertising budget. There isn't much sense in spending extra money on advertising to bring people into your store, only to have them met by inadequately trained salespeople. Too often, poorly trained, incompetent salespeople are unable to handle additional customers. A well-managed company must put money into its people.

4. HOW MUCH IS A COMPANY SPENDING ON ITS ENVIRON-

MENT TO STAY CURRENT? In the case of a retailer, it must provide a fresh environment for its customers. For instance, a 1997 store which hasn't been refurbished since 1987 will lose its appeal to today's shopper. Likewise, every business must keep its environment fresh and upbeat for its employees, whether or not customers pass through its doors. In this regard, even such businesses as candy wholesalers, stock brokerage firms, and building supplies distributors should provide a pleasant atmosphere for the sake of employee morale. Poor working conditions do, indeed, affect people's attitudes and productivity.

5. WHAT INFORMATION DOES THE COMPANY MAINTAIN REGARDING ITS CUSTOMER? You must have a clear understanding about your customer. When I first meet with a prospective client, I examine what the company is doing to build a strong customer relationship. Is its mailing list on a sortable database to enable it to correspond with specific groups of customers? Does it use an online computer system for instant communication with its branches, vendors, and customers? Are its customer communications perceived to be sincere? For example, many companies send special offers to their customers, yet our research reveals that as many as 40 percent of those consumers don't believe these mailings represent legitimate savings. Consequently, these companies are destroying the goodwill of their own customer base.

Other obvious things to look for include: Who do your customers think you are—are you the first company they talk to? The second? The third? And when a customer needs something out of the ordinary, are you able to respond? How do you stack up against the competition in fixing problems?

An example of how this works is given by David Finkel, who is currently president and CEO of Signature Home Care, Inc., in Irving, Texas. "Several years ago, as CEO of a hospital in Columbia, Missouri,"

Finkel explains, "I wanted to find out how to attract physicians in the area to use our new 350-bed facility, in spite of the fact that most of those doctors already had their own hospital beds. When I'd ring them up, because they had a hint why I'd be calling, they avoided talking to me. Later, when I discovered that a lot of physicians in the area had an interest in woodworking, I came up with a novel idea. I invited Ian Kirby, a world-renowned British woodworking expert, to Columbia to conduct a series of seminars, limited to twenty persons per session. Invitations went out to six hundred doctors with instructions to call my secretary for reservations.

"We were besieged with calls," Finkel says. "We couldn't accommodate everybody, so I instructed my secretary to say, "I'm sorry, but the seminar is full and we can't take any more registrants. However, if you call David Finkel, I'm sure he'll be able to find some way to accommodate you.'

"Then, when they called, I'd say, 'I'd like to give you a tour of the hospital, and while you're here, I'll personally give you your seminar tickets.' Once I had them on my own turf, I was able to get valuable feedback from them about how we should market our services."

It doesn't require deep pockets to find out what your customers think—but when the feedback comes, you have to be willing to listen, not defend.

CONSUMER MIND READER #1

Twelve Financial Factors That Cause Consumers to Postpone or Cancel a Major Purchase

For this book, we conducted a study to find out what financial obstacles would prompt American consumers to postpone a major purchase of $1,000 or more. The survey also covered the question of what would cause someone to cancel the purchase of an item that had been special-ordered but not yet purchased. The following information was learned:

Reason for response	Percent to postpone or cancel
1. (tied) You owe the Internal Revenue $1,500.	52.5%
1. (tied) Your parent(s) need special medical care.	52.5
3. You just learned your house has termites and needs repairs.	49.3
4. Your spouse requires diagnostic tests at the hospital, necessitating out-of-pocket payment to cover the insurance deductible.	41.6
5. Your roof leaks and needs minor repair.	40.5
6. You need new tires for your car.	39.8
7. There are rumors about more job cuts at work.	36.5
8. You made an error in your checkbook and have less money in your account than you thought.	36.3

9. Your credit cards are at their limit.	36.1
10. You need major dental work.	33.7
11. Your family pet requires expensive veterinary treatment.	33.3
12. Your child needs braces on his teeth.	31.5

During this survey, out of forty-five financial crises tested, these dozen responses above a 30 percent level are significant enough to move consumers to defer a major purchase. Note the two tied for the number one spot—reflecting Americans' great fear of their government and respect for their parents. Our research reveals Americans spend a lot of time taking care of their elderly parents—anywhere from five to twenty-five hours a month is quite common. In third and fifth place, the study showed that Americans place a very high priority on taking good care of their homes because they want to protect their equity. Interestingly, rumors about more job cuts at work used to rank among the top three on the list but now rank in only seventh place. Consumers told us they've heard so many rumors about job cuts that they no longer panic, because too often the rumors have proven false. To be expected, number four, ten, and twelve are health-related emergency expenses for family members, which explains why health care costs are a major political issue. Number eleven can be put in the same category—it also is a health-related emergency expense for a loved one—the family pet!

What can manufacturers and retailers do to prevent the above reasons from reducing sales revenue? Although the occurrence of these factors is often beyond their control, merchants can ask wholesalers and manufacturers to speed up the time to process special orders. What will this accomplish? The shorter the time between the placing of the order to the actual time of delivery, the less chance there is for one of the above emergencies to occur. Likewise, manufacturers can cooperate with their dealers in expediting special-order requests.

CHAPTER TWO

EVERYTHING YOU NEED TO KNOW ABOUT TRENDS

The corporate graveyard is filled with companies that failed to recognize the whims of the American consumer. Among the star-studded list are former giants such as Studebaker, Packard, Eastern Airlines, Railway Express, and Gimbels. These represent only a handful of enterprises that have been laid to rest.

A glaring common denominator is shared by those corporations that have gone belly-up: their management failed to respond to trends. For reasons ranging from poor execution to a resistance to change itself, they were unable to compete effectively in the marketplace.

In our high-tech, fast-changing world, trends come and go at a more rapid pace then ever before in the history of civilization. And trends know no boundaries. They occur in every industry, regardless of product, and they can happen at any time.

Those business leaders who are capable of spotting a trend and, equally important, who can swiftly react to a trend have a decided edge over their competitors. And, at a higher level, there are those rare individuals who actually set trends—they are the real masters of the world of business. It is they who attain a dominant position in the marketplace and stay at the top.

A word of caution is in order, however, before you read this chapter: Becoming the trendmaker in your marketplace is not for the faint of heart.

Even once you have spotted a trend, it is no piece of cake to react. There are risks. If, however, you plan to remain in business, you really have no other choice. Getting market share is synonymous with getting and keeping customers.

ANTICIPATING TRENDS

When Wayne Gretzky, the greatest hockey player of all time, was asked to explain his success, he answered, "I skate to where the puck is going to be, not where it has been." Business leaders would be wise to heed Gretzky's advice. Trend-spotting is anticipating what to expect in the future rather than acknowledging what has already been.

But, unlike hockey, every business has some historical perspective. What has happened in the past cannot be ignored; just the same, it's dangerous to presume everything will reoccur at the same time and place. Still, the past does afford us some guidelines. A consumer trend is more easily anticipated when we know what consumers were doing before, so spotting trends requires knowing consumer habits over a long period of time. Hence, by studying consumer patterns, we can develop a historical perspective.

Once a trend has been around for a while, it's only a matter of time before the consumer gets bored. Although the forces that drove the customer, say, three years ago may have been strong, other factors eventually arise. By knowing where the customer has been, a trend can be spotted at least three to nine months before it becomes commonplace.

To anticipate a trend, we at ARG begin by observing little factors that become indicators of how consumers will react in the future. By creating a research time line, we view how consumers respond to certain issues over a period of time. In the beginning stages of a trend, we notice a tiny bleep that starts to get a little bigger. If it begins to pick up momentum, a trend is probably developing. Rather than a single major factor indicating an upcoming trend, generally a lot of little clues signal its arrival.

For instance, in an early May 1988 window, we observed consumers saying, "I want more service when I shop at a retail store." This observation prompted me to write a 1988 article stating the membership warehouse clubs in this country would not see the year 2000 if they continued having a non–customer-service policy. I was the first in the nation to express this concern about their problems. Not until late 1991 and early 1992 did other analysts and industry experts pick up on it.

As things turned out, we've witnessed the demise of several membership clubs in America. In the early 1990s, Kmart's membership club, Pace, was bought out by Wal-Mart's Sam's Club, and the Price Club merged with Costco. Consequently, we now have only two nationwide membership clubs remaining in the United States.

Of course, the service issue is important to every business in America. In our consumer research, we asked consumers, "What do you think most importantly influences you when you shop at a retail store?" For the previous seven years, nearly 6 percent of the consumers responded they wanted someone to give them extraordinary service when they walked in the door. Now this may not be a significant number of responses to some people, but when we suddenly realized that this number had jumped to 9 percent in late 1988, it had a great deal of meaning to us. Without that historical perspective, 9 percent wouldn't have seemed significant to us either. But compared to 6 percent, we saw a 50 percent increase, which we considered meaningful.

We also observed in our surveys that more and more people were telling us, "Because I have less time to shop, I need more assistance more quickly so I can achieve other things that are more important to me in my life." Currently only 31 percent of Americans say they can easily get away from work to handle a problem in their homes. Well, if a consumer buys a product that proves to be faulty, and has to leave work several times because a store doesn't take care of it efficiently, the consumer jeopardizes his or her job.

This research illuminates what's driving today's consumer to say, "I want to go to a store where if I have a problem the retailer will take care of it for me the first time. And I want a store that takes care of my problem based upon what my needs are, not based upon that store's inflexible schedule." So because consumers can't easily get away from work, timely service becomes a more important factor in deciding where to shop for certain products. Then, when we factor in how many households in this country have both spouses working, these numbers become even more significant. Consequently, we believe the reputation perception of a company is becoming a bigger and bigger force. Consumers are saying, "If something goes wrong after I purchase a product, I don't want to take time to deal with an aftermath of problems."

In the personal computer industry, we surveyed consumers who told us they expect to spend about thirty-five minutes in a store to shop. Yet when they are actually making a purchase, they are willing to spend up to sixty minutes.

Our research also indicated that today's consumers are looking at 4.5 ads before shopping anywhere. This reflects a trend—that consumers now place a higher value on their time. They want to get very well educated on the front end of their shopping experience, to avoid having the retailer make their lives any more complicated.

While the research time lines my company produces are based on regional and national trends, it's possible to compose do-it-yourself time lines for a small business. This requires keeping good records on your business and tracking a lot of things that may not seem significant at the time, but over a period of years will provide you with important information. You begin by keeping track of such things as your company's daily sales activity by the hour. You can also record such information as the number of individual shoppers versus shopping groups who come into your shop each day; the average time each customer spends in your store; how frequently each customer shops at your store; and the average time compared to the amount spent per customer. The data you measure can run the gamut—including such information as your customer's time constraints, your marketing efforts, your advertising program, your service to customers, and so on. In three to five years, patterns will emerge which will show you what to expect in the future.

Still another trend we picked up in 1994, which continues on in to today, involves the way consumers react to advertising based upon their perception of a retailer's reputation. We learned that if they don't trust the store, they won't look at or notice its advertising! This knowledge sends a strong message to retailers that they had better concentrate on their reputation in the marketplace. For those who don't, their advertising efficiency will take a nosedive.

A trend we spotted resulted from a study we did on newspaper reading habits. A few years ago, we noticed the abundance of inserts appearing in the Sunday newspapers offering coupons for supermarket-related products. By asking readers probing questions about most-read sections of the newspaper, we learned it was not actually the newspaper itself but the Sunday inserts that piqued their interest and provided the most effective advertising.

Our 1988 study revealed that 39 percent of American consumers were reading Sunday inserts—however, after the supermarkets initiated double-coupon programs, this number dramatically increased to its present 74 percent readership. With all those people clipping coupons to get a double discount at the supermarket, I immediately advised my retail clients to insert their circulars in Sunday newspapers to sell furniture, appliances, sporting goods, and so on. We advised our clients to act within a two-week window to go heavy with this form of advertising. Did we ever get the jump on the competition! Depending on my clients' marketplace, they placed themselves anywhere from three months to three years ahead of their competition.

Interestingly, when this Sunday insert information first became known to me, I predicted Montgomery Ward would have a very successful year. My prediction was based solely on the fact that the company had always been a major advertiser in the Sunday inserts and thereby had an edge over everyone else. Anyone who bought stock in Montgomery Ward at that time knows its department stores' sales volume soared, benefiting from additional readership driven by the supermarkets' push on double coupons every Sunday.

A while back, we had a head start on another trend—this time in the banking industry. This one was a result of a major bank that hired me to study the impact of signage that appears *inside* the bank. This particular bank wanted to test the impact of its signs placed throughout its interior. Could people who personally came inside to make deposits be sold other bank services by effective "billboards"? Our client was especially interested in the effect four-color signs had on customers. Would full-color signs generate more business for services such as home equity loans, opening an IRA account, or financing a recreational vehicle or boat?

When we interviewed bank customers, our survey revealed that four-color ads were indeed very effective. Our report indicated that the signs positively impacted 20 percent of the people who walked into the bank—one out of every five customers. During the course of a year, that's a lot of new business resulting from that bank signage.

OTHER TRENDS

Something interesting is usually happening when an answer to a question reappears with increasing frequency. This occurred in 1983 when I asked consumers, "When thinking about electronics and appliance stores, does any store first come to mind?" I addressed the same question to consumers concerning drugstores, tire stores, sporting goods stores, and others, always asking, "Does any one retailer come to mind?"

At first, as many as 38 percent of the responses were "No," meaning that no particular store came to mind. Let's say that 30 percent of the people said XYZ Store is the first store to come to mind. This means that if you owned XYZ Store and ran a big weekend promotion, you could expect to draw as much as 68 percent of the marketplace, because, including the 30 percent of the customers you already had, in theory, another 38 percent were up for grabs. In 1989, the percentage of customers up for grabs kept dropping, and by 1996, when I asked the same question, only 6 percent of the consumers said, "No store comes to mind."

This means that XYZ Store had a shot at getting 36 percent of the shoppers with a big sales promotion versus 68 percent only a few years ago. In the eyes of retailers, this is a significant trend, because it means that in order to increase your market share, you must be more focused and more on target than your competition—you must take customers away from somebody. Certainly, it was a lot easier with so many undecided customers a few years ago, but today, there are not nearly as many up for grabs. As you can see, a trend of this nature is bound to influence aggressive retailers who want additional market share. This is the finding that inspired my concept of predatory marketing strategy, which is explained in detail in Chapter 7.

It is important to realize that trends are not necessarily confined to a particular industry. In fact, once a trend is identified, several companies in unrelated industries may pick up on it. For example, as discussed above, research revealed that consumers working longer hours are looking for ways to get more out of their time. Knowing this, I will cite examples of two entirely different products to illustrate how two companies successfully reacted to this information.

For starters, Pert Shampoo was floundering in the marketplace until its marketing and research people got together and came up with a new all-in-one shampoo and hair conditioner. The new shampoo/conditioning product did in one step a job that formerly took two separate steps. The idea was right on target with the consumer's desire to conserve time—giving Pert a home run and a new market position.

Along the same line, Bruce Wax came up with a floor wax that did essentially the same thing that Pert did with shampoo. Bruce Wax introduced a new wax to the marketplace that required only one coat of wax instead of two or more coats. The company cashed in on the same trend—with an entirely different product. (Another wax company, Simonize, did this with its one-step car wax.) Of course, time-saving products are not new and revolutionary—for many years, fast-food restaurants, one-hour dry cleaners, quick lubes, Express Mail, and many other services have catered to hurried consumers.

The early 1980s earned the name "the decade of price," meaning the consumer was driven to the retail stores that offered the lowest prices. In January 1986, however, our research indicated that, because of growing limitations on consumers' time, stores providing the most selection were beginning to be a significant consideration. And by the end of the 1980s, what had started out to be the decade of price ended up being "the decade of price *and* selection." This trend created the rise in the category killers, which, in turn, inaugurated the "big box" retailers. It also led to the building of 25,000-to-75,000-square-foot stores across America—retailers such as Home Depot, Circuit City, Best Buy, Office Max, Office Depot, Sports Authority, and Bed Bath & Beyond. This was a reaction to the consumer who began to say, "I want a great price, but price becomes irrelevant if I can't find what I want to buy in your store." Category killers have brightened an otherwise dreary retailing scene in the 1990s. They generated about $550 billion in sales in 1995, a third of total retail sales nationwide.

Store size began to increase because consumers began to "cherry-pick" the merchandise in small stores, meaning they'd only buy a small store's goods with the low prices. This practice produced a dramatic drop in profit margins. By opening larger stores with more selections, big box retailers generated additional profits because of larger sales volume. In larger stores, the retailer also had the advantage of offering more choices of merchandise in "steps." "Steps" is a term used in the retail community; a special is advertised, but once in the store, the customer is told, "This is what we've advertised, but here are other good alternatives for you to consider." While the small store didn't have enough space to carry all the steps, the big store did, generating better profit margins. Our research tells us that by the year 2000, the American consumer will be three times more selection-driven than in 1990. This is vital information for planning what size stores to build or lease to meet future needs.

Now, in the mid-1990s, as I mentioned earlier, consumers are becoming more service-driven. This does not mean they no longer want good prices or selection—they want good prices, selection, *and* great service. Because of the time constraints placed on today's consumer, still more trends have emerged regarding shopping habits in the big superstores. Today, as much as 70 percent of the purchases made in these stores occurs on weekends, versus only 40 to 50 percent a decade ago. Consequently, today's consumer is demanding faster checkout. While a checkout line for five or fewer items was acceptable in the 1980s, consumers now want an additional checkout line for ten items or less, so when they have eight purchases, they don't have to stand behind somebody who's buying thirty.

And, again because of time constraints, 1996 research reveals that more than 95 percent of consumers say: "If you advertise a product, you'd better have it in the store when I get there." Not only this, but 90 percent of the consumers insist that the store highlight exactly where the merchandise is located, because they don't want to waste their time looking for it somewhere in the back of the store. After a sale is made, 94 percent of consumers want a thirty-day satisfaction guarantee. Here the consumer is saying, "If I have a problem with what I buy, I don't want you to waste my time making me battle you to get my money back. So I want you to make the return process easy and simple for me." A decade ago, none of these demands would have exceeded 40 percent.

Levi Strauss & Co. has grown by leaps and bounds during the past decade because it cashed in on a trend. Recognizing a more casual America with an increasingly unpretentious lifestyle, the company simplified its business by closing forty factories between 1983 and 1986, and in the process reduced its workforce by twelve thousand workers. Its purpose: to rid itself of all apparel operations unrelated to the jeans business. Gone were its divisions such as Perry Ellis America, Koret of North America, menswear manufacturer Oxxford, and hatmaker Resistol. By focusing only on its main business, Levi Strauss increased sales from $2.6 billion to almost $7 billion in 1995, a nearly threefold growth rate. During this period, in the late 1980s, the company introduced Dockers, a line of casual trousers targeted for an older consumer—to reach the Baby Boomers with their expanding waistlines. Dockers is considered one of the most successful brand launches in American apparel history, approaching the $1 billion range in 1995 sales. With more and more companies relaxing their dress codes, companies like Levi Strauss will continue to cash in on the "corporate-casual" trend.

The American toy industry has also experienced dramatic changes caused by trends. Until the 1970s, products were made to appeal to parents, and manufacturers enjoyed the luxury of demonstrating the introduction of expensive toys in department stores where most of them were sold. But when the big discounters such as Kmart and Wal-Mart began to enter toy retailing in the 1970s and 1980s, they didn't employ salespeople with the time to demonstrate or explain toys. This meant the toy manufacturers bore the burden of the heavy cost of advertising their wares on TV. The annual budget for TV advertising for all toys in the United States shot up from only $9 million in the early 1960s to nearly $1 billion by the late 1980s.

This led toy manufacturers to invent games with the senior toy buyer of big discount retailers in mind—a toy was more marketable if it could be explained in a thirty-second TV commercial. Because of these heavy marketing costs, few new toys are being introduced today. Instead, rehashes of older products are being sold to America's children—old staples such as repackaged Barbies and G.I. Joes. Of course, there are the new licensed products based on movies and TV shows; the success of these toys relies on the heavy publicity generated on the small and big screens across the nation. In 1995, half of all U.S. toy sales were based on such tie-ins.

Changes apparent in the area of play are matched by others in the realm of work. The trend in corporate America to downsize has caused a big boom in the temporary employment industry. The number of temporary workers in the United States has nearly doubled over the past five years from 1.2 million to more than 2 million. This record job creation beats just about every other industry in the country. Meanwhile, the temp industry has undergone dramatic changes. While it is true that most temp workers are still filling low-wage clerical, secretarial, and light-industrial blue-collar positions, fast-growing segments of the temp-job market are professional and technical fields. These high-skill areas now make up about 20 percent of the total temp payroll. Hiring temps today now, more than ever, allows employers to try out a worker prior to offering a permanent job. According to a survey by the National Association of Temporary Staffing Services, three-quarters of respondents said they became temps as a way to look for a full-time position; 40 percent were made permanent offers.

EXTERNAL FACTORS

Trends can be dramatically influenced by numerous factors over which you have no control, ranging from government regulation to changes in the weather. Because the forces that create trends come from so many sources, they are difficult to forecast. These outside conditions obviously vary from industry to industry. Astute trend-watchers scrutinize fluctuations and movements, understanding that by their nature, trends are fortuitous. Trends that are easiest to spot are those started by consumers, and we focus most on those trends. On the other hand, external trend-influencing factors are not so predictable.

Sometimes an external factor's impact can generate not one but a series of trends in the marketplace. Certainly, Egypt's attack on Israel on the eve of Yom Kippur, October 6, 1973, was unpredictable. And what followed was even more astonishing. When the tiny Jewish state struck back, it totally annihilated the enemy that greatly outnumbered it, deeply humiliating the entire Arab world. Who could have predicted the effect of that embarrassment on the American consumer? This military defeat led the Arabs to retaliate with their most powerful weapon: an oil boycott, aimed primarily at the United States, Israel's supporter.

The November 1973 boycott lasted until the following March. It caused several trends in America, starting with the rush to the automobile showrooms selling subcompacts, fuel-efficient models in particular. The gas shortages across America resulted in a forecast that small-car sales could capture 50 percent of the market by the end of the year. For several months, small car models were in tremendous demand. American Motors, which manufactured only small cars, enjoyed an immediate 28 percent increase in sales by the end of 1973. Meanwhile, the Big Three were frantically designing their 1975 models, making substantial reductions in weight. Unquestionably, the demand for smaller cars resulting from the oil boycott began a new trend.

Gas prices, however, which had been 30 cents a gallon, leveled off at 60 cents by the spring of 1974, and a fickle America abruptly became disenchanted with little cars. By the end of the third quarter in 1974, huge inventories of small cars began to pile up. Ford had a ninety-six-day supply of Pintos, while the demand for Lincoln Mark IVs skyrocketed. Similarly, General Motors was sitting on a 105-day supply of Vegas, yet its Cadillac Division inventory had dwindled to twenty-six days. Likewise, Chrysler accumulated a 105-day supply of Plymouth Valiants, and its Japanese-made minicar, the Dodge Colt, was up to a 113-day supply.

This induced a trend within the automobile industry to offer huge rebates on small cars. It even caused Henry Ford II to go to Washington to persuade the federal government to place a 10 percent tax on the price of gasoline, which would make small cars more appealing. John Sawhill, President Gerald Ford's new energy czar, went so far as to propose a $1-per-gallon tax in an effort to induce the nation to conserve energy. Meanwhile, the American public debated whether the 1973 gas shortage was a hoax engineered by profit-hungry oil companies.

Big, expensive cars continued to sell well for Ford and General Motors for several years, and by 1978, it appeared that the United States had fully recovered from the 1973 oil embargo. But then who could have foreseen that the Shah of Iran, who had ruled since 1953, was about to lose power? The Ayatollah Khomeini's overthrow of the Iranian government led to a holy war which caused the Shah and his family to exit abruptly from Tehran on January 16, 1979. The handwriting was now on the wall— the world must brace itself for another energy crunch.

Once the Ayatollah seized control of Iran, he showed his contempt for the United States by denouncing anything connected with the Western world. Khomeini turned off the spigot and created a second oil crisis, and in a matter of weeks, the price of oil doubled. How predictable were these events and the accompanying trends that followed? One Big Three senior executive was asked, "Why didn't the company anticipate another oil crisis?"

His reply was, "We didn't hear anyone on the outside saying the Shah of Iran was going to be thrown out." If the United States government, with its vast network of intelligence, was not aware of what was about to happen in Iran, how could the nation's business community be expected to have prepared for a second oil crisis?

Prior to the gas scare we had in the United States, only 10 percent of consumers claimed that the price of gas was a major consideration in buying a car. But when the cost of gasoline skyrocketed, this factor influenced 36 percent of the Americans shopping for an automobile.

Just as oil crises shook up not only the automobile industry but also nonvehicular businesses, often external factors affect seemingly unrelated marketplaces. It doesn't take an international event to create a trend. It could be a small, uneventful occurrence, even something seemingly trivial. A classic example of one such event occurred in 1934 in the Academy Award–winning movie It Happened One Night. In what was at the time considered a risqué bedroom scene, Clark Gable removed his shirt in the presence of Claudette Colbert; to the audience's surprise, he wasn't wearing an undershirt. After movie idol Gable was seen shirtless, sales of men's undershirts plummeted across the nation—and have never recovered!

Many other celebrities have also started trends. John F. Kennedy rocked the men's hat industry when he refused to wear a hat to cover his well-known locks of hair. Only repeated requests from hat manufacturers persuaded him to carry a hat at his inauguration. Until that time, a well-dressed man nearly always wore a hat. But the hatless President of the United States started a trend that has lasted for nearly four decades.

The adored wife of the President was a trendsetter, too. Women began wearing their hair like Jackie's, and that trend spread across the country and around the world.

Advertisers realize the influence movie stars and professional athletes have on Americans, so, for good reason, these celebrities are paid top dollar for their endorsements. Consider the impact of Michael Jordan on millions of young boys when he appears in commercials endorsing athletic shoes.

More recently, in the early 1980s, while Chrysler was recovering from its near bankruptcy, CEO Lee Iacocca appeared as a company spokesperson in television commercials, wearing a colored shirt with a white collar. The shirt started a new fashion, and to this day, it is called an Iacocca shirt.

Social issues can be a force that spawns a trend. When the crackdown on drunk driving became a national issue, sales of wine with lower alcoholic content increased, and nonalcoholic beer-like products were introduced.

THE RISK-TAKER

In the world of business, trends and change are synonymous. And change of any kind is likely to be accompanied by the element of risk. Although new ventures require some risk-taking, there is perhaps an equal danger in remaining too long with the status quo. If you stand still, you're likely to get buried by your competitors. Leading-edge companies do not wince at new trends.

Of course, hitching your wagon to the wrong trend, or, for that matter, to a short-lived trend, can have dire consequences. For example, the owner of a woman's apparel shop who goes with the wrong fashion trend when selecting next season's merchandise may find herself in serious trouble. And so would a furniture retailer who remerchandised his store with only low-end goods, thinking there was a movement away from his former middle price points.

Every retailer must work diligently to spot trends that determine what he or she should stock. A restaurateur must keep abreast of eating habits and dietary fads. A home builder must be aware of present mortgage rates as well as how they might fluctuate. A manufacturer must be alert to color trends likely to affect the demand for its product.

When analyzing a trend, it's difficult but essential to determine how long it might last. Depending upon many variables, a trend's life span can range from weeks to years. In the woman's apparel industry, for example, color and style trends are particularly fickle, and may run their course in only a matter of months. Fashion changes from season to season, and the right look for this winter may not be stylish next winter.

With large chains such as The Limited and The Gap, the difference between one store doing $5 million a year in business and doing $10 million is how well management can zero in on next season's trends. For many years, The Limited was an industry leader because it offered the "on-trend" look at a lower price. Today, however, the field is considerably more competitive; a dozen or so other women's apparel companies offer similar merchandise at discounted prices. Many of these companies now wait until a color trend is identified by an industry leader; next, they quickly produce a similar line of merchandise in a third-world country, stocking their mall-based stores with copied goods. These knock-off experts have lessened their own risks and have reduced the edge The Limited enjoyed for many years. As a consequence, retailers like The Limited take more upfront risks, but are denied the lengthy forerunner's advantage they once enjoyed.

Once a trend is underway, too much competition can saturate the marketplace, reducing everyone's profit margin. For instance, when Mexican-food restaurants first became popular in the United States, they enjoyed tremendous success. This demand resulted in more and more Mexican restaurants opening. However, once the nation became inundated with them, the Mexican restaurant pie was sliced into so many pieces that, as in the woman's apparel industry, profit margins dropped.

A similar thing happened to the membership warehouse clubs trend. Several years ago, I did a research study that showed from a competitive position, a marketplace could support only 1.8 different membership warehouse clubs. This meant that if two stores competed in the same marketplace, even an equal split meant each competitor would be equivalent to only nine-tenths of a store. With a low-margin operation, this meant neither store could operate in the black. Had a market been able to support 2.2 different clubs, it would have been doable. Two competing warehouse clubs could succeed, even with one at 1.0 and the other at 1.2. Yet in some marketplaces, there were even three clubs—no wonder we've seen the demise of these operations.

Just as short-term trends can be risky, so can betting the future of your company on a long-term trend. But such risk-taking is sometimes necessary. An astute businessperson must make certain long-term plans in order to guide a company into the future. As mentioned earlier, investments in buildings, machinery, and merchandise require large sums up front, and meanwhile, trends change. Management must address the $64,000 question: "To stay ahead of a trend, do I build a store today that will have a larger rent factor, and be a bigger box than the customer presently wants, on a gamble that in a few years it may be exactly what the customer wants?" The same risk exists in every industry where large capital expenditures are required to anticipate future demands.

The risk of some brief trends is that unless you are the actual trendmaker, by the time you get into it, you may be too late and miss it altogether. And if you are the leader of a trend with a very small window, even as the trendmaker you may not realize a profit.

The complexity of trends can increase their risk. For instance, two more trends may simultaneously occur. I've already mentioned that today's consumer is driven by price and selection. The price customer says, "Whatever I buy, I want a low price." Then there is the sale price customer, who wants a low price, too—but on a brand name. The price customer says price is number one and selection is number two. The sale price customer may say that selection is number one and a great price on a brand name is number two. The difference between these two similar consumers is the importance they place on selection and on name brands.

Our studies further indicate that Americans in different regions of the country are not alike. For instance, in New York City, consumers generally prefer the lowest price—period. This preference is so strong, they care very little whether they've ever heard of the brand. However, in the Midwest, consumers value both brand name and price. Midwesterners say, "I believe a brand-name product will last three to four years longer, so I am willing to pay a little more—but not a lot more." These regional differences mean that national companies must design different merchandising strategies—one for each region.

REDUCING THE RISKS

As you learn more about the inherent dangers of trends, allow me to point out that many of these risks can be substantially reduced.

First, before you dive in headfirst, you can test the waters. For instance, in the early 1970s, McDonald's operators complained that while their restaurants opened every morning around 10:00, there wasn't much activity until lunchtime. At the time, nobody in the fast-food field was offering a nutritious breakfast. That's when Herb Peterson, a franchisee in Santa Barbara, came up with the idea of grilling eggs, Canadian bacon, and cheese, and serving it on an English muffin. Thus was born the Egg McMuffin. After testing his new product in his own restaurant and seeing that his customers bought into it, Peterson passed his idea up to the franchisor. McDonald's test-marketed the Egg McMuffin in a few limited areas; after it proved to be a winner there, in 1977 it appeared on the menus of every McDonald's.

With the advent of the Egg McMuffin, a new trend in fast food was introduced to America. Ten years passed before Wendy's and Burger

King followed in McDonald's footsteps. Because McDonald's was the trendmaker, its breakfast success far surpasses its competition throughout the United States. Today, one out of every four Americans who breakfasts away from home is dining at McDonald's.

Before something new is universally available throughout the McDonald's chain, new products are test-marketed at a small number of its more than twelve thousand restaurants. Products that have been test-marketed include such hits as the fish sandwich, the Big Mac, Chicken McNuggets, and the salad bar.

Of course, large companies have the advantage of test-marketing a new product in a handful of areas before introducing it worldwide. But a one-store operation or a small restaurant can test-market, too. For example, a small supermarket can test the reception of a new product by giving out samples to its customers. Or the store may simply pass out coupons with discounts or two-for-one offers. And if you own a Mexican restaurant, you probably wouldn't test-market Chinese food by having it replace half your menu overnight. One new appetizer can be added to the menu for a brief time; if customers are receptive, it can become a standard item. When you test the shark-infested waters of risk, just stick your little toe in.

Many companies conduct focus groups before introducing a new product. A company can bring a small number of people together in a focus group, show them a product, ask them lots of questions, and then talk and talk with them about it. Based on the group's reaction, the company begins to have an understanding about what the consumer is thinking. Some large manufacturers, such as General Electric and Whirlpool, actually put the new product into consumers' homes for ninety days. The problems these people encounter help the company get all the bugs out before introducing the new product nationally.

Companies with small budgets give away small-ticket products to conduct test-marketing. A candy manufacturer, for example, can pass out free samples to window-shoppers in a mall, or to pedestrians on a downtown sidewalk, while asking their opinion. A toy manufacturer can do a mailing of its products to a few hundred people and conduct a follow-up telephone survey to get their reactions. You can even display a new product at your local Rotary Club or Kiwanis meeting and pass out questionnaires to find out what people are thinking. Likewise, you can "test-market" an advertising campaign (radio, television, newspaper, direct mail, etc.) by running several different advertisements. Keeping good records of the results will help you determine which ad generates the most favorable results, and that's the one to go with.

THE TRENDMAKER

With the risks that abound, you may question why anyone would want to be a trendmaker. After all, with considerably less on the table, you can play follow the leader and still cash in—somewhat—on a trend, can't you?

There is good reason, however, to be the trendmaker! The first company to offer a product to the consumer can demand a premium. Toward the end of a trend, profit margins go down; those who get in late don't enjoy the same prosperity reaped by the leader. As the great industrialist Andrew Carnegie once said, "The first man gets the oyster, and the second man gets the shell."

In the beginning, the law of supply and demand allows the trendmaker a bigger profit margin. Conversely, as other competitors participate, prices generally drop. Several studies demonstrate that 50 percent of a trend's profits occur during the first third of the trend; approximately 35 percent occur in the middle; and as a trend enters the final stages, more and more people climb on the bandwagon, producing a lower-priced product with correspondingly lower profits.

While high profit margins attract trendmakers, there are other benefits. In the number one position, you set the pace. Those who are not the trendmaker would do well to remember that when you're not the lead dog, the view is always the same. As the trendmaker, a company will enjoy great jumps in sales while the rest of the field just bumps along.

Perhaps the biggest benefit of being an industry trendmaker is that you are put in a leadership position. *If you're in the number one spot, the consumer thinks of you first.* As I mentioned earlier, with consumers having less and less time, it's becoming more important for your store to be the first store shopped.

And whether you're a retailer or a manufacturer, as the trendmaker, you are also perceived as the information leader. People come to you for your ideas and input. This permits you to build a partnership with the purchasers of your product. In this relationship, you are certain to enjoy repeat orders from those customers.

BUCKING TRENDS

Those who choose to buck a trend are the real crapshooters; they take risks of either losing big-time or winning big-time.

In the 1980s, the automobile tire business found price to be the driving force throughout America. While its competition sold price to the American consumer, Michelin bucked the trend by refusing to get into the price war.

Michelin, knowing it could never sell the cheapest tire in the marketplace, created a market with safety as its number one feature. In the company's ad campaign, television commercials informed the American public that when they drove on Michelin tires, their children would be protected, at a time when women were buying more tires for the family car.

By bucking the price trend by selling safety instead of economy, Michelin became the market leader in the quality tire industry, a position it holds to this day.

(In a research survey I conducted for the Audit Bureau of Circulations, a firm that certifies the readership of newspaper and magazine publications for advertisers, we found out that 73 percent of all Americans claim that television is their number one source of product education to make them smart consumers. Needless to say, the print people were not happy with this information. Most small businesses can't afford to educate their customers with costly television commercials. They could, however, introduce and sell their wares by mailing high-production-quality videos to a *select targeted market.* A three-to-five-minute videocassette is affordable, and when packaged properly, it will generate a 55 percent viewership rate during the first thirty days. And, to induce customers to respond, companies will give a small gift to anyone who returns the video. This also allows the company to recycle the video to more customers. The video return rate often approaches 38 percent—so when the cost per customer is broken down according to what it takes to get him or her to your store, the videocassette can be a real bargain.)

BEING A MOVING TARGET

If you're a trendmaker, it's difficult to maintain your number one position because, as the trend continues, others join in, offer lower prices, and take away market share.

Ideally, at the height of the trend, an aggressive trendmaker identifies and starts a new trend, and by the time the competition picks up on it, still another trend is in the works. What makes being a trendmaker an increasingly arduous task is that the window for developing a new trend keeps getting smaller. In some industries, it has decreased from six months to sixty days. This requires the trendmaker to recognize quickly when its present trend is fading, and, simultaneously, to identify and start a new trend.

What's to prevent other companies from copying a trend? Trendmakers may say, "The company that we are today will not be able to compete with the company we're going to be in the future."

Comments like this remind me of a quote from Rudyard Kipling's nineteenth-century poem "The *Mary Gloster,*" which reads:

They copied all they could follow, but they couldn't copy my mind,
And I left 'em sweating and stealing, a year and a half behind.

What happened to Zenith in the early 1980s demonstrates that market share can be lost when a leader ceases to be a moving target. Years before Japanese electronics companies came to our shores, Zenith and RCA were the market share leaders in the U.S. television industry. The American consumer perceived Zenith according to its famous slogan, "The quality goes in before the name goes on." Zenith's crisp, sharp-contrast picture quality compared favorably to RCA's slightly softer picture. And to the American consumer, a television set was measured by the quality of its picture.

Zenith was a market leader, but it became a stationary target once America's trend toward buying high-quality Japanese products emerged during the early 1980s. Then Sony entered the marketplace with a product boasting an even sharper picture than Zenith's. When consumer tests demonstrated that consumers preferred the picture quality produced by Sony, and later Mitsubishi, Zenith found itself in a weakened position. Although the company's number one selling feature still existed, it was no longer an advantage. In the 1980s, my firm's research showed that 60 percent of Sony television owners admitted they were formerly Zenith customers. The quality of Zenith's product had not lessened—it simply was no longer unique or clearly superior. Once the company could no longer claim a real advantage over the competition, the American consumer stopped perceiving Zenith as a market leader.

WHERE HAVE ALL THE TRENDMAKERS GONE?

All too often today, businesspeople tell me, "I'd rather be a profitable number two than a trendmaker who is right 60 percent of the time and wrong 40 percent of the time." This attitude holds back many companies.

A problem that exists within corporate America today surfaces when the consumer is asked, "What's new today in the marketplace?" All too often, the reply is "There's very little new right now."

Consumers who don't find anything new stay home. We live in a consumer-driven country, meaning that new products are what keep our economy strong and healthy. When American management resists taking chances because of a fear of failure, great successes are eliminated. Sure, there will be lukewarm successes, but that's all they are—lukewarm.

It's a bad sign when companies lose the desire to be a trendmaker. Weak managers find it easier to let the competition invest in research and test the consumer, while they sit on the sidelines. "We'll let them have the lead up front, and we'll copy what they do once the trend is established," they say. A company that doesn't assume the leadership role puts itself in a position where it can never be the consumer's first choice. Remember, the year 2000 is closer ahead than 1990 is behind us. And consumers in the year 2000 will seldom buy from their second choice.

In a 1980s study, we learned that when people went out on a particular day to make a waterbed purchase, if they didn't find what they wanted, more than 55 percent of them bought something else and never bought a waterbed.

So what does this mean? In analyzing the buying decisions of the consumer, I think the waterbed analogy represents how tomorrow's consumers will respond to buying decisions of most products. I envision the American consumer as a juggler who, at any given time, is juggling eight balls in the air, each ball representing an item costing $500 or more. These items could be a television set, a vacation, or a set of four tires. When the consumer shops for one of these items and doesn't find exactly what he wants, that ball gets dropped, and it is no longer a consideration. For example, an emergency might come up on his way home, say, during an oil change. The service station attendant points out, "Have you looked at your tires lately? The steel belts are showing, and that's dangerous."

Now the consumer has no choice but to spend his TV or sofa money on the emergency. A decision is made to buy something he wasn't in the market to buy, and some other discretionary purchase is replaced. A trendmaker can withstand a lot of discretionary distractions, because when the consumer comes back to the marketplace with his money, he checks out the trendmaker first. If you're not the trendmaker, consider yourself lost in the shuffle.

SHIFTS IN CONSUMER ATTITUDES

The following chart illustrates how the American consumer has changed over the years:

Years	Period of Time for Consumer Attitudes to Change
1950s	fairly constant; without major shifts for 3–5 years
1960s	3–4 years
1970s	3 years
1980s	2–3 years
1990s	12–18 months
by year 2000	9–12 months

Notice how consumer attitudes toward home use of personal computers has dramatically changed from 1985 to 1995. When households were asked whether they were considering a personal computer for their home or had already purchased one, they responded positively as follows:

Year	Households
1985	18%
1987	23
1989	37
1991	48
1993	57
1995	63

In 1995, in those households with children ages seven to fourteen, 87 percent said they already purchased or were considering purchasing a personal computer.

FIVE REVEALING TRENDS

Customers Making Their Complaints Known

Of consumers who experience a problem, the number who would either call, write, or go in person to complain to that company:

1985	3%
1990	9
1995	18

Of businesses that experience a problem with a vendor/supplier, the number that would make their displeasure known by notifying the rep, customer service department, or corporate executive:

1985	11%
1990	32
1995	45

It's interesting to note that in both the consumer and the business example, between 1985 and 1990, the ratio increased 300 percent.

Consumers' Negotiating Technique

The percentage of customers who try to get a lower price from the salesperson by mentioning other stores, whether or not they have actually shopped there:

1990	48%
1992	53

1994	55
1996	59

As consumers shop fewer and fewer stores, this negotiating technique has risen in major purchases of $500 or more.

Sunday Newspaper Inserts

Customers looking at the Sunday newspaper inserts on a regular basis:

1988	36%–43%
1992	58–61
1996	74–78

When supermarkets adopted double-coupon marketing strategies, the number of consumers reading the Sunday inserts doubled. The number of insert readers has not decreased, even though some supermarkets have dropped the double-coupon promotion.

Concerns About Crime in America

In 1996, in response to concerns about crime, the following percentages of Americans expressed concern about:

Driving through a high-reported-crime area	68.6%
Carrying a large amount of cash	65.4
Walking in a large parking lot	48.7
Walking anywhere at night	65.3

The above concern about crime has impacted, directly or indirectly, 35 percent of shopping in America. *While 30 percent of all retail sales in 1990 occurred on weekday evenings, by 1996, it was less than 20 percent.*

Crime, less time to shop, and the need to spend more time with children/family are dramatically changing the retail landscape.

Average Per Visit Expenditures at Nearby Enclosed Malls by Teenagers

The following dollar amounts indicate changing spending habits of teenagers, ages fourteen through eighteen, who live at home. Their primary purchases per visit (excluding meals and entertainment) at enclosed shopping malls amounted to:

1990	$32
1992	35
1994	38
1996	44

Many teens say they feel that mall security personnel treat them like criminals. Mall owners must not discourage this important shopper group. Mall owners should also endeavor to keep retailers catering to teens.

CONSUMER MIND READER #2

Today's Technology That Americans Most Appreciate

When significant advancements in technology make new products available, not all American consumers view these changes positively. In a special study that asked consumers which products have improved their lives most, the following were shown to be the ten most well received products in the United States:

Product	Percent totally positive
1. Microwave oven	77.3%
2. Universal remote control (a single-unit remote-control device to operate both television and VCR)	66.6
3. Garage-door opener	64.6
4. Telephone-answering machine for the home	61.7
5. Ear thermometer	59.5
6. Breath analyzer	59.2
7. Programmable thermostat for heating and air-conditioning a home	58.3
8. Call-waiting telephone service	56.4
9. Automatic deposit of payroll/government check	55.1
10. Supermarket price scanner	55.0

The big surprise on the list is the breath analyzer. Although some people use it for medical purposes, it is mainly used by police. Simply put, Americans rank the breath analyzer number six because they want to get drunken drivers off the road. The supermarket price scanner was in tenth place. It would have ranked higher were it not for the fact that, too often, it scans the wrong price.

The Top Three ''Wish-It-Was Never-Invented'' Products

During the past ten years, some advancements in technology have not been viewed by all consumers as positive changes. In the following survey, these three products were viewed negatively:

1. Electronic answering service (machine that instructs the caller to follow a series of directions and press different keys, and which may or may not lead to conversation with a "live" person)

2. Shopping on the Internet

3. Cellular car phone

With the exception of the cellular car phone, each of the above products provides a function in which a person is replaced by a machine. The impersonal feeling that results makes people feel uncomfortable and lacking control. Americans are negative about the cellular car phone due to hazardous driving concerns.

The electronic answering service infuriates people because it makes them endure a long process that may not help them and often wastes their time. The major objection to shopping on the Internet is the fear of disclosing one's credit-card number, which, in the wrong hands, could cause financial harm.

CHAPTER THREE

IMPLEMENTING A MARKETING STRATEGY

Every company claims to have a marketing strategy in place, but ask a business owner or CEO to explain his or her strategy to you, and chances are you'll get only a vague explanation—if you're lucky. In most cases, companies can't explain a marketing strategy because they don't have one.

And even those that do don't always execute it. As somebody once said, "Ideas are a dime a dozen, but the men and women who implement them are priceless."

There's a lot of truth in those words. The best research and greatest marketing strategy—with poor execution—are worth zilch.

Over the years, I have observed so many marketing strategies I've lost count. Some had terrific concepts, while others were conceptually mediocre. While ideally you want to begin with a tremendous concept, the concept doesn't guarantee a marketing strategy's success. Many strategies fall short because of poor implementation. In my opinion, an ordinary plan that's brilliantly executed will always beat an extraordinary plan that's poorly executed.

Of course, the real leaders who dominate the marketplace are strong in both concept and execution. They are the Coca-Colas and Disneys of this world. These number-one-market-share companies do everything right, leaving nothing to chance. They understand that their competition is out there doing its best to take away market share. So even though they may be miles in front of the pack, they're always aware somebody is getting closer.

Many people associate marketing strategies with the management of big corporations. But you don't have to be a General Motors to have one. Big or small, every company needs a good, solid plan to follow. It isn't just a nice option—it's the heart and soul of a sound business.

FIVE COMPONENTS FOR IMPLEMENTING A SUCCESSFUL MARKETING STRATEGY

There's a story of a Miami stockbroker who is visited by his New York client. The brokerage firm's office, located next door to a marina, has a magnificent view.

Looking out his fifth-floor window, the broker points out the marina below. "Do you see that huge yacht docked over there?" he asks the client.

"Yes," the client answers.

"It belongs to our CEO. The one docked next to it is our senior vice president's, and the one two rows over is our top broker's. Oh, yes, the one right next to it is mine."

Without blinking an eye, the customer asks, "Yes, but where are the customers' yachts?"

This story has a good lesson. A stockbroker's client isn't interested in how much money the members of the firm make—he's interested in *how much money they make for their clients!* Or even more specifically, *how much money will his broker make for him?* I've related this story to my clients, so they know exactly what I mean when I turn to them and say, "But where are your customers' yachts?"

When advising my business clients, I emphasize the following five attributes essential to implementing a successful marketing strategy:

1. IDENTIFY YOUR CUSTOMERS' NEEDS AND FIND A WAY TO FULFILL THEM. You must begin with this foundation—or your marketing strategy is doomed to fail. If the competition has already succeeded in meeting the number one need, you must decide to address it better or become a niche player.

2. ESTABLISH YOUR OWN IDENTITY BY CREATING A UNIQUE SELLING POSITION. You must clearly communicate to your customers at a level they understand what you offer that makes you different from your competition.

3. EDUCATE THE CONSUMER THAT YOU EXIST. Here, you must cut through the clutter to communicate to your targeted customer that you have something to offer that he or she wants. When you introduce a new product, you must inform the consumer of its benefits compared to the other choice out there.

4. DEVELOP A DISTRIBUTION PLAN. To accomplish this, you must determine the suitable channels to sell your product to the end user. The right product in the wrong store will never reach its potential.

5. UNDERSTAND THAT YOU EXIST IN AN EVER-CHANGING MARKETPLACE. Remember that no marketing strategy is going to last forever. Since change is constant, you must be continually adapting. At the same time, you must be anticipating that change, knowing that the wrong plan will hurt your company. But doing nothing is a defensive position that always results in failure in the long term.

A BLENDING OF MARKETING STRATEGIES

Some analysts thought Quaker Oats overpaid when it dished out $1.7 billion for Snapple, a tea-and-juice-blends company whose 1995 sales were only $640 million. What Quaker wanted was a sexier, higher-growth business, but some Wall Street observers thought the asking price too high for a brand pitted against some awesome competitors. If Quaker, however, can implement its planned marketing strategy, the company will demonstrate to the world that it got a bargain. Similar doubts were expressed in 1983 when Quaker purchased Gatorade's parent company, Stokely–Van Camp, for $240 million: at the time, the sports drink company's sales hovered around $100 million; today, Gatorade's sales exceed $1 billion.

At present, Snapple's market share in teas is 15 percent, and in fruit drinks 24 percent. With the backing of Quaker, whose sales were at $6.3 billion, the brand is believed to be better positioned to fight off the big soft drink competition in the fruit drinks business, where Snapple currently holds the number one spot. To implement its marketing strategy, Quaker identified its customers' needs when it purchased Snapple. Secondly, Snapple already had an established identity; thirdly, the consumer was aware of Snapple's existence. Since Snapple already had these attributes, Quaker had to pay a hefty premium to acquire the company. This costly route is frequently taken by large corporations that wish to avoid creating a company from scratch.

Quaker made one major faux pas, however, that was realized only after the acquisition. The parent company initially believed the same distribution system was shared by Snapple and Gatorade, hence a probable synergy would be mutually beneficial to both subsidiaries. Only after the sale, however, did Quaker realize the two distribution systems were completely different. Snapple's three hundred distributors deliver directly to stores, while Gatorade's distributors deliver to warehouses. When Quaker attempted to turn over Snapple distributors' big supermarket accounts to the Gatorade reps and instructed Snapple distributors to concentrate instead on convenience stores and small accounts, the distributors objected, and sales fell 5 percent during Snapple's first year with Quaker.

Quaker management has since agreed to alter its marketing strategy and work in harmony with Snapple distributors. Since then, Quaker has instituted several other major changes. By processing orders faster and running bottling plants more efficiently, Quaker has reduced delivery time to distributors from three weeks to three days. Pleased distributors say their inventory costs have since been halved, and they can now deliver goods to stores within forty-eight hours. Quaker made taste improvements and reduced Snapple's fifty flavors to a more manageable thirty-five, which included six new flavors and seasonal products such as a cider tea for Halloween. Packaging has also been improved; four-packs, twelve-packs, and plastic thirty-two-ounce and sixty-four-ounce family-size bottles were introduced. By tapping into its sales database, Quaker will automatically replenish Snapple inventories, just as it does with Gatorade.

In October 1995, Snapple distributors attended a two-day convention in San Diego, where they were entertained by comedian Bill Cosby. To fire up the troops, General Norman Schwarzkopf delivered a motivating speech on leadership. The distributors were further inspired when they heard the announcement that the company planned to place twenty thousand highly visible Snapple coolers in supermarkets, convenience stores, and schools—going head-on against Coca-Cola and Pepsi. They were also informed that in the spring a fresh new ad campaign would be launched.

Although it's too soon to grasp the final outcome, it appears that Quaker has developed a superior distribution plan—one that promises to succeed in a knock-'em-down, ever-changing marketplace. While reasons for acquisitions and mergers run the gamut, more and more deals such as the Quaker and Snapple deal are taking advantage of synergies that ensue from the blending of marketing strategies. This is especially true in fields that require investments in high technology or research and development. Note, for example, the mergers of pharmaceutical giants, such as Glaxo Holdings' 1995 acquisition of Wellcome, and the 1996 merger of Sandoz and Ciba-Geigy. In the rough-and-tumble world of drug marketing, huge savings can be realized by combining overlapping operations, and, in particular, distribution costs. Other savings result from combining research and development. For similar objectives, Chase Man-

hattan Corp. and Chemical Banking Corp. consolidated in 1995 to become the nation's biggest bank. In the past, many proposed empires were
viewed as too complicated or cumbersome to be managed effectively on
a large scale or over far distances. Yet now, everyone from producers of
goods to distributors of goods is forming networks coordinated by computers and communications technologies. Their joint service functions
include advertising, marketing, information, transportation, inventory
management, sales, and billing.

Neither of these mergers—one in pharmaceuticals and another in
banking—could have taken place had it not been for today's advanced
technology. In a technology-driven business environment, however,
multibillion-dollar corporations are enjoying marketing synergies created
via skillfully orchestrated mergers and acquisitions.

IMPLEMENTING A LOW-COST MARKETING STRATEGY

One of my favorite illustrations of a startup company implementing a
marketing strategy on a shoestring is TeleMagic, founded by Michael
McCafferty. The firm produced the world's number one sales software
program. In 1983, McCafferty had already logged some twenty years in
the computer industry, after experiencing some major ups and downs. "I
had just gone through a period of political infighting in a company I
founded that left me on the outside of my own company," he explains.
"Consequently, I had not worked for a year and was living on credit cards
in a state of depression. Then a personal bankruptcy took away my plastic."

McCafferty was living in a tiny studio apartment, sleeping on a used
mattress. "I was so broke, I didn't even have a car," he says. "So what
did I do? I decided to become a consultant, just like a million other broke,
unemployed guys. A wooden folding chair and a door laid across a couple
of two-drawer files became my office furniture." This is when he thought
about providing a software program to small business owners to help them

keep records of their inventories and billings to their customers. With no money to advertise, and not even a car so he could make calls on customers, McCafferty was in a bind. "I had to come up with an idea to drum up some business that didn't require a bundle of cash," he explains.

This is when McCafferty took out a yellowed, tattered piece of newsprint he had carried in his wallet for over a decade. "It was an article I had torn out of *The Wall Street Journal*, which gave advice to entrepreneurs. Based on my past business experience, I personalized some of the information, and several revisions later, I said, 'Boy, this is the kind of stuff I wish I had been taught a long time ago!' I christened it 'The Ten Commandments for Managing a Young, Growing Business.'"

McCafferty persuaded a local printer to produce two hundred copies of his list on a 17 × 11 cardboard poster, with "Michael McCafferty & Associates" and his phone number at the bottom. Next, he hired a friend's pretty girlfriend to help him. Marianne was a full-time waitress, her income based on tips, so she had no problem agreeing to work for McCafferty on a commission basis. He instructed her to stop in at every business in a certain large industrial park in Sorrento Valley, on the north side of San Diego. Her job: to give a poster to every business owner in the area.

Marianne asked, "What am I supposed to say to people?"

"Just one word," her employer instructed her. *"Computers."*

"Computers? But I don't know a thing about computers."

"That doesn't matter. Just say 'Computers?' as if you are asking a question. Have a question mark in your voice. Also don't forget to give 'em your beautiful smile."

McCafferty explains that he wanted to keep it simple, realizing that there would be a problem if she attempted an explanation.

"What do I do next?" she asked.

"Don't say a single word after you say 'Computers?' Wait for them to reply. If somebody says 'Yes,' point down to the bottom of the poster and say, 'Call this number if you have any questions,' and then turn around and leave."

"What if they say 'No'?" she asked.

"Point to my name and phone number and say, 'Call this number if you have any questions.' And again, don't say another word. Just leave."

Marianne passed out the two hundred posters in two days, and then McCafferty's phone began to ring. While some people simply called to get another poster, twenty-five genuine prospects responded. This got McCafferty's consulting business off the ground. Marianne earned $2,000 in commissions, and from that time on, the Ten Commandments posters generated enough repeat business and referrals that it was never necessary for McCafferty to make cold calls. This was the start of TeleMagic, which, in 1992, less than ten years later, was sold to Sage Group, a British company. McCafferty received $7 million in cash, plus 15 percent of the company's sales for the next twenty seven months—a potential worth of an additional $6 million.

CHOOSING THE RIGHT MARKETING STRATEGY

Earlier, I pointed out how a business decision to switch to merchandise that is priced wrong for the customer is apt to cause disastrous results. Obviously, a company that selects an incorrect marketing strategy is programming itself for hard times. For this reason, operating under the "If it ain't broke, don't fix it" theory, some management tends to shy away from changing a marketing strategy already in place. After all, the wrong move can indeed break the bank!

To avoid heading in a direction that could devastate your business, a good marketing strategy must anticipate how and why the customer will react to the strategy. This is accomplished by clearly understanding your customer's needs and problems, and consequently fulfilling a need that your competition is not addressing.

As discussed, Michelin Corp.'s decision to focus its marketing strategy on women buyers illustrates my point. When safety was discovered to be one of their biggest concerns, Michelin regeared its advertising campaign to appeal to safety-minded women. To achieve this, the company broke a longtime tire tradition that had dictated placing ads mainly in male-dominated TV programming or in newspaper advertising in the sports section. Instead, Michelin's advertising campaign focused on television commercials appealing to women. As you may recall, those commercials showed babies inside the Michelin tire, with a message stressing their security. Appealing to a mother's instinct to protect her offspring, they sold peace of mind.

Volvo is another company that devised a marketing strategy based on safety to appeal to women buyers. Its commercials demonstrated that its cars could withstand a crash better than those of its competition. Consequently, Volvo's core customer base is women with a family who are the decision-makers for the car. In this case, the family unit is not necessarily defined as a traditional husband-wife family, but instead, as one with children.

In addition to emphasizing safety, Michelin's and Volvo's marketing strategies share another important feature. In both cases, the company had to educate the consumer on what made its product unique. I accentuate this point because uniqueness by itself is not enough. If the consumer is not aware that a company has a unique position, it is the same as not having a unique position.

It's interesting that Michelin and Volvo have both focused their marketing strategies on women. Both companies are right on target, because women are increasingly becoming the chief decision-makers influencing the buying of big-ticket items. Our studies reveal that in the 1960s, women were the chief decision-making influence in 23 percent of major electronics and television purchases. In the 1970s, these numbers increased to 38 percent; 1980s—47 percent; 1990s—53 percent; and by the year 2000 the figure will reach 58 percent.

Likewise, in 1975, 19 percent of the time, women controlled the choice of which financial institution was selected to finance a home. In

1985, this figure rose to 31 percent, and in 1995, it hit 46 percent. In 1995, men controlled only 36 percent, leaving 28 percent where they both have equal say.

One of the most interesting research studies we ever did involved a brilliant marketing strategy for a Broadway musical. (While this show was a huge success—and a name you'd immediately recognize—I am unable to divulge its identity; my reasons for secrecy will be apparent when you read what follows.)

In the mid-1980s, a play producer and an investment group invited me to meet with them in New York City. One of the show's investors had heard me speak, and at his recommendation, the group offered me a challenge. They wanted to know if it was possible to do marketing research to increase the chances of success for their show.

I met with the group and asked them a series of questions. When I was informed there were seventy eight Broadway critics in the United States, and fewer than ten were truly influential, I decided to conduct a thorough study of those ten individuals plus as many of the sixty eight as we could reach, to solicit their views on Broadway plays. ARG's telephone interviewers told each critic: "The survey is being conducted for the purpose of understanding how plays are critiqued and reviewed."

Our telephone interviews included questions ranging from "What do you think are important ingredients of a successful Broadway musical versus a drama?" to "What factors cause some shows to bomb and therefore are things to avoid?"

The purpose of the survey was to discover what critics liked and disliked; with this knowledge, we made sure our show would appeal to these seventy eight individuals. Since a Broadway critic can make or break a show, our marketing strategy was to concentrate on obtaining favorable reviews.

Based on what the critics told us, three major adjustments were made in the show: (1) A different female lead was signed. (2) Four songs were scratched from the show. (3) The show was shortened by twenty minutes based upon their opinion of the ideal length.

This marketing strategy worked extremely well. The show received rave reviews and did extraordinarily well on the road. It was, in fact, one of the most profitable Broadway hits in the past two decades!

THE COMMITMENT

Once a marketing strategy is in place, you must get your organization committed to making it work.

Of course, a majority of CEOs simply declare to their people, "This is what we are going to do." This approach usually works when a strong leader communicates his game plan and everyone knows he is determined to make it work. A story about Abraham Lincoln and his seven Cabinet members comes to mind. "Each of you has an equal vote," the president said to the men, "which is a combined total of seven votes. You should remember, however, that I have eight votes."

Lincoln was right. But I've seen many good game plans fail because management was unable to reach a consensus within, and consequently, nothing got done.

The commitment must start at the top. A strong leader must demonstrate to his people that he has the will to go forward. With this kind of leadership, everyone in the organization can be expected to rally around him. Of course, there may be dissenters—and they should be listened to. Perhaps the plan isn't doable after all; honest debate is healthy. But once a commitment is made, everyone should be expected to support it. Doable marketing strategies that fail generally do so because they lack strong support. Having 80 or 85 percent support within the organization is simply not enough. Today, a 100 percent effort is required for successful implementation.

Great marketing strategies are never easy, and the most innovative ones involve the most risk. I once told a client, "If it were easy, you could hire some high school students part-time to do it."

The game plan implemented must cater to the buyer of your product. In this respect, *it must be user-friendly* to the customer—customer-friendly.

To achieve this is hard work. No matter how many hardships are placed upon the organization, your new system must be easy for the customer. Your marketing strategy should never be built around what's convenient for you. If it's easy for you, it's also easy for your competition.

For instance, ARG has counseled several of our retail clients to implement a thirty-day complete satisfaction guarantee. Some of them reacted to this advice by telling us about all the risks and difficulties their stores would encounter in implementing this policy. "It may not be easy for your operation to do," I told them, "but because this is what your customers consider most important, it will win customers for you."

Along the same line, Bill Rowland, founder and CEO of American Appliance, which has twenty-seven electronics and appliance stores in the greater Philadelphia area, wanted to know what could be done to generate additional market share.

"I recommend offering next-day delivery to your customers," I told him. "And furthermore, back up what you say. Tell your customers, 'If we don't deliver it by tomorrow, it's free!' "

Bill looked at me with raised eyebrows. I could tell he was thinking that it's possible for any delivery to be late.

I told him, "If you really want to do what your customer wants, you'll figure a way to do it at his convenience, not what may be comfortable for your people."

"What if the weather is horrendous, or a truck breaks down?" he questioned.

"The more exceptions you place upon your guarantee," I explained, "the more watered-down it is, and the weaker it becomes."

"Well, it's going to require us to make some changes," Bill replied.

"It's the right thing for your company to do, Bill," I assured him. "Sure, your organization will have to stretch itself. But that's okay. You'll have to figure out what changes are required to guarantee next-day delivery, and then put in a lot of work and effort to carry it out. But since this is what your customers want, there really isn't any other choice, is there?"

After Rowland reviewed what our study had shown, he recognized how important it was to offer next-day delivery. In particular, it provided an edge against Sears, an American Appliance competitor that did not offer next-day delivery.

At first, Rowland encountered resistance from his people, who didn't think guaranteeing next-day delivery was possible. "We'll be forced to give away too much free merchandise," they warned.

With some major effort, however, American Appliance was able to incorporate systems to make next-day delivery so automatic that the company decided to go one step further. "Our customers were so pleased with next-day delivery," Rowland explained, "that we figured if we could deliver merchandise the next day, why couldn't we push ourselves to guarantee delivery on the *same day*? And once we proved that if we really stretched ourselves, there was no limit to what we were capable of doing for our customer, we decided to also do installation on delivery. Now we even give a three-hour time window, which means we'll pinpoint when our delivery truck will arrive at the customer's home within a three-hour period. To make it even more convenient, we telephone the customer at his work twenty minutes before delivery, to say we're on our way. This is a real time-saver, because it allows the customer to meet us at the house, while reducing the time he or she has to spend away from the job."

Of course, not every merchant can offer same-day delivery as American Appliance does. In the beginning, even Rowland was unsure his company could do it. And did it put a strain on Rowland's organization? Certainly. But, as I told him, when a marketing strategy is based on fulfilling the customer's needs, it doesn't matter if the organization likes it or not—you must do it.

Naturally, it took a commitment. And it required a major risk. Had the company been unable to implement its marketing strategy, ill will could have resulted when the company failed to live up to its promise. Likewise, American Appliance could have ended up giving away a lot of free washing machines and refrigerators.

THE "YES BUTS" WILL KILL YOU

Implementing a new marketing strategy, as I previously mentioned, requires that a consensus be reached. It is certain that pressure will be applied from the outside by the competition; what isn't needed is additional resistance from within.

To quote the comic strip character Pogo, "I have seen the enemy and he is us." Too often, organizations are riddled with the "Yes Buts." These are a result of doubting Thomases who say, "It's a great strategy, and we should do it, but . . ." With every aggressive marketing strategy, an element of risk exists, which compels people from different areas of the organization to voice reasons why a plan—any plan—won't work. Often these rebuttals come from the financial side of a corporation. The bean counters name all the reasons why the operating budget won't accommodate the plan. Or the in-house attorneys cite possible legal repercussions. Their oft-heard comments range from "It could invite product liability" to "It might be interpreted as a false claim." Other "special interest" departments include people from warehousing and shipping who may express the opinion that the plan is not logistically sound. Operations people will say, "It is great in theory, but I doubt that our stores could handle the volume." Merchandising people, advertising people— the list goes on and on. With every manager having a different perspective, consensus is no easy matter.

It takes courage for a CEO to move forward with a marketing strategy after one or more department managers warn of grave consequences. Since each of these highly paid executives is the most informed individual in that area of expertise, a wise CEO must carefully listen to all opinions. But if 100 percent consensus is always required, few new ideas will ever be implemented.

Then too, some marketing strategies must be put into place swiftly to react to certain trends with short-term windows. Sometimes an opportunity requires a quick response, such as implementation of a plan within a three-to-four-week period. Conflicting opinions from obstructionist department heads can mean some organizations are unable to execute a swift response. And while some others do react more quickly, one or more of their special interest groups may fail to buy into the program; consequently, the marketing strategy is never fully implemented.

What adds to the difficulty of the decision-making process is that the "Yes But" people are not necessarily Milquetoast stereotypes incapable of decision-making. On the contrary, they are often astute managers whose opinions are respected throughout the organization. So strong conviction is required for a business leader to push forward with a marketing strategy. It requires making change and taking risk—occasionally against the judgment of stalwarts of the company.

For years, the Michigan-based F&M Drugstore was hailed as one of the first successful discount super drugstore chains. The company's strength evolved around its ability to make exceptional deals and pass the savings along to its customers. You might walk into an F&M store, for example, and find the lowest price on a brand-name toothpaste, although it might come in an odd size. The company had established a reputation for being the lowest-price store in its marketplace.

When Wal-Mart began opening stores in the same markets, for the first time, F&M customers were given a choice to shop at another extremely well-priced store; undoubtedly, this tarnished F&M's low-price identity. As more Wal-Mart stores came into its market, F&M scrutinized each of its existing stores, and its management started to look at different markets and began to consider an array of marketing strategies. But no matter how many options the company explored, its management was unable to reach a consensus on what action to take. "This location doesn't have the traffic to support an F&M store," someone would object. "Let's expand our merchandise lineup and carry different categories," another would interject. Each time a marketing strategy was presented, someone would voice a rebuttal. As a result, this once-successful company is no longer in business.

There are three ways the Yes Buts will kill a business: (1) Management is unable to reach a consensus, so the company is unable to respond and therefore remains stagnant. (2) Management may reach a consensus, but is unable to react quickly. (3) Management reacts quickly to everything, but is unable to develop an overall strategy. When this happens, the tyranny of the urgent replaces the kingship of the important. In the case of the F&M Drugstore chain, its management never addressed the issue of its identity in the face of competition. It never answered the question "Now that we have intruders in our marketplace, what should F&M's stance be?"

THE BUREAUCRATIC SHUFFLE

Closely related to the Yes Buts is what I refer to as the bureaucratic shuffle. While it exists mainly in large organizations, small organizations are not immune. Many think bureaucracy is confined to giant corporations with layers upon layers of vice presidents. While often a great marketing strategy is thwarted by a collective group of people, sometimes it takes just one person to kick it off target. For instance, a quagmire of bureaucracy could thrive in a tiny company, perhaps helped along by a single individual in charge of warehousing and delivery.

In general, however, bureaucracy is associated with big firms. Small, independently operated businesses are usually headed by one or two owners who make all the decisions. In this respect, these enterprises are normally focused, and in such an environment, little politicking goes on.

However, large organizations may have employees who help justify their existence by creating bureaucracy, which, in turn, spawns politics. In an attempt to prove their worth to the company, these people either nitpick other people's marketing strategies to death or offer to "upgrade" any program or idea that passes their desks. While some of their suggestions may represent slight improvements, with everybody putting in his or her two cents' worth, implementation can be delayed, even to the point where the plan gets shelved!

The bureaucratic shuffle is alive and well in those organizations that promote people for no reason other than longevity. According to the Peter Principle, such promotions elevate managers to their level of incompetence. For instance, someone who performed superbly as an executive secretary will not necessarily be as effective when promoted to office manager. An individual like this could become a bottleneck, creating problems rather than expediting solutions. Likewise, in some corporations, a manager who has risen to an executive suite position over his coworkers' heads may find he doesn't feel comfortable making high-level decisions. As a consequence, someone in that spot could delay or even withhold consent for new ideas.

Within bureaucracy-ridden companies of all sizes, people resist change simply because it doesn't fit their personal agenda. Some individuals are so narrowly focused on their own areas within the organization that they are blinded by tunnel vision. In a case quite different from that of American Appliance, a warehouse manager for another retailer struggles with the physical inventory problems he imagines would result if his company initiated a same-day-delivery guarantee. While the added value would be well received by the store's customers and stimulate new sales, the warehouse manager might refuse to support a new procedure simply because it threatens to make his life more difficult.

In other cases, resistance is based on personal likes and dislikes, as well as customs or habits. For instance, a while ago, I advised a particular client that his store should be open over the long Memorial Day weekend, which, in the retailing industry, is typically a great time of year to run a sales promotion. After he surveyed his employees' opinions, he told me, "Britt, here in Wisconsin, everybody goes fishing over Memorial Day weekend. My salespeople have assured me it's no use being open that weekend, because we'd just have an empty store."

"*Everybody* goes fishing?" I asked.

"Yeah, in this town, everybody fishes that particular weekend," he replied.

"Well, it may be that your salespeople want to go fishing Memorial Day weekend," I answered. "But, for the record, I happen to know this particular weekend is one of the best of the entire year for your competition."

In a 1996 study on consumer shopping habits exhibited during three-day holiday weekends, we learned the following:

1. Consumers are shopping at a 60 percent higher rate. This means if a thousand customers normally came through a store's front door on a normal Saturday and Sunday, there'd be sixteen hundred during a three-day holiday weekend.

2. The number one reason why an increase occurs is that there is more opportunity for both spouses to shop together.

3. There is a trend toward people's taking shorter trips during three-day-weekend holidays. We also found that when trips are taken on three-day weekends, people often take an extra day off work. Money saved by a shorter trip or an eliminated trip is often put into a day of shopping during their vacation.

4. People are thinking: "A vacation lasts only a few days, but a new purchase or a home improvement lasts a lifetime." These consumers are staying home and putting their money into a new computer, a remodeling job, and so on.

Speaking of weekend shopping, another study showed that when a retail store opens at 8:00 or 10:00 on Sunday morning rather than noon or 1:00, its Sunday sales revenue increases by a whopping 40 percent. This trend toward earlier Sunday hours evolved in the last few years, when many retailers began to notice that their Sunday-afternoon sales were equal to their all-day Saturday sales. So, they reasoned, if they could do in five hours the volume that normally was done in eight hours, they could do even more business by being open longer hours on Sundays.

With weekends being such important days for retailers, we conducted still another study to find out what happens when a store plans a big event such as a reduced-inventory sale and then something happens to make customers stay home. This "something" could range from a bad ice storm to the seventh game of the World Series. We found that only 15 percent of those consumer dollars that would have been spent are, in fact, spent on the product that the consumer had targeted. The reason is that today's consumer has many priorities, and if his or her money isn't spent today to purchase a particular item, several other items will pop up that are also important priorities. Hence, the consumer who doesn't get around to buying an item now may postpone buying it altogether.

RAISING THE BAR

One of the major milestones in sports was the breaking of the four-minute-mile barrier. Many runners and even physicians believed it was actually physically impossible to run that fast. Even though a few of the fastest milers in the world began to approach this incredible time during the early 1950s, it was still considered impossible.

Finally, in 1954, Great Britain's Roger Bannister broke the four-minute mile. Even more amazing was what happened only three months later. In Vancouver, Bannister was pitted against John Landy in what was billed as the mile race of the century. Incredibly, Bannister clocked in at 3:58.8 minutes—and Landy at 3:59.6 minutes! Once the barrier had been broken, other runners raised their expectations, and soon the running of a four-minute mile became almost ho-hum. At present, the world record for the mile is down to 3:46.32.

I believe the single greatest challenge in today's competitive market-place is for companies to continue to raise the bar so everybody has a chance to jump higher and higher. Like those mile runners and the four-minute barrier, it's just a matter of raising one's sights. Great plans are never easy, but with hard work, they are attainable and produce great return.

After hearing me speak at the 1994 national convention of the Associated Volume Buyers, a man named Jon Holzgrafe invited me to visit his store. In 1978, he founded Jon's Home Center in Quincy, Illinois, and he had operated the successful appliance and electronics store ever since.

When I arrived in Quincy, one of the first things I noticed about his 10,000-square-foot store was its appearance. Jon's Home Center was operating in the 1990s out of a 1970s-looking store. It looked like a run-down Quonset hut—which, actually, it was. "You've either got to build a new facade on the store and expand it, or move into a new location," I told him.

Jon had been considering a new store before we met, and I suppose one reason he was interested in talking to me was that he wanted me to confirm such a move. After conducting a research study in which we interviewed not only his customers but other consumers in the area, we verified what I had suspected when I first laid eyes on his store. While Jon's own customers never told him face to face that the faithful old store's appearance was a turn-off—remember, customers aren't confrontational with business owners—our interviews confirmed that his customers indeed viewed the store as unattractive. When we analyzed comments from the people in the area who *didn't* shop at his store, they expressed an even stronger dislike of its appearance.

Our study also revealed that the people in the marketplace most likely to shop his store were in the fifty-plus age group. This told us that in the short run, younger people would shop his store only as long as there was no alternative in the marketplace. "A serious problem with your present store, Jon," I said, "is that every time you read seven names in the obituary column, five of them are your customers!" He didn't realize it, but he had a dying business.

Quincy, which has a population of forty thousand, is situated in the tristate area where Illinois, Missouri, and Iowa meet. For good reason, Jon was interested in knowing whether a larger store would draw customers from across the river on the Missouri side. I confirmed a superstore would bring in people from the larger driving radius around the area. "Yes, you'll attract new customers from Hannibal and Carthage, Missouri," I assured him. "And since younger people are even more interested in selection, a larger store will help you capture a bigger share of the under-fifty age group."

At that time he had only a 9 percent market share of the area's washer and dryer business. Jon's eyes lit up when I told him, "A larger store offering greater selection can increase your market share to as much as 30 percent."

Since his existing store was mortgage-free and a new location would require considerable debt, building a new store with a brand-new mortgage was a big step for Jon Holzgrafe at age forty-five. But Jon was convinced there was greater risk in staying at his run-down location. How well he understood that a store with a poor appearance limited his growth. In fact—even mortgage-free—in the long run, it could eventually put him out of business.

"Britt, your study convinced me to build the new store," Jon told me later. "Also, having the in-depth research in hand was influential in getting my local banker to make the loan.

"My six commissioned salespeople were also behind the move," Jon added. "In addition to having a much nicer working environment, they understood that a higher-volume store would mean better income for them. And when your research showed their commissions would increase anywhere from 10 to 20 percent the first year, you were right on target."

In November 1994, just eighteen months after I met Jon, his new 28,000-square-foot store opened its doors. As forecast, it is drawing customers from the tristate area, and its sales volume has since reached the $6 million mark—double the volume of his former store.

Jon Holzgrafe is an excellent example of an entrepreneur who took a bold step forward, daring to raise the bar.

THE OTHER GUY CAN THINK TOO

Lest you forget, you are in a highly competitive marketplace. Once your marketing strategy is in gear, you'd better face up to the fact that *the other guy can think too!* When your plan kicks in, the competition is going to react, one way or another. You can be sure a competitor won't lie down and play dead. He will react. And believe me, he's going to try to retaliate. No competitor worthy of the name is going to stand still while you take away his customers.

I have seen many marketing strategies fail because while the initial plan was good, nothing effective was done afterward in response to the competition's reaction. Often what you do in the beginning puts you just slightly in front of your competition—so you do have a running head start. But that's all it is, only a small amount of lead time, while your competition is busily planning a countermove. It is like a game of chess in which each player makes countermoves against the moves of his opponent. You must continually modify your plan, improving it in response to your competition's countermoves.

Above all, don't abandon your marketing strategy when your competition comes out with an improvement on it (which is inevitable). To do so would place you in a defensive position—an undesirable situation. Instead, you must continually regroup and move forward with even more improvements. In anticipation of your competition's reactions, you must have prepared a contingency plan, perhaps several—Plans B, C, D, and so on.

An underlying theme of this book is the necessity to embrace constant change. This means that when your competition responds to your strategy, you must be ready to implement your contingency plan immediately. Sometimes, even before Plan A is implemented, you must be planning ahead to introduce Plan B and Plan C, always staying a few steps ahead of the competition. In the most competitive industries, this often involves having three sixty-day plans, all to be implemented within a period of six months! Remember what Harry Truman said: "If you can't stand the heat, get out of the kitchen." One thing is for certain—you can never be satisfied with the status quo. If you stand still, you'll be passed by— maybe even run over.

CONSUMER MIND READER #3

Top Advertising Turnoffs

In a survey we conducted for this book to determine what is most offensive to Americans about the printed advertising they read and the television commercials they watch, we came up with the following seven serious/major objections:

1. The ad contains vulgar language.

2. The fine print is too small to read.

3. The ad sells "sex" instead of product.

4. No prices are shown.

5. Ad presentation is jumbled and hard to understand.

6. Discounts are not believable (70 percent range and up).

7. The ad does not include a customer satisfaction guarantee.

At the top of the list was advertising that contains vulgar language. While foul words have not yet been expressed in mainstream advertising, they are already starting to creep into advertising directed at Generation X, appearing on some cable channels. "Vulgar language" is more than just dirty words; it also includes obscene body language and movements that communicate vulgar activity. Many people associate advertising that features vulgarity with a low-class company. Furthermore, indecency insults them. If, in the future, lewd advertising becomes even more of a trend, you are advised *never* to use it.

Ads with fine print too small to read is the second top advertising turnoff. Simply put, when consumers read these ads, they think the advertiser is hiding something. Consumers believe that such a company would take advantage of them if it could.

Consumers object to ads that sell sex instead of the product. While this might not be as objectionable to Americans under thirty-five, it definitely is offensive to the older consumer. With the over-forty audience, sex-related advertising makes viewers feel a company is trying to direct their attention to sexy images and away from the actual product. "Using overt sex is the only way you think you can get my attention," they claim. This is interpreted as treating them with a lack of respect. Many advertisers can subtly use sex in their advertising very successfully, but "taste" can be a fine line.

When no prices are shown in an ad, consumers say, "What's the retailer hiding? Are they ashamed of their prices? Are their prices so high that they don't want me to be able to compare them to another company's?"

When a television commercial has many cuts and multiple messages, it is often described as jumbled or difficult to understand, and the viewer becomes confused.

Five years ago, in a similar study, offering discounts at 70 percent off was listed as the number three turnoff. However, while it is still questionable to many Americans, it has dropped down to number six on the list. It's not considered as incredible today because many retailers such as major department stores are marking merchandise at 50 percent off, and even offering another 10 or 20 percent off those prices. Still, consumers believe these discounts are not true values; they believe retailers have inflated the regular prices of their merchandise in order to give such large discounts. Hence, these "great" savings don't seem credible.

Finally, today's consumers want a retailer to take care of them. Our studies confirm that a thirty-day customer-satisfaction guarantee is the number one way consumers measure whether a store is reputable. Today, consumers say value is no longer defined only as price and quality. Value is now defined as price and quality *plus* a store's reputation.

CHAPTER FOUR

THE NUMBERS BUSINESS *IS* A PEOPLE BUSINESS

In every business, numbers must be scrutinized. That's because numbers tell us a great deal. They tell us our day's sales, as well as what our profits are. Whether we stay in business in the future is determined by the sum of these digits. Success is measured by numbers.

In my field, everything I do embraces numbers. Without the numbers in my business, there would be no black and white; everything would fall into a gray area. Without the numbers, instead of guiding my clients, my services would engender confusion and doubt. The numbers eliminate ambiguity.

As a survey research firm, we collect data on people's attitudes and use these numbers to create a composite of a specific marketplace. In this respect, *the numbers business is a people business!* What it boils down to is this: By understanding what the numbers say, we can not only identify, but really *get to know* the consumer. Bear in mind that while research does not highlight an individual customer, it does provide a valuable profile of customers in general.

While customer profiles are based on numbers, each customer is a unique individual who must never be treated as a number. A customer is a being with emotions. A customer has needs. A customer is a person with whom you must develop a relationship. *Numbers have no emotions, no needs, and no relationships.* This chapter helps you understand what the numbers tell about customers—yours and your competition's.

ONE CUSTOMER AT A TIME

Zeroing in too closely on the numbers can result in losing sight of the customer. And while a good marketing strategy is based on a composite of customers, *nobody ever sold anything to a composite.*

Too often, business executives get so caught up in their charts and graphs they stop paying attention to individual customers. I'm reminded of the old riddle "How do you eat an elephant?" The answer is *one bite at a time.* Like the riddle, a marketing strategy must focus on a long-term game plan to capture market share, but never lose sight of the fact that market share is captured *one customer at a time.*

When a top sales manager rallies his troops to meet and break their quotas, he cautions them to concentrate on one sale at a time. How well he knows that quotas are never achieved in one fell swoop. And sales-people who think only about making their sales quota rarely excel. A salesperson with dollar signs in his eyes is a real turnoff to prospects. A salesperson anxious to finish one sales presentation and rush on to the next fails to generate confidence. His lack of conviction comes through loud and clear.

It reminds me of a time when I was sitting in a restaurant with a life insurance agent. While he gave a professional presentation, I wasn't con-vinced that he was truly interested in my welfare. The agent's gaze drifted toward the door each time a successful-looking businessperson entered the room. His eyes even followed the attractive waitress as she walked by our table. I thought to myself, "Obviously, I'm not his number one concern." He lost the sale.

SUCCESS IS 95 PERCENT UNDERSTANDING PEOPLE AND 5 PERCENT PRODUCT KNOWLEDGE

Another life insurance agent, a top producer in his field, once told me, "Understanding people is far more important to my business than how much I know about my product." This highly proficient Chartered Life Underwriter knew the life insurance field, but that's not what made him do so well.

"The universities and insurance company home offices are full of experts who know much more about what I sell than I do," said this successful man. "But I don't have to know all they know. I just want to know more and more about the people I deal with."

In the early 1980s, I was asked to do a study for Seabrook Island, a large upscale resort development just south of Charleston, South Carolina. This planned community had condominiums and houses priced from $100,000 and up—some in excess of $1 million. These beautiful residential properties were built along the marshes, around the golf course, and on the oceanfront.

I was called in because a group of condominiums called Marsh Cove weren't selling. "Marsh Cove was developed outside of the security gate," a marketing vice president informed me. "That's the reason we can't sell these properties. So we want you to find out how we can convince prospective buyers that security will not be a problem."

After visiting the area, I realized Marsh Cove was in such a remote area that it wasn't possible to move the main security gate to surround it. (Later, however, a mini-gate was installed so that only residents with a security card could be admitted into Marsh Cove.)

After conducting a poll of both the people who purchased property in Marsh Cove and scores of prospects who had been shown these properties but did not buy, I met with my client to present my findings.

At the meeting, I told the group of executives around the conference table that, contrary to their assumption, the security gate was not the biggest factor in the poor sales. "Our study indicates that a person considering resort property in this price range is planning a casual lifestyle that includes sprawling out in the living room," I explained. "These condos aren't selling simply because the living rooms are too small."

The senior executive at the meeting disbelieved my report. "You completely missed the boat, Beemer," he told me. "All our other properties are selling well, and these should too. We already told you that the big difference in these properties is that they are outside the main security gate."

"That's not what the people we polled told us," I replied.

"No way!" he exclaimed. "I'll call the same people you interviewed, and I promise you, they will verify to me the security gate is the main issue."

"You can't call the same people, because our survey was confidential," I pointed out. "It wouldn't be ethical."

"You're off base," he said. "I'd stake my reputation on it. Let me talk to them and I'll prove it."

I remained calm. "Here's a list of people we tried to contact, but didn't reach," I answered. "If you're going to call, I recommend you say you're calling from our firm." I handed him the list of names, as well as a list of questions to ask.

With that, he walked out, went into his office, and closed the door. A half hour later, he came back, his head hanging low. "Beemer's right," he said.

"I reached three people. I told them, 'We're doing a survey of people who visited Seabrook Island. I noticed you looked at the Marsh Cove property, and I wanted to ask you the number one reason why you didn't buy.' "

He read each of their comments he had penciled on the file cards:

" 'Living room too small.'

" 'Living room too small.'

" 'Living room too small.' "

The above example is clearly a matter of not understanding what the customer wanted. Losing sight of the customer's needs can frequently happen, when the pressure is on to generate sales, or, as with Marsh Cove, when large numbers of sales must be made to compensate for hard times. Situations of this nature can leave management thinking more about solving problems at home rather than serving the customer's needs.

In the above story, the Marsh Cove senior manager could have called the same people we surveyed, and certainly many companies that can't afford to hire a marketing research firm do conduct their own surveys. If you choose to go that route, here are two tips:

First, be sure to put a lot of thought into the questions you ask; the quality of the answers will depend on it. And ask questions that are not confrontational. In analyzing consumers, our research reveals that 88 percent will avoid confrontation, voicing defiance only when forced to. What's more, 44 percent of consumers *always* avoid confrontation. I mention this because if you ask questions that confront them, they'll tell you only what they think you want to hear.

Second, don't identify yourself as being from the sales or marketing department. It's preferable to say "research department," or better yet, say you're with an outside firm. This way, people will be more willing to open up and be honest with you. In order to accomplish both of these recommendations, depending on your budget, you may want to hire a research firm to make up the questions, and then ask it for permission to use its name when your people make the actual calls.

All too often, business owners and top management are either so close to or so far away from their customers that while they *think* they understand the consumer, they are, in fact, clueless. When management makes marketing decisions despite the fact that no new information is coming in, watch out!

THE PEOPLE DIFFERENCE

Often management attempts to emulate its competition without even knowing the reason for the other guy's prosperity. A case in point involves Southwest Airlines and the spectacular success it enjoyed in recent years compared to the rest of the industry. While the airline business as a whole lost $12 billion between 1989 and 1993, Southwest alone showed a consistent profit. No wonder the competition tried to emulate the more obvious traits of the Dallas-based firm by cutting fares and offering no-frills service.

On the surface, the competitors' reactions seemed logical. After all, Southwest's planes were filled with customers while their seats remained empty. It seemed obvious that travelers preferred lower fares even if it meant sacrificing such niceties as assigned seats and meal service. Coping with what they believed was Southwest's marketing strategy, several Southwest competitors began playing follow-the-leader. In just a matter of time, they figured, the bargain fares would attract customers, and with reduced overhead, they'd soon be turning a nice profit.

But it was not to be. They failed to realize that the success of Southwest is not just about low prices. It's about people. Several low-priced airlines have failed to survive—most notably, People's Express. Cheapness alone does not make a successful airline. Only Southwest knew how to make travel cheap *and enjoyable*. That's what makes it a great airline.

The real secret of Southwest's success is its people—something the copycats failed to take into account. In order to offer low fares, the competing carriers downsized not only administrative staff, but also support people in the field. After this critical mistake, it wasn't long before passengers felt the lack of customer contact. And the personnel reductions diminished the loyalty of those employees remaining on the payroll. Surviving employees had witnessed the dismissal of large numbers of fellow workers, which negatively impacted their perception of their own longevity. If their employer had no loyalty to those employees who got the boot, they figured, their own jobs were in jeopardy. Employers who are not loyal to their employees receive no loyalty in return.

When workers feel this way, it is no secret. Customers can sense the morale level at a company, whether high or low. And at Southwest, employee morale is high. *This is the people difference!*

The lesson learned by those airlines that tried to emulate Southwest's success is obvious: Price-cutting isn't what makes Southwest work—it's the employees' conviction that they work for a wonderful organization. The company treats its people with respect, and they return that respect. In my opinion, it's basic human nature: Treat people well and they will treat you well. Evidently, in the world of large corporations, some managers get so caught up in numbers, products, and machinery that they fail to realize people are the most important factor in the success equation.

When you board a Southwest airplane, you notice the employees are enthusiastic and cheerful. Their enjoyment of their work makes Southwest a fun airline to fly. You feel a warm feeling when you fly Southwest. The friendly atmosphere these employees create cannot be found in a company manual. I don't believe it can be taught in a training course. It's an intangible quality that is not a result of low prices or no frills. Clearly, the Southwest management team has earned the respect of its people. This is what differentiates Southwest from its competition.

THE REFLECTION

There's an old saying in the retail business: "If the boss screams at a store manager, how many customers will feel it?"

Temperament has a snowball effect. If the store manager takes out his frustration on his employees, they transfer it to customers. But it also works in reverse. A manager can have a strong positive influence on a workforce. Certainly a manager who has pride in his company will hand down that pride to his people. And a manager who treats his employees fairly can expect a fair day's work from them.

Much of this reflection starts at the top of an organization. Personality and temperament permeate from top to bottom, from the CEO's office to department after department. If the CEO is a shouter and screamer, senior managers will shout and scream at subordinates, and shouting and screaming will be heard all the way down to the very lowest person on the totem pole. In contrast, CEOs who are warm and sensitive generate a caring feeling emulated by other company employees.

I am constantly meeting with top CEOs and business owners of both large and small companies, and invariably the head honcho's personality sets the mood for the entire company. A meeting with a dry, formal CEO practically guarantees that when I confer with his subordinates, an obvious lack of humor and informality will be present. Likewise, when the top dog is affable, a friendly atmosphere is manifested throughout the company.

Integrity also starts at the top. When a highly principled CEO sets the pace for his people, a sense of pride prevails. People feel good about themselves when they think highly of the company they work for.

You don't have to head a big company to instill these qualities in your staff. On the contrary, in a smaller company, the leader is more likely to have one-to-one relationships in which he or she serves as a strong role model.

Although the investment firm Bear Stearns is by no means a small company, its CEO, Alan "Ace" Greenberg, is one business leader who works closely with his "fellow" workers. Not one to believe in ivory towers, Greenberg spends most of his workday not in his private office but at his desk on the trading floor, working side by side with the firm's 375-plus traders. He blends in well with the other traders—if you didn't already know he was CEO, it's unlikely that you'd single him out from the other men and women. "I love being on the floor doing the same things my associates are doing," he says. "I am extremely accessible, and they know that. Anyone who wants to see me for whatever reason doesn't have to go through a secretary, or for that matter even knock on a door. Everybody here can just walk up and talk to me. It doesn't bother me at all. In fact, I love it."

Greenberg's form of open communication works well because Bear Stearns people feel comfortable approaching a boss whom they perceive as personable and caring. His dry sense of humor puts subordinates at ease. Through his famous inner office memos, Greenberg circulated one of his favorite quotes: "A man will do well in commerce as long as he does not believe that his own body odor is perfume." This he sent out to managers at a time when profits were at a record high, adding, "We must not get cocky or overconfident."

On the subject of keeping expenses down, another memo read: "I have just informed the purchasing department that they should no longer purchase paper clips. All of us receive documents every day with paper clips on them. If we save these paper clips, we will not only have enough for our own use, but we will in a short time be awash in the little critters." Several days later, a second memo was dispatched: "The response to the memo on paper clips has been overwhelming. Bear Stearns will no longer purchase rubber bands."

While Ace Greenberg has a reputation for being frugal and running one of the tightest ships on Wall Street, this can be misleading. His philanthropy is equally legendary. *New York* magazine has described Greenberg as "the biggest giver on the Street." For nearly two decades, under his leadership, all Bear Stearns senior managing directors—about 150—have been required to give 4 percent of their total annual compensation to charity. "We don't care what charity they give it to, what we think is important is that they give. We think it sets a tone for the whole firm." Most of the managers exceed this quota, and Greenberg leads by example. In addition to personally giving away millions of dollars, he gives a lot of his time. Known as one of the best fund-raisers in New York City, he says, "What charitable organizations need is people who will call for money. I don't want to be on the boards or committees; I'm interested only in fund-raising."

Since people crave a leader who is available to them, has integrity, and is caring, no wonder people rally around Ace Greenberg. He epitomizes the kind of leadership that makes his associates feel good about themselves, and, in turn, proud to be associated with Bear Stearns.

A SALESPERSON'S INFLUENCE

Just as a CEO's strength is reflected throughout the organization, a company salesperson greatly influences the customer. We've conducted research studies on just how much the American consumer relies on a salesperson for guidance in making a purchase, and the strength of a salesperson's influence is surprising. We measured that influence, by which I mean the ability of the salesperson to sway the shopper to buy one brand over another or a particular model over another.

While the amount of influence varies from industry to industry, it remains substantial overall. Here is what we discovered through our studies:

- The salesperson influences the customer's buying decision in 80 percent of all furniture purchases.

- When buying a mattress and box springs, the salesperson's influence is 60 percent.

- When buying area rugs, a salesperson's influence is 75 percent.

- When buying electronic products, it is 60 percent.

- When buying audio products, it is 80 percent; with car audio sales, it runs 90 percent.

- In the travel industry, a travel agent sways 40 percent of all customers on their choice of which airline to travel.

Since your salespeople have such a strong influence on your customers, it makes good sense to recruit and train a superior sales force. In big-ticket retail industries, research studies estimate that it costs $18,000 to train each salesperson. Obviously, at this figure, high turnover of personnel is very costly. One way to keep them is by providing them with a pleasant environment—including a well-lighted, well-decorated workplace, clean restrooms, healthy and well-prepared food in the cafeteria, and so on. How does this add to a healthy bottom line? Research shows that customers sense when employees are happy and want to be at their jobs—and the customer's perception of the morale of the employees directly influences buying decisions.

KNOWING YOUR COMPETITION'S CUSTOMER

Most top managers are long removed from their customers. What they think they know is based on personal experience early in their careers, when they were in daily contact with customers—days now long gone. Even the rare manager who continues to have direct contact with the customer may be misled. As we have seen, most customers, wishing to avoid confrontation, are reluctant to express feelings, especially adverse ones.

Even more misled are top managers who claim they know *all* the customers in their marketplace—including their *competitor's* customers! They assume the people who don't buy their products or shop their stores are no different from their own customers. False assumption! If they were identical, they would be their customers. Plainly, differences exist.

Certainly, the better you know your marketplace—your customers as well as your noncustomers—the more effectively you can position yourself to improve shopper share and closing rates as well as to impact your competitors' market-share position.

How vital is it to understand competitors' customers? I advise clients that between the two, it's more important to know theirs than yours! For this reason, when a client hands me a list of his customers and says, "Call these people," I generally discourage such a study. Such a project would present limited data, telling the client only what his customers thought during a limited window of time about a particular product category.

In today's business world, there is an alarming turnover of people. For this reason, it's likely that a want ad in the employment section of the newspaper will be read by one of your competitor's ex-employees who is looking for a job. Such an applicant provides an often overlooked opportunity to ask all sorts of questions about the former employer. It's highly probable that these job interviewees will volunteer valuable information. It is not unusual to find that over the years, an enduring friendship has formed between a sales rep and his customers. Those customers may feel their loyalty is to the salesperson rather than to his former company. Should this be the case, a newly hired salesperson may bring several accounts to a future employer. You might go a step further—and take the interviewee to lunch, in an away-from-the-office setting where he or she can relax and talk freely. Preparing a list of questions in advance can maximize this opportunity to ask what you *really* want to learn about your competitor.

One time you can learn a great deal from a customer is during a sales presentation. Good salespeople know to ask a lot of questions about the customer's needs. And when the time comes to ask for the order, they're not shy about it.

Still another way to reach your competition's customers is to hire a list broker who can create a list of your noncustomers. There are several quality database lists available that can be rented for a relatively small fee. After a list is created, a database marketing firm can do an analysis of the list to determine what your competitors' strengths and weaknesses are within specific customer groupings. For manufacturers and distributors, these groupings can be broken down by industry, geographical area, credit rating, size of company, and so on. This data can show you a very complete profile of your noncustomers.

YOUR INTERNAL CUSTOMERS

It has traditionally been the salesperson's job to sell the company's products and services to customers. The function of everyone else in the organization was simply to support the sales effort. But today, more and more companies have expanded their definition of "customer" to include viewing others within the organization as "internal customers."

For example, a retired vice president of quality of a large heavy equipment manufacturing company said, "When we talk about quality, we're not just talking about machinery, but about every process having an output—product—that goes to someone. This means that within the company, there are internal customers. And each individual seeks to deliver a quality product to his or her customer. For example, a designer's product goes to an engineer, and an engineer's product goes to a manufacturing person, and the manufacturing person's product goes to the marketing person. Similarly, public affairs people have internal customers, and so do the accountants, attorneys, and so on. With this mind-set, everyone strives to produce a quality product and everyone is customer-driven."

Instilling this spirit is easier said than done, particularly with employees who have little or no actual contact with external customers. It must be done early on with employees, starting with a job description that clearly spells out the job's "customer connection." This means *everyone*—from people on the shipping docks to clerks in accounting. Every single person in the organization has customers—even though he or she may never actually contact the "traditional" customer.

Employees in tune with serving customers within can more easily relate their jobs to external customers. Being a customer-driven company depends on more than just the frontline salespeople.

UNGUIDED MISSILES

Suppose a retail store located in a medium-sized market has a sales force of ten people. Now let's give this retailer an annual advertising budget of $200,000. You could say the store owner is actually investing $20,000 in each salesperson, in an effort to bring customers in the front door for him to sell.

With this much investment in a salesperson, wouldn't it make a lot of sense to provide proper training? Yet, few retailers spend the time or money to guarantee a decent return on their advertising investment in each salesperson.

Without that training, "unguided missiles" are being placed on the sales floor—salespeople who aren't knowledgeable about the product they sell and know even less about the customer. Consequently, people stroll in the front door—consumers ready to buy something now—and they walk out disappointed, with their money still in their pocket. Frustrating, isn't it? Not only for the store owner, but for the customer as well.

This is happening all across America, even with companies who send sales reps to make personal calls on their customers. In this case, the rep may be the company's only contact with the customer—the company's ambassador. If this individual is one of those unguided missiles, imagine the ill will created when he or she comes into contact with eighteen to twenty-four customers every day.

An ARG study revealed that more than 70 percent of all Americans view a salesperson in a retail store as *the store*. This means their impression of the store—positive or negative—depends on how they were treated by *this single individual*. Remember, now, that the customer who walks into a store sees considerably more than the prospect who is contacted by a sales rep at his or her home or place of business. After all, the in-the-store customer sees the actual store, its physical inventory, other employees, and so on.

A company such as Prudential Insurance, for example, can have tens of thousands of employees and agents. A life insurance prospect, however, meets only one of them—the agent who sits across his dining-room table to make a sales presentation. Because he is the sole representative of Prudential, the professionalism or unprofessionalism of this single agent leaves a lasting impression on the prospect's image of the entire company.

You don't want any unguided missiles in your organization. An unguided missile can do a lot of damage.

THE OBVIOUS IS NORMALLY WRONG

Writer Anatole France once commented, "If 50 million people say a foolish thing, it's still a foolish thing." Often what appears to be obvious turns out to be wrong.

Employees' opinions about a store's customers may be misleading because they're based on biased views—like the retailer whose employees tried to talk him into closing during the Memorial Day weekend. In another situation, a retail client said his employees protested vehemently when they learned the store would remain open on Saturday evenings. However, the owner persisted, and it turned out to be the store's best nighttime sales of the week. Likewise, in Portland, Oregon, a home furnishing retailer's employees expressed disapproval when the store announced it would open Sunday mornings at 10:00. They had a legitimate reason; after all, Sunday morning is not a desirable work time for an employee with a family. But it proved to be a wise choice for the store, because 60 percent of its Sunday sales are now made before noon. What this means is that your employees' wants may not reflect your customers' needs. Nonetheless, your first allegiance is to do what is easy for your customers, even though it is difficult for your employees, or, for that matter, for you.

A while ago, a retailer informed me of his plans to open a new superstore in a "hot shopping area" in Pensacola, Florida. It was the "ideal" site, I was informed. "In addition to having the highest traffic count in town," he excitedly told me, "it's surrounded by many of the leading national retailers. If they think it's a good area, Britt, it must be. They can't all be opening there without knowing what they're doing."

Although he was convinced he was right, I was still asked to do a study of the area, if for no other reason than to safeguard his sizable investment in real estate for that project. Well, my study showed that opening a store in the area would be disastrous for him. His store catered to elderly customers, and our survey of these people indicated they didn't like to travel on congested roads to shop. Our study recommended another location with less traffic—where the new store thrived. Meanwhile, sales volumes of several of the retailers in the highly congested area are running 30 percent lower than comparable store figures.

When your industry is all going in one direction, it takes courage to go against the grain. But then a company that isn't willing to take risks can never become and remain the market leader.

DIFFERENT STROKES FOR DIFFERENT FOLKS

During the tax season, I meet with my CPA to review my annual expenditures. In what seems like hundreds of questions, he asks for minute details.

"Was this credit card charge for entertainment with a client or was it personal?"

"Was this travel personal or business?"

"Was this payment a charitable contribution?"

"Now let's review your interest deductions, Britt. Tell me about . . ."

I know he drills dozens and dozens of other clients with the same questions, always writing down notes to himself to verify certain figures, to check with my bookkeeper on this and that, and so on. During one cross-examination, I blurted out, "I don't know how you do it. It would drive me crazy to have to deal with the numbers and details you do."

He put down his pen and removed his glasses. "You know, Britt," he said, "when I go over your travel expenses and see how you're constantly far from home, boarding airplanes and traveling around the world, I think to myself, 'Thank heaven it's him and not me!' "

Sometimes I think about what he said. It's great that we're all different, isn't it? After all, it would be a very boring world if we were all the same, don't you agree?

It's a serious mistake to lump all people together and treat them identically. While there are qualities we all share, no two people are identical.

A national and international company must realize that people in different markets have different buying habits. Of course, some of these differences are obvious. In fashion, for instance, people wear different clothes according to climate, and urban and rural people dress differently. A while ago, there was one identifiable uniform prevalent across corporate America. Official or unofficial, this dress code separated management from the working class. Today there are many dress codes, some quite distinctive— and they can vary by industry as well as by region. Owing somewhat to Bill Gates, in Seattle, for example, there is a significant group of Microserfs donning baseball caps. Business folk dress differently according to whether they work in the Northeast or Northwest, Silicon Valley or the Motor City; whether they are investment bankers, entertainers, or advertising executives.

For instance, once we found out that Midwesterners tend to be quality-driven, compared to New Yorkers, who are more price-driven, we applied this information to print advertising. We discovered that Midwest retailers who insert four-color circulars in the Sunday newspapers do better when they use better-quality paper. Buyers typically associate higher-quality paper and full-color ads with better merchandise. Conversely, New Yorkers respond at a lower level when retailers raise the quality of paper for Sunday inserts.

These differences send a message to companies that do business on a regional and national basis. Americans in different parts of the country respond differently to the same marketing strategy. Therefore, an effective marketing strategy in one part of the country must be customized to be useful in other parts of the country.

NO SINGLE REASON

Lumping people in the same category, expecting everyone to think alike, is nonsensical. Since no two people are alike, there is an array of reasons why customers buy. This is why a marketing strategy requires enough flexibility to permit tailor-making it to fit individual customers.

Otherwise, you'll start out selling a one-size-fits-all and end up with a one-size-won't-fit-anyone.

To illustrate how this works, let me take you back in time. In 1983, I stopped at a local restaurant in Charleston with a close friend of mine, David Ivey, a periodontist, to enjoy a late-night snack. On this one particular night, I happened to ask David how his day went.

"I had a frustrating day," he sighed. "A woman who came into my office desperately needing gum surgery left after deciding not to get the work done."

"Every now and then, I imagine you must get a patient like that," I sympathized.

"How about every other one?" he volunteered.

"Boy, that must be frustrating!"

"You can't imagine! I'm supposed to help people with their dental problems, but when I don't communicate with them well enough, and they walk, I feel I've let them down. I've been in my practice for five years, and I'm still not used to this part of my work."

"Tell me, why would anyone who needs gum surgery turn down your services?" I asked.

"People have all sorts of reasons," he told me. "Vanity is a strong reason why one person may want surgery, yet another person who doesn't want to appear vain may say no. Many people are afraid to undergo surgery because they fear the pain associated with the dentist's chair. With others, it's a money issue. And some people just like to procrastinate, thinking the problem will go away by itself."

"And what are the reasons people consent to have the surgery?" I inquired.

"Mainly because they want to keep their teeth. Did you know that more people lose their teeth because of poor gums than because of tooth decay?"

"No kidding! And what are the reasons why people don't want to lose their teeth?" I asked, as if I didn't already know.

"For a variety of reasons," my conscientious friend replied in a serious tone. "With one person it may be strictly appearance, for another fear of having difficulty chewing with dentures. Somebody else may have a gag reflex and can't stand the thought of putting something into his mouth. And, of course, losing one's teeth is a sign of aging. In our society, the accent is definitely on staying youthful for as long as possible."

Since the source of all of David's patients is referrals from general dentists, I asked, "Is there a difference in how each dentist refers someone to you that makes it easier or more difficult to persuade that person to follow through with the recommended procedure?"

David's eyes lit up. "You bet there is! Some dentists do a terrific job explaining why it's necessary to see me, and they create such a sense of urgency that the patient is presold before he gets to me. Other dentists talk about the need for gum surgery in such a casual way the patient isn't convinced he has a real problem, so he never gets around to seeing me. And a lot has to do with the confidence level the referring dentist generates. Say, for instance, you went to a fence-straddling doctor who told you, 'You know that last time you had a chest pain, Britt? Well, it might have resulted from blocked arteries. Maybe. You may have that problem. When you get home, why don't you look up a cardiologist in the yellow pages, and see what he thinks.'

"Now another physician tells you more firmly, 'Britt, you've had this pain twice now in the last month, and it concerns me very much. I have somebody with whom I work a lot, and he's an expert diagnostician. I'm going to personally call his office right this minute and set up an appointment for you to find out exactly what the problem is. I'll ask him to report his findings directly to me as soon as possible afterward, so we can figure out what our options are without wasting any time.'

"Just like these two doctors handled it, Britt, there are different ways a dentist can prepare a patient to see a periodontist."

I inundated David with questions before making my recommendations. "When you meet with a referred patient," I said, "do you go through the same routine with each one? In other words, are you saying pretty much the same thing to your prospective patients, as if you are giving a canned presentation?"

He thought for a moment and said, "Yes, I guess I am, but I do make adjustments based upon their reactions."

"I suggest you classify your patients according to their needs," I told him. "You could do this by asking specific questions at the beginning of your interview, and based on the response, you should address each patient's major concern. For instance, if a patient talks about a bad experience with a previous dentist, you could explain that there is no need to worry about pain and discomfort. Say, 'I assure you there is nothing that's going to bother you about this surgery. In fact, when we're through, you're going to tell me that you could kick yourself for waiting so long to get this done.'

"With another patient, who expresses concern about the procedure's cost, you might say, 'As far as expense goes, it's like anything else. If it's a value to you, we'll work with you so you can pay for it over a period of time. The main thing is to do what's best for your health.' "

In time, David was presenting his special services in the same manner a professional computer representative or an investment adviser would give a presentation. He'd ask a lot of questions pertinent to his patient's needs, and then offer the best solution to fix the problem. It's the same approach I take when I first meet with a prospective client.

As David later explained to me, "With today's HMOs and managed health care, all too often somebody other than the provider of care is making decisions for patients. When this happens, the doctor is reduced to being a mechanic. By questioning my patients and listening carefully to them, I establish a healthy relationship—and they know I truly care about them. When I get to know them, they feel as though they're more than just a number referred to me by another dentist. You know, there is such a boom of information in the field of medicine today, too much time is spent on the technical side of it, causing neglect of the human side. In my office, now I can make sure that doesn't happen."

I feel that David's genuine concern about his patients had a psychological effect on them. He shows them he cares, and they care back. When you stop to think about it, it's a remarkable thing to convince people to have gum surgery. After all, they have to spend a lot of money on something they don't want, that they'd like to put off, and that they think will hurt them.

In addition to working on his presentation to his patients, David focused on how he could work with his referring dentists so they could better prepare their patients to visit him. After all, they had a vested interest. If their patients lost their teeth because of gum problems, they'd have no need for future dental work. In this area, it was a matter of having David's referring dentists provide more information upfront on their reasons for the referral, motivating patients in a positive way to visit a periodontist, and creating a sense of urgency to do it soon.

It was only a matter of time before David's closing ratio on referred patients rose from 60 percent to 90 percent. Today, he is the most successful periodontist in Summerville, a town just west of Charleston.

Other professionals who rely on referrals, say from accountants or attorneys, should do what Dr. Ivey did when he instructed his referring dentists to prepare patients to see him. Of course, proper preparation by the referrer is necessary for all businesspeople relying on referrals as a source of new business.

Before making a recommendation, a good stockbroker will, like Dr. Ivey, conduct an in-depth fact-finding session with a prospective client. The broker has to know such things as the individual's long-term goal—whether it is the accumulation of capital or income-yielding holdings—and what is in the present portfolio, particular personal financial objectives, and so on. Only after carefully evaluating his prospect's needs can the stockbroker give counsel accurately. Likewise, professional salespeople ranging from real estate agents to life insurance agents should tailor-make their sales presentations to fit their customer's needs.

It gets more complicated. Along the same line, people make shopping and buying decisions for more than one reason. For example, a computer store may want to know why a shopper decides to consider a particular computer. While the customer may have one main reason, several other strong reasons may also influence the decision. Today, it's not entirely realistic to ask, "What's the most important reason?" because people don't live in a vacuum. Sometimes they may not even be aware of their true reasons.

Interestingly, while consumers may say selection and price got them into a store, in making their final purchase decision they are often influenced by the salesperson's explanation of quality. So while selection and price created the foot traffic, it was the value perception that created the final decision to purchase. It is news to some retailers that the factors that drive consumers into the store may be totally different from the factors influencing their final decision.

ABOUT VOICE MAIL

It doesn't take a genius to recognize that voice mail, while useful, epitomizes how impersonal business can become. This progressive, efficient form of communication is so commonly used today that you expect it whenever you call for anything—from making an airline reservation to obtaining information on your bank statement. Yet one friend says he gets so frustrated with voice mail he has to restrain himself from throwing his telephone out the window.

Of course, it's understandable why voice mail is used. It replaces many telephone operators—and it works twenty-four hours a day, around the clock, 365 days a year. In short, voice mail is a tremendous money-saving convenience for a business. There is only one catch. It's not always convenient for your customer.

A recent study revealed that 40 percent of Americans are strongly against voice mail. Now when I say "strongly," this means either they hate voice mail or they dislike it very much. Another 25 percent or so can tolerate it, which means they are not enthralled with it. The remaining 35 percent are saying, "It's okay and I can live with voice mail," but by no means do they love it.

In the past five years, our research shows that the numbers strongly opposed to voice mail have risen from 20 percent to the present 40 percent. This sizable increase in a relatively short period of time indicates that within the next five years, the number can be expected to rise to 70 percent.

Today we can quantify the irritation level a customer experiences when he calls a retail store's service department and finally speaks with a person after being forced to go through voice mail. Companies that treat people like numbers, and that do what's convenient for themselves, not their customers, may reduce operational costs upfront, while their voice mail is driving customers away. So, in my estimation, it doesn't work.

Much voice mail simply is not customer-friendly. It sends the message "Because our company can't solve its problems, we're going to pass some inconvenience along to our customers."

Perhaps a better mix of voice mail usage with live-operator usage would be the answer.

When it is not used sensitively or in the appropriate contexts, voice mail can be seen as an example of the way many businesspeople think today: It's easier to cut employees than to improve sales. If a company has a problem with its telephone operator(s), it should strive to correct that problem before it institutes a computerized program that alienates customers.

We did another study for *US Banker* magazine, and we found that 80 percent of Americans trusted a human teller to an ATM machine. This reconfirms what we learned from the negative response to voice mail. While a certain efficiency is gained by today's technology, people don't want to be handled by a machine. They'd rather deal with a human being.

It may look like I've zeroed in on voice mail and ATM machines as the epitome of impersonalization in corporate America, but my reason for selecting them is their increasing usage. I could just as easily have focused on airlines, hotels, and car rental agencies which are notorious for putting their customers on hold. And what about the mountains of paperwork with which hospitals and health insurers burden their customers; the hassle it takes to renew automobile license plates in some states; the unnecessary waiting that physicians subject patients to in reception rooms? Unfortunately, the list goes on and on.

DECLINING CUSTOMER LOYALTY

Customer loyalty is becoming a thing of the past. Here's what has happened to it in America in the last 45 years:

Year	Customer Loyalty Level
1950	66%
1960	50
1970	33
1980	25
1990	16
1996	12

The major reason customer loyalty is dropping is companies' refusal to meet today's consumers' expectations. They demand certain things from a company they deal with and the products they buy, but their expectations are not always met. Even when they are, that may not be enough, because today's consumers are loyal only to a company that goes *beyond* their expectations. So it's no longer sufficient to give your customers what they expect. For them to come back to you, you must give them even more. In today's marketplace, you have to supersatisfy them— you have to do something exceptional. It's easy to be average. It takes work to understand what your customer expects and exceed it each and every time.

CONSUMER MIND READER #4

What Employees Strongly Dislike About Their Jobs

Our survey of Americans identified their top ten work-related pet peeves. Interestingly, each of the top ten complaints focused on American workers' perceived mistreatment by management.

Complaint	Percent who strongly dislike it
1. Verbal abuse/raised voice	39.0%
2. Sexual discrimination	37.2
3. Racial discrimination	34.5
4. Favoritism	29.4
5. Salary cuts	27.7
6. Undeserved promotions of boss's "friends"	27.5
7. Employer/supervisor "talks down" to employee	24.2
8. No compensation for "extra work"	24.1
9. Being blamed for boss's error in front of a client	24.0
10. Constantly being pressured to hurry	23.0

Recent studies suggest that today's productivity levels in the workplace have been driven up by fear of job loss due to downsizing. While fear may keep an employee working longer to demonstrate job commitment to an employer, it does not improve morale or job satisfaction.

What Employers Strongly Dislike About Their Employees

We surveyed employers with ten or more employees to find out their top ten pet peeves about their employees. There were eleven major frustrations above a significant level where employers "really dislike" a problem. In order for a frustration to be considered serious, a 33 percent or higher negative response was recorded.

Response	Really dislike it
1. Habitual Monday or Friday illness	40.6%
2. Coming in late	39.4
3. Completing only a portion of task, leaving rest to others	37.9
4. "That's not my job" attitude	37.9
5. Hygiene	37.7
6. Vulgarity	37.6
7. Unprofessional attitude toward clients	37.5
8. "Slacking off," resulting in tasks completed by others	37.2
9. Cheating on expenses	35.3
10. Overstating abilities/experience in job interview	34.9
11. Continuously failing to meet deadlines	34.6

According to those surveyed, when an employer has a "really dislike" perception exceeding 33 percent, employees had better watch out! At this level of frustration, an employer is likely to terminate problem employees.

CHAPTER FIVE

THE VISION

Having a vision is where it all begins. All great marketing strategies start with a vision.

It's a sign of good leadership when this vision is clearly defined and communicated throughout the organization. High-level executives don't have a patent on vision, since even fledgling entrepreneurs have dreams of developing Fortune 500 companies. Unfortunately for many people, their dreams are only that—just dreams. But the man or woman who possesses a vision can turn mere dreams into reality.

A major advantage people with a vision enjoy is that their standards aren't measured by what others consider acceptable. Visionaries have no predetermined boundaries. As business leaders, they don't try to base their growth rate on their peers' performances. Instead, their personal standards are higher than—or different from—the norm. To these individuals, average growth is often considered failure. Likewise, their perceptions are closely in tune with those of their customer. Fixing this vision firmly in your mind consistent with customer needs is prerequisite to its success.

WHAT'S IN IT FOR THE CUSTOMER?

Note that the vision isn't "What's in it for me?" The emphasis is always on the customer. Always. The vision of every leader of a successful marketing strategy addresses the question "What's in it for the customer?" While the Walt Disneys of this world may or may not have consciously addressed this question, it was the focal point on which their marketing strategy was based.

If your prime concern is how you will benefit—you won't! Doomed from the start are those who focus solely on the bottom line. People who visualize attaining personal wealth or building a successful business are badly mistaken. Acquiring prosperity is the by-product, the reward that naturally follows when you do all the things that are right for your customer.

One woman who had a vision to build a company that would do good for others is Lane Nemeth. In 1978, Lane started Discovery Toys, Inc., from her garage in Martinez, California. She chose the toy business because she considered manufactured toys based on violence unsuitable for her two-year-old daughter, Tara. Formerly director of a child care center, she wanted to provide parents with developmental toys for their children; doing so, she felt, would make the world a better place.

"I thought it was important for parents to understand," Lane explains, "that playing with their children is a way to say 'I love you.' You can't say it by calling your child from your office. You have to say it by doing positive things with your child. This is how I raised my own daughter—playing with her—and it's a very positive experience. As a parent, you feel good; it's fun and you laugh together. And later, your child goes off less prone to negative behavior, because you shared that positive play time.

"A prime purpose of Discovery Toy games," she continues, "is to get kids and their parents away from the television set and video games, so they can interact with other human beings. This way they develop valuable social skills. When a parent and child play a game, it's a wonderful way for them to communicate with each other. You'd be surprised how much conversation takes place over a game board that wouldn't surface at the dinner table."

One of Lane's criteria for selecting a toy for her company is that there must be more than one way to play with it. "This helps develop the child's imagination," she explains. Another "must" for a Discovery toy is that it has to have a purpose in the child's development, whether educational, creative, physical, or all three. "And naturally," she adds, "it has to be fun!"

Discovery Toys has a national direct-sales organization of 45,000 women who sell their products primarily by organizing parties. Lane decided to market her products via direct selling versus traditional retail outlets because her toys needed to be demonstrated to customers. When the company was first founded, she lacked the resources to educate her customers via television commercials. And she knew that without a presentation by trained sales reps, her products were unlikely to sell off the racks in retail outlets. So Lane's vision to get her educational toys in the hands of children required her to take another course, the slow, painstaking route of recruiting one woman at a time and training her so that she, in turn, could recruit and train other women. While only a handful of direct sales organizations have succeeded on a national scale, Discovery Toys is one of them. Today, the company's independent sales reps—often mothers with a college education—truly believe in what they sell. And they sell a lot of toys. Company sales now are in the $100 million range.

Another woman who had a vision to start a company with a child-centered product line is Gun Denhart. In 1983, she and her husband, Tom, founded Hanna Andersson (named after Gun's grandmother). Based in Portland, Oregon, Hanna Andersson is a catalog company that distributes high-quality 100-percent-cotton infants' and children's clothes. Gun envisioned a company that would sell baby clothes that had a comfortable softness—like the kind that small children wore in her native Sweden. Gun's motivation to start a company to fill a void in the marketplace came when her son, Christian, was born in 1980. "Everything out there was polyester," she explains. "I wanted my baby's clothes to be soft to the touch, and I wanted something that, unlike some other baby products, would last more than a few washings."

It took three years for the dream to become a reality. In the summer of 1983, the Denharts contracted a Swedish garment company to manufacture the first Hanna Andersson product line. The first Hanna Andersson catalog was shipped the following February.

Later that year, the company initiated an innovative marketing concept called "Hannadowns." It works like this: When a child outgrows his or her clothes, the company will take them back as returns and issue a credit of 20 percent of the original purchase price. These "Hannas" are then donated to needy children. Gun has been amply rewarded for her vision of distributing high-quality merchandise while, at the same time, doing good for others. Today, Hanna Andersson has sales exceeding $50 million, and hundreds of thousands of garments have been donated to charities and crisis centers.

FIRE IN THE BELLY

I used to marvel at how Joe Montana would quarterback the San Francisco 49ers in the playoff and bowl games. Anytime the 49ers were behind by less than a touchdown, his fans knew he'd pull off the winning play in the final moments of the game.

Montana had a special quality I call "fire in the belly." Even on TV, you could see it in his eyes. When he'd come out of the huddle to call the signals to his team, he oozed confidence—his teammates could feel his intensity, and the crowd could see his confidence. Montana was so driven to win he was willing to put everything on the line, knowing that if he did, he'd succeed. Great business leaders who focus their energy on attaining their goals inspire others to exert all-out effort, too.

You don't have to be an NFL quarterback to have this magical quality. That same enthusiasm comes through when Lane Nemeth addresses reps at a Discovery Toys sales conference. And you can hear it in Gun Denhart's voice when she talks about her Hannadowns. The contagious enthusiasm and conviction of leaders drives others to rally around them.

Fire in the belly can't be faked. Anything less than the genuine article doesn't work. For your vision to inspire others, you have to believe it heart and soul.

FOUR CHARACTERISTICS SHARED BY LEADERS WITH A VISION

In addition to fire in the belly, there are at least four common denominators shared by leaders who have vision:

1. THEY WANT TO MAKE A DIFFERENCE. Over and above the promise of financial reward, the desire to benefit others drives these visionaries. In addition to serving their customers, they want their staff and representatives to do well. Since they are not motivated solely by self-interest, they are not afraid to seek out employees who are better than they are. The people they choose tend to be intensely loyal, because they have been invited to share in the vision. It is not uncommon to hear outsiders refer to such employees as "fanatics" or "zealots."

2. THEY'RE DECISIVE. Focused visionaries who are sure about what they seek don't hesitate to make the decisions that attain those objectives. People who are indecisive generally lack direction. And not knowing where they want to go makes it difficult and confusing for them when the time comes to be decisive. When people have a vision, however, they move in one direction, unhindered by distractions. As an old saying goes, "I do what I do best, and I leave everything else to the rest."

3. THEY'RE NOT EMOTIONAL ABOUT CHANGE. When you're obsessed with a vision, you'll discover your emotions won't keep you from accepting change. You know you are focused when what it takes to realize the vision becomes routine. And those who embrace change have no fear of taking risks. With a vision, a person is willing to modify his game plan many times along the

way. Why? Because the particular method for getting there is never as important as simply getting there. Consequently, a dozen or more plan revisions may occur.

4. THEY HAVE AN OFFENSIVE STRATEGY. By its nature, supporting your vision requires taking an offensive position. Just as a football team drives downfield toward the goal line, overcoming any barriers in its way, a person with a vision pushes forward with determination, always striving to achieve that vision. The visionary also understands the importance of momentum. A great leader never puts a defensive strategy into place; a visionary does not assume a reactive position.

ADMITTING A MISTAKE

Having vision does not guarantee success. Even the best of plans can go haywire. And even visionary risk-takers understand that nobody can expect to bat a thousand.

When the public rallied against the newly introduced revamped Coke, Coca-Cola executives realized that their window to respond was short. They quickly reached a consensus: "We're not going to tell the rest of the world we are right and our customers are wrong." Instead, the company said it had blundered and hastily revived its old formula. If management had not responded promptly, the company was on track to lose seven or eight points of its market share.

The American consumer is ordinarily forgiving when companies step forward to admit a mistake. On the other hand, denying impropriety provokes anger and creates ill will. Denial could even be interpreted as an insult, causing people to think, "I know you were wrong. How dare you treat me as if I were stupid by denying it?"

Your own customers, in particular, tend to be forgiving when you make a mistake—as long as you openly admit it. So don't sell them short;

they understand that to err is human. Don't allow false pride to block your path to progress.

A friend who owns a medical center building recently told me about a difficulty he had with a janitorial service company. Each night, the cleaning company dispatched a crew of workers to clean the suites of six doctors. Like many janitorial services, this company experienced high turnover among its minimum-wage hourly employees. And although the company had serviced the building for four years with minimal complaints, of late my friend had been inundated with calls from his tenants lamenting the poor service.

When he called the janitorial company to pass on his tenants' discontent, the owner said, "We have a new crew working at your building, and my cleaning supervisor is still breaking them in. Do me a favor and fax me a list of their complaints, and I'll see that he takes care of them."

My friend followed his instructions; however, several weeks went by and the doctors came to him again.

Once more, he called the owner. "My tenants say there is no improvement, and they insist that something be done."

"Talk to my cleaning supervisor," the owner said. "What you're telling me isn't what I'm hearing from him."

"I don't want to talk to your supervisor," my friend said. "You're the owner, and I expect you to take care of it."

"I'll talk to him and call you back."

Another week passed without word from him, while the doctors' grievances continued. By now, my friend was furious.

When he called, he was told, "My cleaning supervisor says there is absolutely nothing wrong with the way your building is being serviced."

"Nothing wrong!" my friend exploded.

"I've personally talked to the crew, and they say they're doing a good job. Our other customers aren't complaining. But the problem here is *they're dealing with doctors*. There's no way to please them. I'm sorry, but the nature of our business is that you just can't satisfy some people."

My friend disagreed. He canceled the service and contracted with another janitorial service.

When a business owner has a vision, he is possessed with a passion to provide the best possible service to every customer. Had this janitorial company owner had such a desire, he wouldn't turn around and point a finger at his customer. Instead, he would have insisted that his people adhere to his customer's standard of excellence.

DARING TO DEFY CONVENTIONAL WISDOM

Somebody once said, "A successful person learns all the rules and follows them to the letter. A supersuccessful person learns the rules and then breaks them, one by one."

A visionary is not afraid to sail on uncharted waters. To be innovative, you must be willing to do things differently. You'll never hear a visionary say, "We can't do it because we never did it that way before," or "We can't consider it because it's against our policy." Such lame pretenses alienate internal creativity and, worse, antagonize customers.

This does not imply, however, that a visionary refutes conventional wisdom for the sake of being obstructionist or defiant. Being independent does not mean being a maverick out to change the world for the sake of change. A visionary is not too proud to use what has already been proven. Still, a free-thinking spirit drives this sort of individual to challenge what he believes doesn't work. And once convinced he is right, he is not easily swayed by the opinion of others.

When Tom Monaghan founded Domino's, pizza restaurants were already quite common. Monaghan made a fortune by merging two existing ideas into a new one. Back in the early 1970s, when he opened his first pizza shop in Ann Arbor, Michigan, the pizza industry was considered saturated. Pizza parlors were everywhere; the turnover rate was incredibly high. But by adding a new twist to his business—delivering pizza to the buyer—Monaghan struck gold. What was so new and creative about Domino's? At the time, Monaghan recognized that people wanted pizza to be served while it was still hot. It didn't take a genius to come up with the technology to send a delivery truck to somebody's home. His concept was simple: Make good pizza and deliver it hot.

Back in 1952, when Kemmons Wilson founded Holiday Inn, the first motel had already been "invented"—Wilson merely found a way to provide more comfort and convenience to the traveler. Wilson had just returned to Memphis from a family vacation to Washington, D.C., when he conceived what was to become the world's largest hotel chain. After being unable to find decent lodging for his family, Wilson wanted to build a chain of clean, family-oriented hotels. He visualized Holiday Inns across the nation, even around the globe, offering this service to the weary traveler.

When Bill McGowan founded MCI Communications in 1968, he had a vision. At the time, people thought it ridiculous to attempt to lock horns with AT&T, America's largest corporation, which had a monopoly on the nation's telephone service. People questioned McGowan's judgment when he talked about raising capital to form a nationwide network to compete against AT&T, which had been around for more than a century; why, its billions of dollars in assets exceeded the wealth of most countries! But by taking technology from the computer industry, McGowan believed he could leapfrog over AT&T, which he considered antiquated and complacent. McGowan's vision led him to raise $100 million, at the time the largest venture-capital underwriting in the history of Wall Street.

Still another remarkable story of vision concerns Bill Rasmussen, founder of ESPN. The idea of ESPN first came up when Rasmussen and his son, Scott, were stalled in a massive traffic jam on the Connecticut Turnpike. Bill, a public relations director, had just been fired by the Hartford Whalers hockey team, which had just finished its worst season ever. He needed a job. During the traffic tie-up, father and son talked about the huge boom in sports across America. With the emerging satellite technology, they envisioned a cable television station featuring sports—just sports—on a twenty-four-hour basis, 365 days a year. It took the Rasmussens just fourteen months to make their vision become a reality. In the beginning, their sports network met with enormous resistance. It's ludicrous to think you can broadcast sports—just sports—twenty-four hours every day of the year, they were told. Conventional wisdom decried the idea that people wanted sports around the clock, every day of the year. And even if they did, it was felt there weren't enough major sports events to broadcast twenty-four hours a day. The Rasmussens were forewarned of the impossibility of getting contracts with professional teams and major colleges. Supposedly, the networks had already locked up those contracts. You'll never find anyone to sponsor small college sports events, others cautioned.

To launch their network, Rasmussen invested an initial $8,000, borrowed from his credit card. Then came the hard part—negotiating rights with the NCAA, securing interim and long-term financing, assembling a staff, and completing production facilities in time for a September 9, 1979, launch. From their vision evolved cable TV's largest network, today reaching more than 62 million U.S. homes and delivered in eleven languages to 120 countries.

SHARING THE VISION

Truly exceptional successes are rarely a result of individual effort. In the world of business, great organizations are, in particular, built with people. Those who reach the highest peaks say time and time again, "Nobody does it alone." While a vision may begin with a single person, only when it is shared with others does it begin to blossom.

It is a sign of good leadership when a leader shares his vision and invites his people to participate. Those who are included from the beginning tend to be more supportive throughout the entire implementation. When it becomes *their* vision, it becomes a focal point of the corporate culture.

It is essential to communicate the vision properly to all members of the organization. In this respect, I like to use the analogy of a carload of people vacationing together. What would it be like if the route to be taken was not communicated by the driver to each passenger? If the driver doesn't mention that he's taking the scenic route, a passenger may become confused, thinking the driver is lost. Perhaps in the passenger's mind, the only route to follow is the interstate, the fastest and most direct way to get to their destination. Traveling through small towns and over back roads may seem like unnecessary detours.

Like the driver, a CEO may want to look at the scenic route, but the company's financial officer may want him to race down the interstate at seventy miles an hour. He wants to arrive at the destination in the least amount of time because the CEO hasn't communicated the importance of the scenic route. When this happens, everyone is pulling in different directions and the organization is thrown off course.

Isn't it better to have a unified effort exerted by everyone? The vision must be shared with everyone from salespeople to financial people. Even the company's vendors should be invited to participate. Nonsales personnel must be informed of their important roles in serving customers: Receptionists, telephone operators, shipping and receiving personnel—every employee within the organization—must understand how his or her job contributes to serving the customer. The vision belongs to everyone.

A LACK OF VISION

In a company without a vision, lack of direction sends every staff member running off helter-skelter to do his job. Without vision, companies drift because they have nowhere to go.

A classic example of a retailer that went under because its management lacked vision is Highland Superstores, an electronics and appliance chain store based in Detroit. For years, Highland was a leader in its marketplace, but it met its Waterloo trying to become a national power player by opening stores in Indiana, Louisiana, and Texas. Although Highland never had what were considered "ideal" superstores in Detroit—stores of the future with large selections of merchandise—its edge was having great salespeople. Its new stores in out-of-state markets were formatted after its original Detroit stores—simply inadequate to go against competition such as Circuit City and Best Buy. The last straw was when the company started transferring its great salespeople out of Detroit to run new, faraway stores. With its base watered down, Highland lost its edge in its own hometown, enabling ABC Warehouse, a local low-price electronics and appliance retailer, to take over its number one spot in the Detroit area. Meanwhile, because Highland failed to do adequate marketing research in its new markets, it misjudged the business climate in Texas. Then when bad times struck the oil industry in the Southwest during the 1980s, Highland was unable to weather the financial storms. The once highly successful electronics and appliance retailer is now out of business.

THE DEMISE OF THE AMERICAN DEPARTMENT STORE

In case you haven't noticed, many of the nation's best-known department stores have fallen by the wayside. Once-proud Gimbels no longer exists. Macy's filed for protection under federal bankruptcy laws, although it has since been bought out by Federated. And Federated, the largest of all department store chains, has only just recently emerged from its own bankruptcy filing. Others that have also closed their doors are Allied Stores, the parent of Gimbels and Jordan Marsh; Associated Dry Goods, parent of Lord & Taylor and Joseph Horne's; and Carter-Hawley-Hale, parent of Neiman-Marcus and Broadway Stores. Bonwit Teller, Bloomingdale's, and Saks Fifth Avenue have suffered severe financial strain. Cleveland's Halle's is gone, and Washington, D.C.'s leading department store, Woodward & Lothrop, has also fallen. Also departed are such great retail landmarks as Garfinkel's in Philadelphia, Wanamaker's in Philadelphia, and I. Magnin in San Francisco.

In New York City alone, thirty-one major department stores thrived

in the 1950s, yet this number has now shrunk to just eight. Only one—
Saks Fifth Avenue—has managed to avoid either being acquired or de-
claring bankruptcy. (Bloomingdale's has experienced both.) Gone is their
era, one which most New Yorkers imagined would last forever.

In their heyday, these grand department stores dominated their respective marketplaces; other retailers could do pretty well by merely following the lead of these trendsetters. And it was an awesome lead! These
big stores were more than companies—they were institutions. They
reigned supremely, and their leadership was unchallenged. The community's leading department store was often the heart and soul of the
city's downtown shopping area. In larger cities, where there was plenty
of business to go around, this prestigious role could be shared by two or
three department stores.

In their prime, department stores possessed three major advantages
over other retailers. First, they were the original occupiers of the big
boxes. And their big boxes were located in the center of the city, most
often on a prime downtown site. In such a big box, a giant store could
offer many products to its customers. Second, these stores were perceived
as trendsetters, particularly in the apparel side of retailing. Also, a certain
amount of prestige was associated with shopping at a department store.
A customer wearing a purchase made at a particular store took pride in
that statement that it made. When it came to color and style in fashion,
few challenged the department store's leadership role. Third, each store
had its own charge card, thereby ensuring an incredibly loyal customer
base. The card was—and is—a powerful sales tool. Our research reveals
that when a person has a store charge card in hand, there is an 80 percent
chance that store will be the first store shopped, and there is a 90 percent
chance that once in the store, shoppers will make a purchase before leaving, if they can find something in their size.

When you're the number one player—which department stores
were—as long as you're doing everything right and nothing changes, you
can, theoretically, maintain your number one position indefinitely. However, this assumes that not only your competition remains static, but your

customer as well. In the real world, this is unlikely; we know now that no company can rest on its laurels. So no matter how superior and comfortable department stores were in the early 1980s, if they were unwilling to adapt to change, their leadership was doomed.

As it happened, specific changes took away the three advantages department stores enjoyed over other stores. First, competition entered the marketplace in areas such as electronics and appliances, categories that were important to the department stores. Since these categories were not the most important part of their mix, they got chipped away. When local furniture stores followed the example set by the electronics and appliance stores and they too opened large stores offering better selection and broader price points, another eroded category resulted.

Second, department stores believed no competition could ever be more on-trend and more fashionable than they. Sadly, they discovered this to be untrue. When stores like The Limited, The Gap, and Benetton entered the scene, these retailers with their offshore resources were able to knock off current fashions quickly, competing very favorably. Then discount stores began opening big boxes in the suburbs; retailers such as Wal-Mart, Target, and Kmart also had offshore resources enabling them to offer current fashion at low prices. This meant that even when the department stores were first to introduce the fashions, within weeks the competition could offer similar merchandise more attractively priced.

Third, while the department stores felt secure in knowing they still had their charge card customers, even this advantage was lost when MasterCard, Visa, and American Express with their huge credit card base started offering perks to their cardholders. Whether it was extra values such as frequent flier miles or points that could be converted into cash credits, the department store's core strength—its credit card customer base—was eroded.

Would it have been possible for the department stores to adapt to these changes? Yes, but with much difficulty. Their big boxes were located in downtown areas and shopping malls, which, in effect, boxed them in. Even with their immense amount of floor space, they couldn't compete in all categories, because they didn't have enough space for everything. This is particularly true when the competition began to specialize, offering tremendous selections of a single type of merchandise in 60,000-square-foot stores. As the American consumer became more selection-driven in the 1980s, department stores, with their finite amount of square footage to allocate to various departments, became extremely vulnerable. For instance, with electronics and appliances being, say, only 15 percent of a department store's sales volume, it wouldn't be feasible to allocate 25 percent of its space to this one department. Had customers been willing to shop in only five thousand or six thousand square feet to satisfy their electronics and appliances needs, a major department store could have continued to be a major player in this area. But when the consumer wants to roam in a considerably bigger store, the major department store is totally inadequate to fight the battle in its smaller showroom.

Something drastic happened when the department stores reduced what their customers considered core categories. For years, most Americans associated major purchases such as electronics and appliances with department store shopping. But because of low profit margins on hard goods as compared to high margins on soft goods, hard-goods inventories got reduced. This had dire consequences. These retail executives failed to realize that the American consumer judged the price image of the entire department store based on its pricing in certain hard-goods categories. With those barometers removed, confused customers were unable to determine whether the store was a low-end, medium-priced, or high-end place to shop. This left the door open for category killers with their big boxes to come in, offering more selection *at lower prices*.

Many customers said, "I expect a department store to carry this product category, this product, and this item." So when the store methodically chopped away those areas believed instrumental to department stores, the customers' perception of "the ideal department store" disintegrated. In many cases, it was a matter not so much of resting on laurels as of the physical inability to respond to customers' perceptions of how big a store they wanted to shop.

If you talk to analysts on Wall Street, you're likely to hear a different explanation of the demise of the American department store. The investment community puts the blame on leveraged buyouts, some of which were financed with junk bonds. It is true that the ensuing high debt service required a reduction both in services and in inventory selections. The leveraged buyouts were a symptom, but not the cause. Department stores failed because when they were making money, they didn't reinvest their profits to create a better mousetrap. Although customers of yesteryear were driven by department stores' displays of merchandise, management began to allow stores to become stale and tired. Department store management had forgotten that the department store customer expected to shop in a nice store. Meanwhile, the competition started selling the same goods at lower prices. By the time department stores recognized their troubles, they had waited too long. They had already started to take out all of the little extra things that made them special. The consumers never thought department stores were the lowest-priced, but they thought they were competitively priced. And while consumers had previously been willing to pay a little more for added value, they no longer perceived the difference to be worthy of the higher price tag. A window was opened for the competition which allowed it to become entrenched. Finally, because of poor performance, the stocks of department stores dropped in price and they became ripe targets for the mergers and acquisitions boys on Wall Street.

If department stores had retained the vision, many might have avoided the fate that awaited them. What happened, however, was that *the customer changed and the competition responded*. And when a business, even a market share leader, is incapable of responding, it doesn't have the luxury of picking up second, third or even fourth place—it is out of business.

THE BIG PICTURE

One of my favorite people who had a vision is a Russian immigrant named Rose Blumkin. In 1937, she opened a small furniture store in Omaha, which is now called the Nebraska Furniture Mart. Today, both "Mrs. B" and her store are well known by cornhuskers and other Mid-westerners who travel from neighboring states. The store reports that the legendary Mrs. B, at age 101, has never missed a day's work. Nebraska Furniture Mart, with floor space of 400,000 square feet, is the nation's largest furniture store under one roof. Its present sales are in the $250 million range. Mrs. B's son Louis, chairman, heads the store, along with her two grandsons Irv and Ron. In 1983, 80 percent of Nebraska Furniture Mart was acquired by Berkshire Hathaway, which is chaired by multibillionaire Warren Buffet.

Mrs. B founded her company on two basic premises: Sell cheap and always tell the truth. Adhering to this philosophy, the business has prospered since its opening day. Following her initial success, Mrs. B's vision was to have a gigantic store—one that would be located in the downtown area of Omaha, and be so big it would serve as a designation store, attracting people from hundreds of miles away. With this ambition, her giant store was built. Her vision has long since become a reality. The Nebraska Furniture Mart is the most popular attraction in Omaha—even tour buses include it as a regular stop.

Mrs. B had a vision, and by focusing on the big picture, this remarkable woman, with the help of her son and grandsons, fulfilled it. While the Blumkins chose the marketplace of Nebraska and adjacent states to achieve their immense success, today's big picture is not restricted to local areas. We truly live in a worldwide marketplace. In this respect, your competition is not the guy across the street or even on the other side of town, but in foreign lands in every corner of the globe. The first sixty years or so of this century were called the American Century—when the United States consumed nearly 75 percent of the world's goods. Other nations are emerging in faraway places from the Pacific Rim to the Common Market in Europe, and with modern technology, the world has been transformed into a global village.

Not long ago, businesspeople placed borders on marketing zones, confining their sales efforts to cities, counties, or states. Regional areas consisted of parts of the United States; lines were drawn that confined marketing areas to the New England states, north or south of the Mason-Dixon line, east or west of the Mississippi, and so forth. Today's aggressive business leaders know no boundaries. Their marketplace is worldwide.

No longer can even an owner of the corner mom and pop shop think only of the local neighborhood. Nowadays, every businessperson must think globally. An entrepreneur doesn't have to run an international company to be affected by what's going on around the world. A drop in currency of the yen or mark concerns a small Midwestern business owner just as it would a banker or travel agent in New York City or London. And even if there are no plans to open an office in Paris or Rome, what happens in the Euromarket still has a bearing on almost every company's bottom line.

When the dollar is weak, for instance, a foreign manufacturer may raise its prices to an American manufacturer. This, in turn, means the owner of a small local retail store can be forced to pay more for the merchandise it sells. This price increase could even happen during a period when times are tough and the consumer isn't willing to pay a higher price. Do you get the picture—the big picture? In today's global marketplace, it behooves every businessperson to keep abreast of world affairs.

Small retailers have said to me, "But Britt, I've rarely seen a foreigner walk in and buy something from my store."

"What you don't see," I reply, "is the foreign company walking into a vendor that sells products to you and saying, 'Can you build a hundred thousand units for our company?' Then, because the company from the other side of the globe pays a premium for the goods, your vendor raises the price on your future orders."

International business today is everybody's business. If the Japanese government subsidizes one of its electronics manufacturers, it makes a difference to a small business—just as it matters to General Electric and Motorola. Likewise, oil prices in the Middle East are every American's concern, as is economic and political strife in Russia.

As more foreign goods are sold on our soil, today's American business leaders aggressively expand their operations abroad. In this respect, every progressive businessperson must think globally. Whereas in years past, local businesspeople confined marketing efforts to their own community, rarely crossing state lines or worrying about the other side of the Mississippi River, today a well-orchestrated marketing plan no longer halts at national borders.

On the home front, every retailer should be concerned about what Wal-Mart and Kmart are doing, including those who do not presently compete head-on against these two giants. Likewise, an astute businessperson keeps current on issues raised by local, state, and federal government activity. Note, for example, that a few years ago an IRS revision had a nearly fatal effect on the tax shelter industry.

In this country, local business owners understand their competition isn't limited to any particular location. A browser in a small exclusive ladies' apparel shop in Pittsburgh, for instance, may be wearing a fashion purchased on New York's Fifth Avenue. And what retailer today does not understand that his customers will go home to find a pile of catalogs waiting in their mail?

What happens in faraway places such as Russia or China is not so far removed from every community—including yours, no matter how small or remote. Don't wear blinders, viewing only what's in front of you. In today's competitive marketplace, you must survey all directions to see the big picture.

HOW THE CEO'S VISION IS PERCEIVED

In a 1994 survey, more than two thousand interviews were conducted with the CEOs of Fortune 1000 companies and their subordinates. The survey was broken down into three groups: Group 1, CEOs; Group 2, managers in senior and middle levels; and Group 3, lower-level and front-line staff workers. Observe how differently these company employees answered the following questions:

DOES YOUR COMPANY HAVE A DEFINED CORPORATE MIS-
SION?
94 percent of Group 1 said yes.
79 percent of Group 2 said yes.
36 percent of Group 3 said yes.

DOES YOUR COMPANY HAVE A CORPORATE MISSION THAT IS
UNDERSTOOD THROUGHOUT THE COMPANY?
65 percent of Group 1 said yes.
54 percent of Group 2 said yes.
19 percent of Group 3 said yes.

DO YOU FEEL YOUR COMPANY HAS A PLAN OR VISION FOR
THE NEAR FUTURE?
91 percent of Group 1 said yes.
59 percent of Group 2 said yes.
26 percent of Group 3 said yes.

DO YOU FEEL YOUR COMPANY HAS A PLAN OR VISION FOR
THE LONG-TERM FUTURE?
80 percent of Group 1 said yes.
44 percent of Group 2 said yes.
13 percent of Group 3 said yes.

There is much to be learned from these responses. Evidently, most CEOs feel they know where they want the company to go. However, farther down the line, their vision is being poorly communicated. Note, for example, that less than one in five staff people who have contact with customers on a regular basis feel there is a clearly understood corporate mission. Also observe how few upper and lower managers feel their company has a vision for the near and long-term future. Imagine how this affects morale. And when only one in eight employees thinks a long-term vision is in place, considerable anxiety about job security prevails, especially for younger employees. Understandably, these employees are consumed with doubts about what will happen to their careers when they reach their forties.

There is a strong correlation between a company's vision and its corporate culture. In two thirds of all studies on the subject, the CEO's personality *is* the corporate culture. Note, for example, that in Jack Welch's early years at General Electric, he was referred to as Neutron Jack. Welch was perceived by many people as having a "slash-and-burn" personality—a cut-your-losses-quickly type of guy. Consequently, this attitude prevailed throughout the corporation. Welch has since changed. He's now perceived as a visionary CEO who is building corporate unity, empowerment, and striving for consensus. Welch has changed, and so has General Electric's culture. Today a greater teamlike atmosphere permeates the corporation.

The CEO's personality and style of management set the pace for his management team, and the team, in turn, passes these characteristics on to subordinates. So while a company may have a certain strong corporate culture, it is subject to change with the changing of the guard.

CONSUMER MIND READER #5

Ten Reasons for Recent Weaker Than Anticipated Retail Sales

1. Americans are saving more.

2. There is nothing new or exciting to buy.

3. There is a fear of crime.

4. Retailers have lowered the quality of merchandise due to price reductions.

5. People are working longer so they have less time to shop.

6. Americans are concerned about their futures.

7. Family debt is a concern.

8. Americans have less disposable income.

9. Americans are taking care of elderly family relatives so they have less time to shop.

10. People are buying more at discount stores, which reduces total expenditures.

Our research for this book reveals that, for the first time, an increase in American savings is listed as the number one reason for a drop in retail sales. To find out why savings have increased in the United States, America's Research Group conducted a survey that revealed that Americans have concluded that to master their destinies, they must take tighter control of their financial future. The following is what we learned in our surveys:

- "While I have several credit cards, I buy only what I need and put the difference into savings or investments for capital appreciation."

• "We want our children to be educated at better universities to enhance their chance for future advancement. To accomplish this, we must save more and invest more aggressively."

• "Our home equity is not accumulating as well as we antici-pated. [We heard this especially in California.] Hence, we are restraining our spending and seeking better financial growth op-portunities for retirement income."

• "Social Security benefits are iffy for our retirement, so we must save more on our own." This concern is especially prevalent among Americans under age thirty.

• For fifteen years, Americans purchased at least 8 items each year that cost $500 or more, but in 1995, this figure dropped to 6.5 items and continued at the same rate in 1996. In the early 1980s, Americans replaced their major appliances after only 1.9 repairs, but in 1996, major appliances are replaced after a whopping 2.8 repairs.

• With personal safety a prime concern, American families are spending more dollars to make their homes secure.

• Concerned about the value of their homes, Americans are spending more time performing maintenance on their homes and yards. Over the 1996 Fourth of July weekend, 50.8 percent of American families aged twenty to fifty-nine worked around their residences. This figure is up sharply from the 35 percent of pre-vious years.

• Americans are concerned about what will happen when they and their family members live longer. The anticipate more med-ical bills and thus the need for more retirement savings.

• In 1996, many Americans upped their expectations from 7 percent as an acceptable rate of return on all investments to 8 percent. This prompted banks and other savings institutions to market mutual funds rather than CDs.

CHAPTER SIX

NEVER UNDERESTIMATE
THE COMPETITION

In any competitive environment, the lesson to be learned is the same: Never underestimate your opposition. In contests from the sports arena to the battlefield, this point is emphasized. Always respect your foe's potential to beat you.

The annals of unexpected upsets have been repeatedly documented in all fields of endeavor, dating back to biblical times when David slew Goliath—indeed an awesome competitor.

How well major league managers and coaches understand this lesson! When the Super Bowl championship winner faces even the most lowly ranked team, players are still cautioned about a possible upset. Leaders in the business arena would be wise to take note. Small competitors grow bigger, weak competitors get stronger, and companies that don't even exist today could become tomorrow's strongest competitor.

New and stronger competition may come from any direction—from foreign shores as well as from your own backyard. A formerly unknown competitor may make a surprise advance in technology, or a formerly weak competitor could receive a financial transfusion from a silent investor. While New York City and Chicago have long been considered the epitome of a fiercely competitive, dog-eat-dog marketplace, even small communities can no longer be considered safe havens. For instance, thousands of small, homegrown retailers were unable to compete against

Wal-Mart when the huge discounter invaded their seemingly sheltered territories. Likewise, after the national fast-food franchises saturated larger markets, their operations expanded into small towns across America. The same can happen in any industry. A giant competitor that never paid attention to your success in the marketplace before may suddenly seize the opportunity to expand into your niche, which you had previously considered your own private world. Your competition is capable of doing things you never imagined!

GETTING *YOUR* SLICE OF THE PIE

The disposable-dollar pie is finite in size. Each consumer has only so much he or she can spend. When it is spent, it is gone. Each time a competitor takes a slice, the pie gets smaller.

Say, for instance, a husband and wife receive a combined bonus totaling $2,000. This money can be spent in many places. He may choose a home entertainment center or a new sofa. She may have different ideas—a new computer, decorating a bedroom, a vacation. That $2,000 is up for grabs; competition for it is by no means confined to a single industry.

What some businesspeople fail to realize is that they are not just competing against the company selling the same thing they do. The competition also consists of the company in a completely different industry. This is true because once the consumer spends his disposable dollar—and he's tapped out—his shopping is over. Only after he has accumulated more disposable dollars can he reenter the marketplace.

A large computer store retailer recently told me he was planning to open a big box store in one of the "hottest" shopping areas in his metropolitan area. "The traffic count is the highest in the city," he said, "and all the category killers are opening there. You should see them lining up, Britt. Best Buy and Home Depot are already open, and there's a Target and a Bed Bath & Beyond, too." He continued to name major retailers, including four major department stores, one super office supplies store, and one giant automotive store. He pointed out that his store would be the only computer store. "If those retailers are coming into the area, that's proof it's hot," he concluded.

I know a lot of retailers use the same criteria to determine the site for a new store opening. But as I pointed out to this person, just because there was no computer specialty store in the area didn't mean his store had no competition. The area had lots of competition, all going after the same finite number of disposable dollars.

The competition for finite disposable dollars is also a factor to be considered by anyone who sells nonconsumer products. A specialty steel manufacturer, for example, may put off installing a new tracking system and instead spend its disposable dollars to purchase new high-tech machinery. Or both buying decisions may be delayed because a section of the plant's roof is in dire need of repair and it can't be postponed another winter. No corporation has an unlimited budget. Like the typical American family, a business also has only so many slices in its pie.

THE "UNKNOWN" COMPETITOR

Deeply embedded in our American culture is the common belief that the number two guy must try harder than the number one guy. The role of underdog brings with it the eternal hope that hard work and perseverance will prevail. This credo warns number one companies to guard against complacency and remain alert. Those who fail to respond to the heat of competition are likely to lose their leadership position.

Of course, sometimes the heat doesn't come from the number two company but instead from some small, unknown competitor, and by the time its presence is first noticed, it has already positioned itself to make its heat felt.

Success not only breeds success, it also breeds competition. It is certain that many entrepreneurs are attracted to a marketplace in which a dominant company prospers. Just observe the start-up companies that initially emulated and later improved upon the performance of their Goliath predecessors—possessors of what seemed to be impenetrable shares of the marketplace. Then, in a relatively short span of time, an industry new-comer appears out of nowhere and becomes a major player, sometimes even forging ahead to capture top spot.

In 1958, when American Express entered the charge card field, its major competition was Diners Club. Once American Express captured the lead in its field, the company's main concern was that the Automobile Association of America might become its biggest threat. Its management believed that if the AAA came out with a credit card, the association's millions of members would sign up for its cards and, practically overnight, AAA would dominate the market. As it turned out, the AAA never came out with a charge card, but the banks did—MasterCard and Visa—and later, Sears produced the Discover Card (now owned by Dean Witter). Even as recently as 1990, AT&T introduced Universal Card, signing up more than ten million cardholders within two years.

So after enjoying a dominant position for two decades, American Express found itself going head-to-head with some colossal competitors—companies that, years before, never could have been envisioned entering the field.

From the 1950s through the 1980s, IBM dominated the computer industry. During this period, the company's stature was unequaled any-where in the world. IBM was hailed as the most admired, best-managed, and most profitable company ever. Known as Big Blue, the company was clearly the bluest of the blue chips.

Throughout the world, computers and IBM were synonymous. In the 1950s, IBM dominated its marketplace in every corner of the globe, before Steven Jobs, founder of Apple Computer, was even born. All the while, IBM's biggest fear was that AT&T (before its divestiture) might become its most awesome competitor.

So how did tiny Apple Computer, founded in 1976 by Steven Jobs, twenty-one, and Stephen Wozniak, twenty-six, ever gain ground against IBM? Apple was able to make its entry into the computer industry based on a brilliant marketing strategy. At its start, Jobs and Wozniak admitted,

"If we're going to build and market computers, we can't compete with IBM." IBM's market share position was approaching an off-the-chart level. When it came to business computers, IBM owned the marketplace. Consequently, Jobs determined that his company should build a computer that wouldn't be marketed to the business community, or, for that matter, even to adults. Instead it would cater to children and young adults. Jobs understood that the potential buyers in this market had no loyalty to IBM; for that matter, many of them had never even heard of the company.

To launch their new enterprise, Jobs sold his VW van and Wozniak his Hewlett-Packard programmable calculator; with the proceeds they raised $1,350 to finance production of Apple's first product, the Apple I board. With an advance order of fifty boards from a computer store, the Byte Shop, the new firm was able to leverage the order so it could get credit to build more machines in Jobs's parents' garage. By July 1976, the first Apple I boards were made available to hobbyists and electronics enthusiasts for a retail price of $666.66. Later that year, Apple's first formal business plan set $500 million in annual sales as a ten-year sales goal. It took just five years to achieve it.

Apple's phenomenal growth was a direct result of its brilliant marketing strategy targeting America's youth. This kept Apple from having to compete head-on with IBM on its own turf, the adult business-oriented marketplace. In 1979, in Apple's fourth year, a major step toward creating brand recognition occurred when Apple Education Foundation was established. Its lofty goal was to grant complete Apple systems to schools wanting to integrate computers into their curriculum. The foundation's long-range strategy was insightful. Over the course of time, America's youth were indoctrinated to recognize the Apple brand and to feel comfortable with its products. The company designed products to be used by young people, unlike IBM's mainframe business, which was designed for corporate America. And to be certain its product would be user-friendly for its customer, Apple introduced the mouse to the world.

In the beginning, so-called computer industry experts scoffed at Apple's interest in catering to its young customer. IBM executives openly ridiculed Apple, saying, "That's nonsensical. Kids don't have the buying power to purchase computers." Businesspeople preferred to buy an IBM computer, they said, not an Apple "toy." What the naysayers failed to understand was the influence kids possess to get their parents to buy computers.

Today, through efforts made by Apple Education Foundation, the company has donated more than $100 million in computers, peripherals, and training programs to elementary and secondary schools across the country. These efforts have since paid off handsomely. When these school-age computer users, having grown up with Apple, became young adults, it was the Apple brand—not IBM—that commanded their loyalty. In a field like computers, where it takes many years to build brand awareness, Apple's success sprang from a marketing strategy that sidestepped the branded position of IBM.

For years, IBM had been regarded as the world's finest marketing organization. No wonder people ask, "How did such a well-managed company fail to see the influence that kids could have on their parents?" Hindsight reveals that IBM had been so focused on marketing of its mainframes to corporate America that it failed to recognize the potential for another enormous market. Of course, at the time, Big Blue was making billions of dollars selling big computers, so the personal computer side of the business looked pale in comparison. When IBM finally did make its move into the personal computer field in 1980, Apple had already become the trendsetter.

In recent years, Apple, too, has fallen from grace. No longer is it the dominant market leader in the personal computer field. The first lesson to be learned from Apple's stumble is that if you live by technology, you must be prepared to die by technology, meaning you have to continue to be the technology leader. In the beginning, when comparisons were made to IBM's personal computer, Apple was perceived as being more innovative and state-of-the-art. "The mouse is user-friendly," people said. Today, however, all companies have some variation of the mouse and Apple's technological advantage has waned.

Second, Apple began with a decision to limit its distribution to computer specialty stores. Its management did not believe the mass merchants could do a good job selling its products. Even though today most computers are sold in office superstores and in electronics and appliance stores, early on this method didn't set well with Apple management. They didn't relish the thought of their computers selling alongside refrigerators or washing machines. Eventually, Apple did distribute its products through various retail outlets, but the company's response came only after it had lost its leadership position in the personal computer field.

Sometimes an entire industry can be caught dozing. This is what happened in the mid-1980s, following the end of the war between independent office supply stores and membership warehouse clubs. After surviving that bout, which could have meant their demise, the nation's small office supply stores were again enjoying growth and prosperity. Their earnings were running at a record high, and there was no immediate cause for concern. It was not, however, a time for celebration. As if out of the blue, three office superstores—Staples, Office Depot, and Office Max—appeared on the horizon. Rather than attacking the existing retail trade, however, these three superstores launched marketing strategies aimed at the commercial side of the office supply business. By sending catalogs offering immediate delivery and charging little or no shipping, they became formidable competition.

The superstores had one other advantage: In comparison to the smaller independent office supply stores, they had much larger inventories. This meant their business accounts didn't have to load up with supplies, since it had become so convenient for them to replenish. The onslaught of competition that hit the small office supply stores now dominates the industry, where it has now captured over 60 percent market share. Without a comeback strategy, the nation's independent office supply stores still have not recovered from the blow dealt by a formerly unknown competitor.

INBREEDING

Some corporate cultures view a company's bringing in top management from the outside as a sign of weakness. This admission of inadequacy, as opponents term it, means the company failed to develop its own people to fill its high-ranking managerial positions. Within the organization itself, those managers who contended for the position and got passed over are quick to point out that bringing in outsiders is damaging to morale. "It signals the other employees that no matter how hard they work, they won't be promoted," they say. "Instead, outsiders will be brought in for key positions."

The flip side of this school of thought is that a prime responsibility of management is to seek out the best possible person to fill its top slots. To promote somebody from within who is not qualified is ultimately unfair to both company and individual. In today's fiercely competitive marketplace, no company can afford to promote lesser contenders out of loyalty. This is simply not the place to put your loyalty on exhibit. Instead, your people need to receive, through your actions, the message that your decision is driven by the company's constant quest for excellence. And if that excellence can be obtained only from the outside, so be it.

While inbreeding is present in corporate America, it is especially widespread within family-run businesses, where emotional rather than rational thinking may be the main consideration. In small, family-operated companies, a father may promote his son knowing he isn't the best-qualified person for the job. The more qualified employee who's passed up may not deem it a fair decision, but lest we forget, a privately owned company isn't necessarily governed by fairness.

Of course, a family-owned business that promotes its own over more qualified employees may pay a big price. Not only could this court financial ruin, but it can emotionally scar the son or daughter who "lost the company business." Additionally, it can result in feuding, causing bitterness among family members.

In businesses that are handed down from generation to generation, several studies indicate that the highest rate of failure occurs during the third generation. One reason is that the vision of the founder has been lost by the third generation. Or the grandson wants to demonstrate that he is better than his father, and to prove it, he insists, "Granddad might have known what he was doing, but Dad was all wrong!" Still another reason could be that while the founder was still running a small business, he insisted that his son learn the basics from the ground up. The grandson who came on board a more grandiose business didn't receive the same exposure and may never have worked in an entry-level position.

In either a large or small business, inbreeding can be an infectious disease of epidemic proportions. All too often, management unwittingly believes it has a monopoly on the best people, who in turn are of the opinion that they represent the best industry thinking. Closed-mindedness of this nature shuts the door on fresh thinking, and, in today's environment, it keeps out people who could bring a much-needed different perspective. Inbred companies are particularly prone to be short-changed in the areas of technology and information, which are changing today at an increasingly rapid pace. The belief that nobody on the outside is capable of conceiving anything comparable to those on the inside puts a company at a serious disadvantage. A management that is lulled into a false sense of security tends to underestimate the competition—putting its company in harm's way.

A DIFFERENCE IN CORPORATE CULTURES

When a competitor gets a jump-start on you with an innovative marketing strategy, you must be careful to evaluate it before attempting to emulate it. Sometimes an attempt to copy or improve upon a competitor's success can backfire. You won't surpass the competition by mimicking it. If you choose that route, the best you can hope for is to be a second-rate version of your competitor.

What another company can easily accomplish with its people may not even be doable within your infrastructure. Certain divisions of your company may not be equipped to emulate a game plan initiated by your competition. For example, your advertising budget may not be as robust as the competition's. Or, for that matter, your shipping department might not be equipped to guarantee next-day delivery as your competition does.

There may also be significant differences in corporate cultures. Just as some Japanese managerial techniques fail to work in the United States (and vice versa) because of differences in culture, among corporations significant cultural variations exist that may not be interchangeable. In short, a marketing strategy that's going great guns for a competitor may not even be achievable by your company. But the flip side is that for the same reason, a competitor may be unable to emulate your marketing strategy.

In most cases, company cultures simply evolve. Here, management doesn't define what its culture should be, it just happens over a period of years. Other companies consciously develop a culture which plays an integral role in how employees and customers are treated and how important decisions are made. The corporate culture has the potential to influence every aspect of how the company conducts business.

In today's best-managed companies, the corporate culture is not a loosely defined, abstract thing. Instead, it is well defined and in written form. It's likely to be referred to as a mission statement, a code of conduct, or perhaps a proclamation of company values. Many companies have wallet-size cards printed containing these messages. These cards, carried by middle and senior managers, can, during heated debates, serve as a guideline on how to make the right decision.

When asked for advice on a slogan that would clearly define what a company's mission statement should be, I advise my clients: *Be first, be right, or be dead!* This advice stems from a revealing study we conducted. In 1985, when new customers had a problem, 65 percent of them would forgive the company after it had resolved their problem. However, our 1995 study disclosed that only 25 percent of customers were willing to forgive and forget. This points up the importance of being the first company the customer comes to, and doing things right the first time so the customer will come back. If you don't, you lose.

KEEPING UP WITH TECHNOLOGY

It is imperative that a company stay on the cutting edge of technology within its industry. With today's rapid changes in technology, a company that falls behind its competition's advances in technology operates under a serious handicap.

Fueled by computers and related by-products, unquestionably, technology has never advanced at such an accelerated pace. Consequently, in the marketing arena, knowing how to navigate the seemingly endless sea of information is imperative.

The banking industry is a prime example of how the use of technology has become a valuable marketing tool. Although personal debt, excluding mortgages, is over the $1 trillion mark and credit card delinquencies are approaching record high levels, banks now relentlessly pursue marginally credit-worthy consumers whom they formerly scorned. At a time when many consumers already languish under the weight of excessive debt, major banks across the country are beating the bushes for their business. To the casual observer, these activities appear to be putting the banks on a collision course with disaster, reminiscent of the 1980s when the banking industry overloaned to finance leveraged buyouts, commercial real estate, and developing countries.

What's different this time around is that today's lenders are more adept at protecting themselves. Their margin of error is lessened by identifying potential losses sooner and charging higher interest rates to risky borrowers. This proficiency stems from the use of powerful computers that slice and dice large amounts of information about potential customers. With this acumen, they can tag not only good customers who are able to afford more debt, but also marginal consumers who are possibly better risks than they might appear on the surface.

By using models of a bank's existing customer characteristics, such as credit usage and repayment history, how long a borrower has lived at a current residence, home ownership, and job tenure, it is easier to predict the likelihood of a customer's loan repayment. Having this kind of information changes the old rules. Now it may not be an automatic disqualification when an applicant has a blemish on his or her credit record, such as a previous sixty-day delinquency, if, say, a period of twenty-four months has lapsed.

In addition to making more prudent loans, technology enhances a bank's capacity to offer its services to loan-worthy prospects. Via computer-assisted mail solicitations, today's bank can identify and zero in on the best risks for credit cards, home equity loans, student loans, and so on. One peril that continues to spur banks deeper into technology is the nonbank competitors steadily invading the banking industry's traditional domain. The average American uses sixteen financial products—including checking and savings accounts, credit cards, home mortgages, and retirement investments—yet less than 20 percent of those come from a single institution. With an average of only 3.3 services per client, a bank has a strong incentive to offer more services to qualified prospective customers.

Every company, big and small, can tap into today's technology to increase its marketing capacity. This is no longer an option; it is imperative. What's more, you can be assured that your competitors are using technology to go after your existing customer base.

WHEN YOUR COMPETITION IS GOING THROUGH ROUGH TIMES, DON'T REJOICE—BEWARE!

When a competitor appears to be in trouble, an initial impulse is to break out the champagne and celebrate. After all, the other guy's loss is your gain. One fewer competitor may seem to translate into your picking up additional customers who formerly shopped across the street.

Instead of rejoicing, however, you should view a competitor's troubles as a warning sign. A formerly worthy opponent's problems can turn against you. When a competitor becomes desperate, he may become dangerous. Why? Because desperation inspires risk-taking. And when people are forced to take drastic measures, they could do creative things they might not otherwise have done. "What do I have to lose?" they ask themselves. As a result of unforeseen setbacks, many companies have instituted changes that ultimately made them stronger companies.

It sometimes takes a down period or lost market share to alert management to a danger signal. When a company gets into enough trouble, high-level management finally begins to raise questions: "How did we get into this mess?" This is followed up by "What do we have to do to rid ourselves of this problem?"

When everything is running smoothly, the "if it ain't broke, don't fix it" attitude prevails. But for obvious reasons, when times are bad, CEOs will begin to listen to other people. After several back-to-back weak quarters, it finally dawns on a CEO that he might not have all the answers after all. With this in mind, be smart enough to give some credit to your competitor: He may have good sources from which to seek advice. Under this assumption, there is some likelihood that he will straighten out his problems and reassume a competitive position.

When trouble brews and management feels pressure to institute change, you never know what your competition will do. During periods when the competition is doing poorly and your business is thriving, although you might not know it, *you* become vulnerable. Why? Because you're riding high and don't see any reason to change what appears to be working so well. When such a feeling of smugness appears, look out! Several years ago, for example, Fretters, the Detroit-based national appliances and electronics retailer, was experiencing some hard times. Although Fretters offered a competitive price range to its customers, its smaller stores were unable to offer selection comparable to that of the big boxes operated by its competitors. When people began shopping fewer stores to make their buying decisions, Fretters realized that its stores were not the first shopped, nor, for that matter, even the second shopped. A desperate competitor is willing to take greater risks, and to turn things around, Fretters replaced its usual mix of media advertising with a brand-new campaign. "Forget newspaper ads and everything else," Fretters management decided. "We're going on TV and run direct price comparisons against our competitors."

To accomplish this, Fretters embarked on a market-by-market TV campaign to inform consumers of its exceptionally low prices. In these ads, Fretters attacked each of its leading competitors in each respective marketplace, informing TV viewers how its prices favorably compared to those of its higher-priced competitors. For example, in Cleveland, an ad named a particular television set model and announced, "This is Sun TV's price—and here's ours!"

While some looked at the campaign as a drastic effort made by a desperate company to win new customers, it did exactly what it was supposed to do. So much so, in fact, that the number of shoppers drawn to Fretters dramatically increased—by 50 percent in some areas and as much as 200 percent in others. Imagine how surprised Fretters' competition was! Just as some of them were standing by anticipating a funeral, they were hit squarely between the eyes by an awesome advertising campaign. In Detroit, ABC Warehouse managed to respond to Fretters' TV ads, and was, consequently, able to hold its own. However, Highland Super Stores, another Detroit-based national appliances and electronics retailer, was not so fortunate. Although Highland ultimately responded, it was too late—not long afterward, Highland closed its doors. (As a footnote, after Fretters enjoyed some short-term prosperity, its management acquired Silo, a much larger electronic and appliances company. Unfortunately, the Silo deal led to the permanent closing of Fretters' doors.)

When your competitor is having serious problems, remember too that you probably don't know how deep his pockets are. And even when you do, circumstances change. When a business is in trouble, somebody may come along eager to bail it out or acquire it. And along with new capital may come new management. When outside people are brought in, anticipate fresh ideas along with a new marketing strategy. Or, for that matter, additional financial resources may enable a second- or third-level competitor to hire strong management from the number one player in the marketplace. And don't overlook the possibility that a competitor might induce one of *your* key managers to come aboard. If so, that individual's knowledge of your company can work against you.

Along the same line, some of my clients have informed me they don't tell their advertising agencies everything about their operation. Because who knows? Advertising agencies change personnel, so somebody who worked on your account may go to work for your competitor's agency. Or, for that matter, if you decide to change agencies, one of your competitors may hire your former agency.

SOME TELLTALE SIGNS

Knowing that top management starts listening when business is poor, you can anticipate that a down-and-out competitor may begin to do things differently. The following are three common early warning signs you may observe from your competition. Consider each signal an official notice informing you, "Don't write me off yet. I'll be back!"

In retailing, for example—and I'm sure this is true in other industries—a common panic reaction is to begin remodeling a store's format. Such changes indicate a competitor may have a new marketing strategy— one that can erode your market share.

Secondly, you should take particular notice when a competitor begins to close a few of its stores. Contrary to what common sense may suggest, such closings do not indicate that it's only a matter of time before every store shuts down. Say, for instance, a retailer has twenty stores in a particular marketplace, three of which are losers. Often a management focused on attempting to turn its three unprofitable stores around could neglect its seventeen profitable stores. Finally, after it becomes evident that "the cancer must be cut," management bites the bullet and closes its troubled stores. When this occurs, the three closings represent a positive step to restore the company's good health, because management was being prevented from putting its efforts and energy into its good stores. So when you see your competitor close down some units, don't start rejoicing. There is always the chance this will produce a stronger, healthier competitor.

And thirdly, when the other guy begins to reduce his general advertising campaign and concentrate on a single media—beware. When Fretters stopped its print advertising to focus on its television campaign, the effect on other electronics and appliance stores in its marketplace was devastating.

Similar telltale signs can be spotted in nonretail industries. A manufacturing company, for instance, might close down its nonproductive plants, or it may even reassess its product line and discontinue what's not profitable. It may also consider robotics, state-of-the-art technology, and downsizing. Clearly, a manufacturer may go through a series of changes that result in a more healthy, competitive company.

Telltale Signs in Retailing

There are certain warning signs that help you recognize when a retailer is in trouble. It's vital to pick up on these signs as a competitor, as a vendor, and as the owner of a troubled company.

1. Sales growth is running at half the industry rate.

2. A store hasn't been remodeled in five years.

3. Management is cutting advertising and/or ignoring market share data.

4. Management is living in the past, always quoting former performance.

5. A different advertising campaign is introduced every ninety days.

Telltale Signs in Big Business Manufacturing

Different warning signs are prevalent when a big manufacturer of consumer products is in trouble. These telltale signs are:

1. The company hasn't brought out a successful new product for three years.

2. Management refuses to acknowledge a new competitor with a different approach.

3. The company's presence at trade shows has been reduced.

4. The company raises its prices in the belief that its competition will follow suit.

5. The company experiences high turnover in the office of vice president of marketing and/or advertising; the company is constantly interviewing new advertising agencies.

Telltale Signs in Small-Business and Service-Related Companies

The warning signs of a small company are not identical to those of the large manufacturing company. The following are telltale signs to watch for in a smaller-size company:

1. The company loses its number one sales representative.

2. Sales growth is running at half the industry rate.

3. Company executives are saying, "That's not my customer."

4. Management is living in the past, always quoting former performance.

5. The company refuses to leave a weak location because the rent is low or because it owns the property debt-free.

CHANGING WINDOWS

The time it takes to respond to a competitor's new marketing strategy is a critical factor in today's marketplace. And because change is occurring at an ever-increasing pace, if you don't act swiftly, you'll be left behind.

Depending upon the industry, the size of the opportunity window varies based on how often the consumer purchases your product. To illustrate how quickly marketing strategies change today, observe the supermarket wars. Rapid change occurs there because the American household shops grocery stores between 3.8 and 4.8 times a month. In the past five years, for instance, 50 percent of American shoppers now patronize one fewer supermarket than they formerly did. This means that to survive, the competitive reaction time had to be reduced, because a supermarket customer is making decisions on a weekly basis. Bear in mind, however, that if you're in a category that's being bought every week, there's no guarantee your window will be open a full thirty days or even two weeks. But it does mean that the farther behind you are—in second, third, or fourth place—when the number one player implements a new strategy, the shorter the window of opportunity for your reaction. This is because the number one company is changing more people's habits faster, since it reaches more people in the marketplace.

A prime example of how a company can respond quickly to make a remarkable turnaround occur is Nashville-based Shoney's. The company was losing so much market share that for a while there was concern it might go belly-up. Founded in 1959, the $1.1 billion restaurant chain with its Big Boy signs is well recognized throughout the Southeastern and Midwestern states. With strong fast-food competition winning over its customers, the 900-unit chain was quickly losing its identity in its marketplace. Many restaurant industry analysts had discounted Shoney's ability to make a comeback. Then company management took a long, hard look at its entire operation. The business had to be revamped, and nothing would be held so sacred that it couldn't be changed. Everything was methodically reviewed, from how to reduce its higher-than-industry-average overhead to consideration of dropping the signage it had used for years—featuring its high-profile "dough-boy" signatory character, "Big Boy." Only after an extensive survey of Shoney's customers did Big Boy remain the company mascot.

After several attempts at changing its menu, Shoney's introduced a low-priced breakfast bar. Offering hearty and healthy buffet-style breakfasts at a reasonable price to an older and senior-citizen customer, the company was on its way to making an amazing comeback.

Shoney's initially focused on promoting its breakfast not only as a healthy meal, but as an all-you-can-eat bargain at just $3.99. On weekends, the price was slightly higher—a dollar more. At first, Shoney's newly introduced breakfast included a large selection of fruits, dry cereals, and bran muffins. Later, the buffet expanded to include eggs, french toast, waffles, sausage, bacon, and turkey ham for the cholesterol-conscious dieter.

In the food industry, as Shoney's proved, it is possible for a company to reverse its misfortunes very quickly. This is particularly true in an industry where customers purchase a product on a daily or weekly basis. Just how quickly a window will open is a reflection of how fast a competitor can change the habits of your customer. On the other hand, in the appliance industry, when a competitor makes a change in its marketing strategy, the time to respond is considerably longer, because a family makes a major appliance purchase (refrigerator, dishwasher, etc.) only 1.2 times every three years. As you can see, it's the consumer's buying habits that determine how quickly you must respond. In an industry where buying occurs more frequently, habits change at an accelerated pace. This applies to everything from buying razor blades to choosing an automobile.

Another factor that has shortened the time frame of the opportunity window is today's consumer's time crunch. As a result of present lifestyles, people are pressed for time, so American consumers are shopping fewer stores. Even with the increase in choices of fast-food restaurants in recent years, American consumers presently patronize fewer different types of fast-food restaurants than they did only three years ago.

In today's retail marketplace, I believe it's essential for a company to risk being different by making a statement unique to its category. Otherwise, a retailer may get lost in the crowd. In a recent survey, we spotted a trend of consumers who think retailers in the same category look alike. In 1985, 59 percent thought all stores looked the same; in 1990, 63 percent felt this way, and by 1995, 83 percent did. This trend delivers an important message: Unless your company stands out within its category, you have no identity and are lost in the shuffle.

PROSPERING DURING LEAN TIMES

A common denominator I've observed with the best-managed companies is that they enjoy substantial gains in market share even during down economic times. This occurs because most companies run for cover when there's a downturn in the economy. Instead of viewing these periods as an opportunity for market-share growth, they choose to simply "weather the storm."

When times are tough, a typical impulse is to reduce overhead, and, in particular, to lay off support people. Marketing, advertising, and research and development are among the first departments to receive budget cuts. When sales are lean, however, it's not the time to cut back in these areas. This does not produce a solution, nor will it turn things around. Instead, if you want to get more people into your store, advertising and marketing research should receive a bigger slice of the company's revenues. Remember that in order to find a cure, you must first identify the symptoms. The symptom is that fewer customers are buying your product.

Reducing your overhead is not necessarily the way to weather a bad economic storm. Since it's probable that your competition is also cutting back, perhaps you should consider taking advantage of a window that has opened. With your competition taking a defensive position, an excellent opportunity is being presented to you to increase your market share.

NEVER TAKE YOUR CUSTOMER FOR GRANTED

Today, more than ever, customers are feeling neglected. In a 1995 survey, we found that as many as 36 percent of all consumers say that the number one retailer in a given category doesn't seem to care as much about its customers as it once did.

In a similar survey, as many as 45 percent of all business owners state that they are considering buying from another source other than their number one supplier. When asked to express why they felt this way, they answered that they fear being vulnerable to the number one manufacturer/supplier, which may become too powerful and thereby able to dictate terms to them. This says a lot about how big companies are taking their customers for granted—and the customers obviously notice, and resent it. Furthermore, they intend to do something about it.

Most interestingly, these studies reveal that you'd better take very good care of your present customers. If you don't, be assured your competition will take them from you. And don't be so eager to get new customers that your old customers are neglected.

WHAT ARE THE ODDS?

Recently we did a study to determine what the odds are that a well-executed marketing strategy will succeed. This study evaluated the chance of success executives could expect based upon their position within an industry. It is further broken down to include retailers and nonretailing businesses (i.e., manufacturers, wholesalers, etc.).

	Chance of Success for a Retail Business	Chance of Success for a Nonretail Business
Number 1 market share company	83–89%	86–93%
Number 2 market share company	76–85	81–88
Number 3 market share company	64–73	76–79
Number 4 market share company	46–48	51–55

What is so interesting about these numbers is that there is a greater chance of success among the Number 1, 2, and 3 companies. But then even the Number 4 company has nearly a 50-50 chance in the retail segment and a slightly better than even chance in the nonretail segment of making an on-target marketing strategy. Another thing these numbers tell: The guy behind you—or if you're a market leader, even the guy three notches down—can come up with a well-executed marketing strategy that can take market share from your company.

CONSUMER MIND READER #6

The Top Twenty-five Reasons Why Advertising Fails

According to our survey, the following list, ranked in order of importance, contains what American consumers state as their top twenty-five reasons why retailers' ads don't work.

1. The retailer offers no reason for the sale.

2. The ad has a weak sale title or lacks one altogether.

3. The merchandise in the ad is unappealing.

4. The customer doesn't like the store.

5. The customer is not familiar with the store.

6. The store exterior appearance turns the customer off.

7. The ad contains too many exceptions and fine print, such as "See store for details."

8. The salespeople are too pushy.

9. The customer isn't interested in a sale unless the discounts are 40 percent to 50 percent to 60 percent off.

10. The store doesn't offer a thirty-day satisfaction guarantee.

11. Items in the ad appear too small—hard to identify the product.

12. The ad doesn't include brand names.

13. The store charges extra for basics such as delivery.

14. The production quality of the ad is inferior to the competition's ads.

15. The advertised prices are no better than the competition's.

16. The store's appearance doesn't change from sale to sale.

17. The salesperson lacks enthusiasm.

18. The same brands are available everywhere.

19. The store's ads look identical from sale to sale.

20. The prices never change.

21. The available store credit programs do not appear in the advertisements.

22. Quick delivery is not mentioned in ads.

23. The store parking area is untidy.

24. The store spokesperson in the ad turns the customer off.

25. The salesperson knows less about the product than the customer does.

Note that several reasons that appear on the above list do not at first seem to relate directly to advertising—such as pushy or uninformed salespeople, store appearance, and untidy parking lot. Remember, however, that advertising goes beyond the message conveyed by newspaper, radio, television, or direct mail—a company's image and word-of-mouth are also factors that influence customers, and these, too, constitute a form of advertising.

CHAPTER SEVEN

A PREDATORY STRATEGY

My years spent running political campaigns have had a strong impact on my business career. In a U.S. Senate campaign, only one day really matters—general election day. For each seat, once every six years, the day of reckoning comes, the day voters step into the voting booth. That first Tuesday following the first Monday in November occurs just once every 2,189 days—365 days times six years minus one day for leap year. In a winner-take-all race, one candidate wins the whole shooting match! There's nothing the loser can do except pack his bags and go home. It's all over.

Some have said, "Had there been a back door, there might not have been an Alamo." Well, come election day, there is no back door. Whether you're behind several points and your back is against the wall or you're just in a tight race, your survival depends on how hard you fight. You've got to muster every ounce of energy for striking the other guy, and you've got to hit him quicker, harder, and more often than he hits you. And even when you're the strong favorite, there's no letting up, because your opponent is always breathing down your neck—waiting for you to make a mistake.

In the political arena, the candidate who assumes a defensive stance is unlikely to win. Almost always, the spoils go to the aggressor—the candidate who launches the strongest offensive front. In a hard-fought senatorial race, I expect both parties to execute a tenacious offensive strategy, and I anticipate a lot of counterpunching from both sides.

My political background prompts me to advocate a predatory strategy in the never-ending battle to win market share. Where I came from, if you didn't win on that once-in-every-six-years Tuesday, you couldn't make a comeback with a Wednesday sale.

After interviewing five to eight thousand consumers every week, and spending thousands of hours in private consultation with top corporate managers across the country, I have concluded that every great company in pursuit of market share engages in a predatory strategy. To my knowledge, there are no exceptions.

I first became interested in developing a predatory marketing strategy for my clients in the late 1980s, when our research revealed an interesting trend in retailing. We noticed that each year fewer and fewer undecided customers were up for grabs. At one time, it was not uncommon to conduct surveys revealing that 38 percent of the customers were up for grabs; over the years, this number has steadily declined—to the current 6 percent. Our research indicates the decrease will continue. This trend delivers a very clear message: To increase market share in today's marketplace, no matter what your business is, you have to take customers away from your competition.

THE PREDATOR'S MIND-SET

In the world of marketing, a true predator always attacks the other guy at his strengths. Interestingly, this strategy contradicts offensive tactics taught on more conventional playing fields. In the world of sports, a boxer must attack his opponent's vulnerability, jabbing away at a bruised rib or perhaps an eye laceration; a football team repeatedly runs the ball through the weak side of the defensive line, or it may launch an aerial attack on a rookie cornerbacker; a tennis player pounds away at an opposing player's weak backhand. The great generals of the world engage in this same brand

⌐⌐ offensive strategy on the battlefield—assaulting the enemy wherever he is weak and unprotected.

If you are going to execute a predatory strategy to capture market share—which I strongly urge you to do—you must rid yourself of any preconceived notion of attacking your competition's weak areas. To concentrate on the fringes of the other guy's business is not productive. *You must attack the competition's core strengths.*

Always remember: The number one objective of a predatory marketing strategy—and you must never lose sight of this—is increasing market share. And since only 6 percent of customers are up for grabs, you must ultimately resort to winning over those customers who don't currently shop you. If you attack your competitors' weaknesses, you won't take many customers away from them. That's because those customers don't shop your competition for its weaknesses. They are driven to shop your competition for its strengths. This means that if you want to take customers away from the guy across the street, you have to give them a better reason to do business with you rather than with your competition that presently has their business.

What this adds up to is that to increase market share—and this is the premise of this book—you must take market share away from the leaders of your marketplace, because they are the only ones with a significant number of customers. Knowing that today's consumer shops at only 1.8 stores for major purchases, you must go after the customers of the number one store. This becomes very obvious when you consider that the no-group—the 6 percent of consumers who say that no store first comes to mind—are too few in number to build a marketing strategy around.

When the American consumer is shopping 1.8 stores, if you're not in the number one or number two position in market share, you're in deep trouble. You can't depend on leftovers—customers who come to your store after a bad experience at the first and second place they shopped. This is why you have no choice but to take customers away from the market leader(s), if you plan to grow—or, for that matter, even stay in business.

Let's play out an example of how this works. Say you operate a women's specialty store featuring Liz Claiborne, and the leading upscale women's sportswear retailer in your marketplace is a local department store with 40 percent of the area's women's sportswear business. By attacking the department store at its weaknesses—let's say it's slow at refilling the racks, and it has part-time, less knowledgeable salespeople—at best, you may get 5 or 10 percent of its business. Remember that those weak areas are not why its customers choose it as their first place to shop. Instead, they shop the department store because it offers a good selection, carries name brands like Liz Claiborne, and offers a store credit card. Since these are its strengths, you have to be perceived as having *even better* selection and, through special purchases, *even lower* prices on Liz Claiborne sportswear. Plus, you can offer your own store credit card with a ninety-day same-as-cash feature to counter its store credit card. If you can do this, you will be able to break the department store in its strengths. Then, and only then, can you realize significant market share gains—it could be as much as one third of the department store's upscale women's sportswear.

Now let me outline for you what such a predatory strategy should encompass. First, because the department store carries upscale, name-brand women's sportswear, you won't make any headway offering low prices on no-name-brand women's sportswear. A no-name, low-price strategy won't have nearly the impact of low prices on Liz Claiborne merchandise. Second, it's important for you to position your store as one that has a larger selection of Liz Claiborne than the department store. Fortunately, the department store with its many departments has limited floor space, which works to your advantage.

So what must you do to beat the department store? For starters, it's imperative that the customer perceive your store as offering superior selection. On this subject, our research shows that 53 percent of American consumers base their perception of a retail store's selection on its exterior appearance. So the bigger your store appears from the outside, the better the consumer will perceive your selection to be inside. If you can't afford to construct an addition to your existing building right away, I recommend you contact a good architect who can design a large facade on your store's exterior to create the impression that it's bigger than it actually is.

Likewise, a manufacturing company can use this approach when going up against a competitor who offers a product of equal quality and price. Let's say that a supplier of automotive components has determined that the other company's edge is due to lower shipping costs. To surpass this advantage, the supplier can use a different parts distributor, one located closer to the customer, resulting in substantial savings in freight for the customer. A predatory strategy can assist the movement of every product, from nuts and bolts to computer keyboards.

This going-for-the-jugular strategy works best when you attack the competition at its core strength. Don't pussyfoot around trying to entice customers away from a competitor by selling your merits over the other guy's weaknesses. Your sole mission is to take market share away from a strong competitor, and to do so, you have to let him have it with both barrels—aiming directly at his strengths.

THE ULTIMATE PREDATORY STRATEGY

As a predator, you'll always attack your competition's strengths. Let me elaborate on how the "ultimate" predatory strategy can be executed.

The first step is to identify your competitor's customers. My firm, ARG, does this for our clients by surveying those customers to find out why they shop there. Our survey questions address the main reasons they are loyal to the competition. "Where have you shopped during the past five years?" "Have you shopped at Store X in the last five years?" "What elements do you like best about Store X?" "What are your other reasons for shopping there?" After asking a large sampling of people dozens of questions, we probably know more about that competitor's customers than he does.

In short, we want to know why they go to the other guy's store versus any other store in the universe. After surveying enough people, we can determine the top reasons motivating these customers, and we can even pinpoint their order, the number one reason, number two reason, number three reason, and so on. This information reveals the exact strengths of the market leader, so we can focus on what our client can do to beat him in these areas, making it entirely probable that these customers can be won over. We try to create a strategy that makes customers reconsider the reasons they shop the competition. To accomplish this, you must be willing to take bold steps. You can't get those customers' attention by doing what you normally do—because what you normally did never got their attention.

There are several ways you can identify the competition's customers on your own. One way is to obtain a list from a quality direct-mail firm and have it purge the names of your customers from the list—and now you have a list of your noncustomers. A salesperson can do this, listing all the prospects in his territory, and then removing his company's accounts. The remainder are the people to be surveyed to find out why they're loyal to the competition. Still another way to find out who your competitor's customers are is to hire someone to record the license plate numbers from cars in Company X's parking lot—in some areas, you can obtain the names of these car owners from the state automobile licensing bureau. Several companies offer this service.

Of course, another way to obtain the names of customers who shop the market leader is to hire a key employee away from your competition. A client who is a wholesale paint manufacturer did this exact thing. When the manufacturer decided to expand its marketing area, we were hired to study the companies that might buy its paint product. When we interviewed the retailers in a new territory, one question we asked was "Who do you think is the best rep that calls on your company?" Over 50 percent of the corporate executives identified the same manufacturer's rep. Some of his customers told us that he was unhappy with his employer. The salesman was paid a straight salary with a small year-end bonus, and he was determined to be paid straight commission. Can you blame him? He was the sales force's number one producer. He felt he was being penalized, since his salary was only 10 percent more than that of the lowest sales rep, while his sales production was three times greater.

The word was out that he had an ongoing fight with his sales manager. We passed this information on to our client, who contacted him before another competitor did, offering him an employment agreement that included being paid straight commission. If he continued at his current pace, the new payment format meant he would more than double his income, and the fringe benefits would also be superior. The client made him an offer he couldn't refuse. Within a month after he came aboard, 80 percent of his former accounts were converted to his new employer.

A word of caution, however, before you consider hiring your competitor's people: You must make sure that your company benefits and complete package are superior to those of other companies in your marketplace. No company is going to allow you to stroll in and take its star employees away without putting up a fight. So be prepared to engage in more than a scrimmage, because you're likely to get an all-out war.

NONCUSTOMER PRIVATE EVENTS

Once a competitor's customers have been identified, the predatory marketing strategist isn't shy about going after them. One way to get noncustomers into your store is by soliciting them to attend special events. A retailer, for example, might have a noncustomer private sale. For this special event after normal shopping hours, he invites only people who do not presently shop his store. It's an exclusive, invitation-only affair, and only noncustomers are invited.

To induce this group to attend, a specific offer should be made. A special sale could feature a one-time discount, or perhaps an added value, such as an extended guarantee or a particular feature available only to those customers at the event. The more extravagant the event, the more exciting and appealing it will be. For this reason, you may want to have a gala affair—with food and beverages served and even small gifts given to attendees. Entertainment can range from a quartet or celebrity to an expert in your field. A camera store, for example, might have a well-known photographer give a brief speech followed by a question-and-answer session.

In nonretailing fields, in a drive to develop new business, a stockbroker might invite a group of investors to a luncheon where the guest speaker is a recognized financial planner. A bank might host a group of real estate brokers at a seminar where topics run the gamut from home financing to interior decorating. A manufacturer might throw an elegant private party at an industry convention and, again by invitation only, entertain a selected group of noncustomers as guests. While some attendees will show up out of curiosity, others may come because their present source is not meeting their needs and they want to shop around. Remember, however, that the people you are courting place a high value on their time, so to induce them to come, you have to make it worth their while.

MOMENTUM

Momentum is an intangible quality that, by its nature, is so elusive it's difficult to execute. In sports, for example, we've all witnessed a tennis match where one player wins 6–0, only to get beat 0–6 in the following set. Then there's the football team that comes from behind by scoring three quick touchdowns in the fourth quarter. Momentum is a consequential factor in many walks of life—sports, politics, business, and so on.

It's hard to stop a locomotive when it's going at full steam, and in the political arena, I've observed that the candidate with momentum on his side enjoys a powerful advantage. As a former campaign manager, I can assure you that if there is ever a time to implement an aggressive strategy, it's when your candidate is trailing by double-digit figures and the general election is only a few weeks away.

I can remember one particular race in which a candidate who didn't appear to have a chance of winning used brilliant strategy to turn his campaign around. I still marvel when I think about how the momentum changed—in a campaign where everyone had written him off.

The 1978 U.S. Senate race in Wyoming pitted incumbent U.S. Senator Gale McGee against Malcolm Wallop. McGee, the front-runner, was a liberal Democrat who had been a major supporter of the Occupational Safety and Health Act (OSHA). His opponent jumped on this issue to implement a highly creative aggressive strategy.

In the way of background, let me say that when OSHA was first created, many zealous bureaucrats insisted that the federal government enact health and safety regulations to protect every working American. At the time, consumer advocate groups across the country prophesied that the passing of OSHA would save tens of thousands of lives and countless more injuries.

McGee was running a pretty typical 1970s incumbent's campaign, focusing on how much he had done for the state and reminding the voters of all of the projects he personally had brought to Wyoming. Meanwhile, Wallop tried to hammer home the idea that McGee had lost touch with the people of Wyoming—which was also your 1970s garden-variety campaign. The incumbent McGee had all the momentum on his side, and as election day edged closer, his numbers continued to rise.

Then Wallop's campaign people created one brilliant campaign commercial, and the momentum dramatically switched. The camera scanned a typical Wyoming ranch scene, showing a large field with a farmer riding his tractor. It opened with the sounds of the engine, and a voice-over told the viewer: "Your senator, Gale McGee, was an active supporter and sponsor of the passage of OSHA. And like many other federal programs, OSHA may have good intentions, but bureaucrats often take things to extremes."

Then, following a brief pause, the announcer's voice continued, "This legislation does not represent the real needs nor does it solve the problems of the people of this state. Gale McGee has lost touch with the people of Wyoming." Pause. "Malcolm Wallop is from Wyoming, knows Wyoming, and cares about the people of Wyoming. He understands the problems."

While the camera focused on the tractor-driving farmer, the voice-over continued, "OSHA says that every working person must be within one hundred feet of a rest-room facility, and we think this illustrates how much out of touch Gale McGee is." As the announcer's voice faded, in full view on the television screen was the ludicrous image of what the farmer was towing behind him: an outhouse attached to the back of his moving tractor.

This single commercial turned the momentum around, and Malcolm Wallop was elected to the U.S. Senate.

Just as an aggressive strategy can change the momentum to win votes, so can an advertising campaign win customers in your marketplace. Over the years, I have designed many strategies to compare the strengths of my client to the weaknesses of the competition. But bear in mind that this differs from true predatory strategy—which would dictate attacking your competitor's strengths, not his weaknesses. In the business world, it's generally the niche player that adopts this tactic—in this case, the objective is not to take away large market share, but instead to take away small chunks of business. For instance, the owner of a small Lexington Avenue men's clothing store, within walking distance of New York City's Bloomingdale's, might offer a better selection of less popular sizes as well as lower prices on a particular brand-name shirt. However, it isn't realistic to expect his tiny 1,000-square-foot operation to make a significant dent in Bloomingdale's shirt department sales.

When you attack a competitor by mentioning him in your commercial or ad, you are, in effect, advertising his name. This means that even when you knock a competitor, you create an awareness of him in your audience. For this reason, never, absolutely never, mention in an ad the name of any competitor who doesn't have significantly more market share than you. To do so is to acknowledge that he is an equal competitor. If, for example, you have a 14 percent market share and a competitor has

17 percent, don't go after him in your ad campaign. The much bigger competitor, however, is fair game. For this reason, it made sense for Avis to advertise, "We're number two, so we try harder," while it would not have been wise for Hertz to counterattack by advertising, "We're number one, so we must be better than Avis."

THREE PREDATORY STRATEGIES

Let's assume your objective is to take large numbers of customers away from a market leader. The following examples portray three ways this can be achieved:

1. A Women's Apparel Chain vs. The Limited

Suppose you own a woman's apparel chain, with stores in the same malls where The Limited is located. You would like to establish a predatory marketing strategy against The Limited. First you must ascertain what The Limited's strengths are. You come up with three: (a) The Limited is a well-known company; (b) The Limited is considered a trend-maker, known in particular for its color trends; and (c) The Limited is recognized for its good prices on high-quality goods.

In light of the above information about The Limited, your predatory strategy must be geared to convince its customers that your store is the place younger women—under thirty-five—should definitely shop. And because a building's appearance can make or break a fashion apparel retailer, your store's entrance area and front window must make a contemporary fashion statement. Inside, your run-down showroom with wood floors is a store of yesterday. It will not support the perception of fashion you want to project. Your location must exemplify a store of today, so you'll be making some cosmetic changes to make it fit your new on-trend image.

The Limited has historically taken a radical position to show its belief in a fashion trend. Your store must do the same. If frost green is presently the designated hot color you are promoting, your store must be committed enough to buy a large inventory in frost green. This means having enough auxiliary pieces to complement other pieces, so a shopper can create a complete outfit with frost green as the predominant color. With a strong selection of this nature, your store will be able to compete with The Limited's on-trend, on-color look.

Next, you must either give your customer *more* quality for the same price, or offer the same level of quality at *lower* prices. Several competitors of The Limited find that they have had to go around the world to find resources that enable them to offer the same quality goods at lower prices, but, consequently, they were able to take some market share away from The Limited.

2. An Independent Mattress Specialty Retailer vs. Sears

Let's review Sears's strengths in the mattress category: (a) Sears has a strong reputation; if there is a problem, Sears will take care of it. (b) Sears offers its own charge card; the customer can finance the mattress. (c) Sears carries brand names.

As a specialty store, your strengths are (a) selection, (b) knowledgeable salespeople, and (c) more convenient locations. Now in order to attack Sears, you must be superior to them, so this requires you to make changes. In the area of selection, it's probable that both Sears and your store carry Sealy, so when Sears advertises Sealy, you must advertise Sealy—but at a lower price. To compete against Sears with its credit card, you can offer six-month, no-interest, no-down-payment, no-monthly-payments promotions, but chances are there's nothing in this area you can give the customer that Sears cannot. You can also offer next-day delivery, but Sears can, too. You can offer to pick up the customer's old mattress, but so can Sears. When it comes to reputation, our research shows that the way you can quickly build a reputation in the marketplace is by advertising on TV, "During the next thirty days, if for any reason you are unhappy with your purchase, we guarantee we will take it back. We will exchange it. We will give you your money back. We will pick it up at your home. We will not give you any hassle whatsoever."

With all of the above, you will equalize your reputation with Sears, create better credit advantages, and offer the same brand-name mattress at a lower price. As you can see, the real tiebreaker is that your store has more locations and your salespeople are more knowledgeable. The secret of this predatory marketing strategy example is that you must, first, match Sears, and, second, come up with a tiebreaker to take away its market share.

3. A Small Carpet Manufacturer vs. Shaw Carpets

As a small carpeting manufacturer, you're up against Shaw Carpets, a company that has approximately 50 percent of the market share in the United States. Shaw Carpets is the giant of the industry, owning brand names such as Salem, Philadelphia, Cabincraft, Sutton, and Evans & Black. Shaw's strengths are (a) a discount program for quantity purchases, offered to the company's dealers; (b) fast delivery; and (c) wide distribution—the company sells to the majority of carpet retailers.

To compete against Shaw, first you must acknowledge that you can't knock heads with Shaw across the board. Therefore, select one narrow price range in which you think your company is strong. For example, you might choose a $15 to $19 per square yard wholesale price where you can focus all your efforts. By concentrating in this area, you might even be able to have a better selection. To counter Shaw's volume rebates, you can offer a once-a-quarter incentive to your biggest accounts, providing deep discounts if they buy during a three-to-five-day or one-week window. You could also tie in an advertising co-op program that could be more attractive than Shaw's volume discounts, and with this, a lower price would always be available.

Second, after analyzing Shaw's delivery program, you could tell your accounts, "We will guarantee to stock these particular products within our line, and if we ever are out of stock, we will waive the freight charges to your store." Here you are making a statement to them that you are committed to a short delivery window. This will be well received by carpet retailers, because it allows them to carry less inventory.

Third, you're not going to be able to match Shaw's wide distribution strategy, but you can counter it with a limited strategy that gives your brand exclusively to one retailer in a particular marketplace. This, in turn, would reduce comparative shopping, and retailers love that because they can get a higher markup.

Of all the companies I have studied, the majority have only two primary reasons why their customers shop them, and rarely are there more than three primary reasons. This is important information, because a company with customers having one or two primary reasons can easily fall victim to a predatory strategy. Let's review two fictitious bicycle manufacturing companies. A survey shows the primary reasons why retailers do business with Company A are:

Established brand name	41%
National advertising program	30
Fast delivery	25

The primary reasons why retailers do business with Company B are:

Low prices in lieu of advertising support	48%
One-year warranty on all major parts	40

Company B is easy prey compared to Company A, because a competitor that has only two areas on which to focus its predatory strategy can more easily take away customers. Not only should you keep this in mind when attacking a competitor, but also note how vulnerable your company is when it has only one or two strengths. In the above example, a competitor could take lots of marketing share from Company B by (a) lowering its prices (i.e., giving advertising allowances, volume discounts, etc.) and (b) giving a two-year, no-questions-asked warranty.

Strong companies that are less vulnerable to predatory strategies tend to be ones with diversity and, consequently, they are more difficult to assault.

THREE REAL PREDATORY STRATEGY CASE HISTORIES

Case History 1

A few years ago, I was called in to develop a predatory marketing strategy for a client who owned a video store. In this Midwestern town with a population of about forty thousand, he was competing against another video store, and at the time, each store was renting a thousand videos a week.

Our research tells us the five reasons people shop a particular video rental store:

1. SELECTION OF CURRENT HITS. The number one reason people choose a video store is that it offers the greatest number of current movies.

2. CONVENIENCE TO HOME. Video renters like stores that are only a short drive from where they live.

3. SELECTION OF NONCURRENT HITS. In addition to a large selection of recently released movies, video renters also want to be able to choose from older favorites.

4. LOW PRICE. Budget-minded people consider low price a major factor in choosing a video store.

5. DEALS. Shoppers are attracted to video stores that offer "specials," such as two for the price of one, a frequent renter's discount, and bargain prices on certain days of the week.

After analyzing this research, we determined the following: My client's competition was perceived in the marketplace as having not only the best selection of current hits, but also the best location. It also had us beat by offering a special deal for selecting more than one video per visit. On the other hand, we had a bigger selection overall, and we saw no significant difference in price.

We knew there was nothing we could do about our location, because my client owned his building and wasn't about to construct a new one. So we devised a predatory strategy to go after the competition's other strengths—the great selection of current hits and the offering of better deals. To break this guy, we tripled our orders of current releases and came out with a midweek special of $1 rentals. On weekends, when we'd get full price, my client almost always rented out all his current releases. But we figured getting $1 per rental during the week was better than having inventory sitting on the shelves.

As a result of this strategy, our client's sales doubled—from 1,000 rentals to 2,000 a week. His competitor's rentals dropped by 50 percent, to only 500. And the total rentals in that marketplace increased from 2,000 to 2,500.

After seeing his business drop significantly, the competitor finally devised a counterstrategy. He began to offer a special deal for weekend rentals. However, it was ineffective, because on weekends, both stores were usually sold out anyway, and when a store is out of inventory, it doesn't matter how much the demand is increased. Our predatory strategy worked well because we attacked the other guy at his strengths—but in his counterattack, he didn't attack us at ours.

Case History 2

A few years ago, a Midwestern savings bank (which will remain anonymous) asked me to put together a predatory marketing strategy. The bank's objective was to take business away from a competing bank that enjoyed a 40 percent share of the home mortgages in its marketplace. The market leader's strengths were (a) it had the lowest mortgage rates in the marketplace; (b) depending on the customer, it took only seven to fourteen days to approve and process a loan application; and (c) it had a good staff who were available and willing to visit a customer's office or home on weekdays from 9:00 a.m. to 6:00 p.m.

First, it was a given that our client had to meet its competition's mortgage rate. Second, a decision was made to invest in technology in order to beat the competition's time for approving and processing loan applications. With this technology, the time was reduced to five days. And third, a program was instituted to meet with customers from 9:00 a.m. to 9:00 p.m., as well as on Saturdays, wherever it was convenient for the customer.

Knowing that real estate brokers control more than 70 percent of all first-time mortgages in the United States, we also put together a marketing strategy for the bank, aimed at the area's real estate brokers. The game plan was to focus on selling the brokers rather than on selling the homeowner. To accomplish this, in addition to sending literature to all the real estate people in the area, the bank's people made personal calls to real estate offices. They also spoke at real estate conferences, invited brokers to attend luncheons, and even conducted classes to educate them on their available services. During this time, they tried to find out what banking services the real estate community most valued. Based on the input they received, whenever a real estate agent called in for a loan's status, our client was able to provide information in less than five minutes, while the competition took thirty minutes to get a loan's status. Our client was also able to preapprove a home mortgage up to $250,000, which, to the real estate agent, was a godsend. This meant the agent could show homes in a particular price range to a potential homeowner secure in the knowledge that the financing would go through. Of course, the processing of the loan would take five days, but as long as the agent knew it would be approved, he or she had only to make the sale. In the past, a sale wasn't a sale until the loan was made—and deals commonly fell through because financing couldn't be obtained.

Once this marketing strategy was in place, my client was off and running. With solid relationships in place with the real estate community, during the next eighteen months my client took away 20 percent of the other bank's market share.

Case History 3

A classic predatory marketing strategy story happened a few years ago when Circuit City, the large appliance and electronics retailer, first entered the Los Angeles marketplace. At the time, Federated Group, an electronics-only chain store operator, had dominant market share in L.A. Its big boxes, which then were 30,000-to-35,000-square-foot stores, were spread across the greater metropolitan area.

At the time, Circuit City was unknown in the L.A. area, while Federated Group was well recognized as the store with the best electronics selection in town. Since Circuit City came to L.A. with smaller, 28,000-square-foot stores that would sell appliances in addition to electronics, it appeared to be no threat. After all, the strength of Federated Group, with its big box stores, was its great selection.

However, the management at Circuit City clearly understood that customers base their perception of selection on how big a store looks from the outside. To bolster this perception, on each of its one-story buildings, Circuit City built a two-story facade with its burgundy three-story tower attached.

Interestingly, surveys have since revealed that when consumers were asked how big they thought the Circuit City stores in the Los Angeles area were, their response was 55,000–60,000 square feet, almost double their actual size. It took only six months for Circuit City to capture the selection image in the marketplace. Today Circuit City is the number one electronics retailer in Los Angeles, while Federated Group has closed its doors. What Circuit City did took away its competitor's dominant market position of selection, and illustrates what can happen when you attack the other guy's strength. Once Federated Group lost its selection strength in the marketplace, its customers headed to Circuit City to shop for electronics—where they *perceived* the selection was greater.

COUNTERATTACKS

When you're under attack by a competitor and losing market share, you don't have to take it lying down. You must counterattack—and make the other guy rue the day he ever messed with you.

In a predatory strategy devised for Perry Drugs, a drugstore chain with stores located throughout Michigan, I advised such a counterattack. Perry Drugs had called me in to devise a plan in response to a competitor, Arbor Drug, which was hitting the marketplace with an extremely strong photo-processing promotion called "Picture-Picture." To drive traffic to its stores, Arbor offered two developed four-inch photos for the price of one; this promotion rapidly made Arbor the number one photo processing drugstore in the marketplace.

After losing considerable market share to Arbor, Perry Drugs called us in to do a study, to create a stronger photo-processing offer that would beat the Picture-Picture offer. Our research revealed that while many people enjoyed getting two four-inch prints for the price of one, some consumers confessed that what they would really prefer to receive was a free roll of film.

With this information, we launched a counterattack called "Perry Pairs." Our media blitz announced, "You can have your choice. Perry Pairs will give you two four-inch prints for the price of one, or you can get two three-inch prints *and* a free roll of film—all for the same price." It was only a matter of time before Perry Drugs recaptured its lost market share to become number one in the marketplace.

Although, oddly enough, Arbor Drugs never did retaliate with its own counterattack against Perry Drugs, I always advise my clients to be ready with a Plan B—prepared well in advance. I make this recommendation because when a market leader begins to lose market share, it's probable that he'll strike back quickly. So if you are called upon to implement a Plan B, it's best to prepare it along with your Plan A.

Although Perry Drugs never had to use its Plan B, it was prepared to go with it if Arbor Drugs retaliated. The company put together a comparative price campaign—commercials were ready to put on television—to inform viewers that in addition to having two options compared to Arbor's single photo option, Perry's was a dollar cheaper. While its predatory strategy, surprisingly, went unchallenged, the company was committed to winning the war it had declared on Arbor Drugs.

If your competitor enjoys the lion's share of the market, just remember that he didn't get it with a defensive marketing strategy, so make sure you have the stomach for retaliation. After you have made your move, prepare for him to launch an offensive attack. Don't expect that he'll just stand there and let you rip his heart out without putting up a fight.

As the expression goes, "Never draw a sword on a king unless you intend to slay him." Be prepared for the other guy to charge back at you, and not only that, be ready to engage in a long battle. A predatory marketing strategy is not implemented on a quarter-to-quarter basis. You don't do it on a whim. A fiercely fought battle may very well continue for the next nine to eighteen months.

MINDING THE STORE

In the political arena, a predatory strategist understands that he must not try to win over additional voters at the risk of losing those already in his camp. A Republican, for example, wouldn't campaign against Bill Clinton by trying to attract the union voter base if that meant turning off his white-collar, small-business voter base. Doing so would jeopardize the assets he already has for the pittance he might gain.

Likewise, a retailer with a high-quality-merchandise-driven clientele would be foolish to lower the quality level of the goods in his store in order to win over a price-conscious buyer. Such a drastic step could very well result in a net loss of business. What this means is your predatory marketing campaign must dovetail with maintaining your existing customer base. If not, you may find yourself taking one step forward and two steps backward.

It's like a game of chess. While you're going after his queen, he's going after your queen, and then you're both after each other's king. Meanwhile, you are taking away each other's castles and bishops. In the game of winning market share, it's a race to see who takes away more customers from whom.

HE WHO STRIKES FIRST

To reiterate, the key to implementing a successful predatory marketing strategy is taking an offensive position. With this in mind, whoever begins the war has an enormous advantage, because, invariably, the other guy is forced to react with a defensive stance. If you've planned carefully, when your opponent reacts to you, you'll have a Plan B and even a Plan C ready to put into action, so that he's continually on the defense.

In a review of fifty of the predatory marketing strategies my company has implemented in the past five years, a remarkable statistic was revealed. Only eight times did the competition respond. We were surprised at that figure of only 16 percent, so we conducted a study to analyze why the response was so low. First, we observed that most successful predatory strategies scoop up 10 to 18 percent more market share than the client enjoyed before. It's a major figure, so when a retailer experiences such a major decline, he's aware that something's happened, but he may not realize it was actually caused by a competitor. Instead, he may attribute it to the economy or some other force outside his control. Consequently, he doesn't know how to react to the competition.

Just the same, never underestimate your competition. You must have a Plan B in place, in the event that you're up against that one-in-six competitor. After all, a revolver has six chambers, but you wouldn't consider playing Russian roulette, would you?

CONSUMER MIND READER #7

America's Ten Most Budget-Conscious Cities

We conducted a survey identifying U.S. markets where consumers are not luxury item or premium buyers. Of all U.S. cities in which there is a disproportionately large number of low-end and middle-end shoppers compared to high-end shoppers, the following ten top the nation:

1. Orlando, Florida

2. Buffalo, New York

3. Salt Lake City, Utah

4. Youngstown, Ohio

5. Johnstown, Pennsylvania

6. Toledo, Ohio

7. Wilkes-Barre, Pennsylvania

8. El Paso, Texas

9. Rockford, Illinois

10. Odessa, Texas

Of the top five cities, Orlando's budget-conscious citizens rank number one in our study. Orlando's top billing is a reflection of the area's huge tourist industry, which employs a large number of people. The immense pool of low-wage earners who work in Orlando's amusement parks, motels and restaurants are not likely to shop higher-priced luxury stores.

In second place is Buffalo, a blue-collar town whose population has a cash-driven mentality. This recent study, as well as studies we conducted in the early 1980s, reveals that Buffalo's economy has been depressed for many years. Consequently, shoppers in the area walk into a store carrying the exact amount of cash needed to purchase a particular item, and they are reluctant to exceed the amount in their wallets; nor are they likely to be tempted by a bigger-ticket item suggested by a salesperson. In third-place Salt Lake City, populated by many large Mormon families, folks work diligently to stretch every dollar. In fourth place is Youngstown, Ohio, a city whose residents have not recovered from the closings of large factories that took place in the 1980s. And rounding out the top five is Johnstown, Pennsylvania, a formerly thriving coal-mining community that has suffered economic stagnation for many years; as a consequence, its citizens are frugal shoppers.

In these ten communities, retailers offering products in lower and moderate price points thrive. Such discount stores include Wal-Mart, as well as off-price apparel stores like Marshall's, Value City, and Target. Outlet malls also do well in these areas. However, retailers that sell high-end products—such as Tiffany's, Henri Bendel's, and Neiman Marcus—do not fare well in these markets. For that matter, automobile dealerships such as Mercedes may struggle in these areas. Likewise, high-priced restaurants and upper-end interior decorators would be wise to peddle their services elsewhere.

Remember, however, that a business selling a big-ticket product that caters to an affluent buyer may not have to rely on large numbers of customers to generate high sales volume. So perhaps a single store of that type could survive, but with one caveat: If competition moved into the area, there might not be enough business to go around, which could result in hard times for both concerns.

CHAPTER EIGHT

THE NICHE PLAYER

John Nesbitt's best-seller *Megatrends* predicted that a few mega-companies would ultimately dominate the world marketplace. Nesbitt may not have taken into account one thing: A vast company that concentrates on the big picture can get a good overview of the forest but is prone to overlook some interesting trees. Because of a mega-company's size, a lot slips through the cracks, paving the way for budding entrepreneurs. Much of this slippage can be picked up by small competitors eager to find their own niches.

Since it takes major resources to operate a business on a large scale, only a limited number of players can be mass marketers. Relatively few can take the route of attempting to offer "something for everyone," so consequently, few companies set their sights on capturing the top spot. Instead, a small player who strives to distinguish his business by focusing on a single niche in the marketplace can thrive in his own small world. Still, he who conducts business on a small scale does not exist in a vacuum. The small entrepreneur also competes in a large marketplace where countless, sometimes Lilliputian competitors vie for customers beneath the towering presence of omnipotent market leaders.

The niche player is a familiar character in business for another reason. Typically, an entrepreneur enters the marketplace with the idea of filling a small void with a product or service not offered by the giant corporation or its well-established competitors. Start-up businesses that do succeed usually continue to operate on such a small scale that the market leader takes little notice. Only a handful of such enterprises ever surface to capture the attention of the top dogs in their respective industry.

THE DEMAND FOR THE NICHE PLAYER

In 1994, we conducted a research study on the consumer's preference for doing business with a niche player rather than a superstore, department store, or national mass retailer. Notice that this demand varies dramatically from industry to industry:

Women's fine apparel	42%
Women's apparel	38
Fine jewelry	38
Major appliances	38
Women's shoes	35
Home audio	28
Mattress	28
Men's apparel	28
Video rental	26
Television sets and VCRs	16
Athletic shoes	15
Small household appliances	14

Although these consumers know they may have to pay a higher price in the smaller stores, they believe certain products are worth the extra cost. They know the small retailer's salesperson will be more knowledgeable—and in locally owned stores, the owner may personally serve them. Therefore, it comes as no surprise that products requiring the highest level of service are the categories with the most demand for a niche player. There are exceptions, however. When it comes to buying a small household appliance or athletic shoes, most people believe the local independent store has a poorer selection. Times have changed: Ten years ago, 56 percent of consumers preferred local appliance stores, but today many smaller appliance stores no longer have their own service departments. Instead, service work is contracted out to an independent service organization. Consequently, the demand for a niche player in appliance retailing is significantly less, even though a knowledgeable salesperson is considered desirable.

While our study was limited to retailing, I believe this thinking applies also to nonretailing industries. There is a demand for a small manufacturer versus a large manufacturer if the customer feels he or she will receive superior service. There's no question that a manufacturer's customers are willing to pay more for value-added services, which range from quicker, more reliable delivery to tailor-made orders.

TO BE OR NOT TO BE

A dry cleaner in a medium-sized Midwestern city decided to specialize in cleaning expensive gowns—in particular, beaded wedding gowns. No one else in the area was able to compete with him. Soon his reputation for that particular type of dry cleaning spread throughout the city. Women from all parts of town who needed to have a special formal garment cleaned felt it was worth it to drive to his establishment. In time, 80 percent of this cleaner's business was dry cleaning beaded gowns. Because cleaning gowns is seasonal, during the busy periods he neglected his regular business.

While his gown service was exceptional, his other dry cleaning work was not much different from the competition's. So while he was the market leader in his specialization, the niche he had established did not by itself generate sufficient revenue for his business to succeed. While these same gown customers stopped by occasionally, they were not willing to drive that far to bring their regular cleaning to his store. After all, there were many other places with more convenient locations for everyday dry cleaning. In fact, our research shows that consumers are willing to drive only 8.3 minutes for dry cleaning services for their regular clothes. Consequently, although he found a niche in the marketplace, he eventually had to close his doors. This tells us that an opportunity to provide a product or service must conform to the patterns of the consumer who is going to buy that item.

Successful niche players find something that gives them an identity that their competitor, the mass marketer, doesn't have. It is ideally something that the bigger competitor doesn't understand or doesn't know how to respond to. But other considerations include: (1) Is the opportunity window for your niche large enough to be viable? (2) What is the area that the competition is missing, that makes your niche viable? (3) Is the customer willing to pay a reasonable premium? These basic questions are predictors of success.

When these three questions are explored, we can see that the dry cleaner clearly misjudged the size of the window for his gown-cleaning niche. Even though he offered a specialized service unavailable in the area—and his service was reasonably priced—there simply wasn't enough business to support his small niche. In Detroit, another cleaner specializes in dry cleaning area rugs; unlike the beaded gowns dry cleaner, he has succeeded, because of the larger market for those services.

In your marketplace, it's paramount to find a niche big enough to make it worthwhile for you to be in business. An idea that works in one particular market might not work in another. For example, the gown-cleaning service might actually have succeeded in a larger metropolitan location in the East—say, New York, Philadelphia, or Boston—but it went belly-up in a midsized Midwest city where evening gowns are worn less often.

The opposite danger lies in finding a niche that's too big! If you choose a niche that's too big and you succeed, you'll attract attention from the big boys—and once you have to go nose-to-nose with them, they will overadvertise, underprice, and outsell you. Our research suggests this rule of thumb: The big players tend to go after a niche when it appeals to at least 33 percent of the category's consumers. With this in mind, a small player should seek a niche that's big enough to serve a marketplace, but small enough to be overlooked by the big players.

YOU NEVER KNOW

I don't think any start-up entrepreneur in his right mind makes a calculated decision to begin by competing head-on with a giant industry leader. Instead, one starts by finding a small niche in the marketplace, and as he succeeds, bit by bit, then he begins to stretch. Only after a series of small successes does he move on to bigger and better things.

For the budding entrepreneur with visions of someday becoming a market leader, this riddle contains a valuable message. While it is important to have a long-range game plan, you must first be focused on short-term objectives. Now don't get me wrong. I'm 100 percent in favor of thinking big. In fact, I don't understand how anyone can start a business venture without wanting it to reach its maximum potential. But having visions of grandeur—looking so far into the future that you don't take care of the business at hand—is foolhardy. For instance, a person who opens a small store may have ambitions someday to spread a chain of women's apparel shops across the country. But his dream of operating a thousand outlets should not cause him to neglect his one store. Only after he has made a success of the first store should he consider opening a second location. And when both are running smoothly and he has acquired sufficient skills to duplicate the same quality in additional stores, he can then consider expansion to a third store, a fourth, and so on.

There's always an opportunity for a small-niche player to find a slot in the marketplace where he can build and prosper. And even the biggest and most successful market leaders realize that somewhere out there, there is probably a small start-up company, still in its infancy, that could grow large enough to eat away at some of its market share.

America seemed to be saturated with fast-food restaurants when, in 1969, Dave Thomas opened the first Wendy's. As Thomas modestly put it, "I saw the chance to have perhaps three or four restaurants in the

Columbus, Ohio, area." At the time, Thomas had no big vision of Wendy's taking large chunks of market share from the fast-food industry leaders. In 1969, when fast-food restaurants were catering primarily to families with small children, Wendy's began by offering a more expensive hamburger targeted to the adult market. Although at that time industry leaders were coming out with larger menus, Thomas focused strictly on selling hamburgers and fries. Thomas found a niche in the marketplace, but in 1969, few would have predicted that Thomas, an eighth-grade dropout, would go on to build a fast-food empire in only a quarter of a century—with an estimated five thousand restaurants around the world.

Likewise, back in 1959, nobody could have guessed that Dan Carney, at age twenty-five, and his brother Frank, nineteen, had started a chain which would someday boast over eight thousand restaurants around the world. But that's what the Carney brothers did when they opened the first Pizza Hut in a dilapidated storeroom next to their family's small grocery store in Wichita, Kansas. It was only because the B&B Lunchroom down the street had lost its lease that the Carney brothers decided to go into business at all, at a time when few people in Kansas had ever heard of pizza, let alone tasted it. Even Frank had eaten pizza only one time previously, although his brother Dan had eaten it many times when he was in the service.

After Pizza Hut was well established as the market leader, then Domino's opened its doors in Ann Arbor, Michigan; its niche was *delivering* hot pizza. Then Little Caesar's came along; its niche was selling two pizzas for the price of one. While Pizza Hut, Domino's, and Little Caesar's are the industry giants, today tens of thousands of small pizza shops have opened across the country, catering to local customers and providing unique products and personal service.

This personal service provided by the niche player wins customers from the mass marketer. The customer's feeling of being honored when an owner personally serves him is the edge the small-niche player has, but this advantage dissipates as an enterprise grows. In order for the niche player to rise to the level where he can compete head-on against the market leaders, a metamorphosis must occur, and only a handful of entrepreneurs are able to make the transition.

In industries such as retailing and fast food, it doesn't take a large capital investment to become a niche player. When it comes to manufacturing such products as airlines and automobiles, however, the cost of entry is considerably higher. Yet, long after AT&T had a monopoly in the telephone industry, niche players such as MCI and Sprint were still able to enter the field.

Innovative entrepreneurs find a window and they make their entrance. Below the surface of the computer industry is a seething substructure of more than fifty thousand small companies, each of which is a niche player. While it's not possible to predict which one will someday become a multibillion-dollar international corporation, it's a safe assumption that some company will come from out there to emerge as a market leader. It's also likely to be a company that doesn't even exist today.

A NICHE PLAYER'S LIST OF EIGHT

In the retailing industry, our research shows that eight characteristics determine the success of a niche player—in this order:

1. PEOPLE COME TO THE STORE FOR ADVICE. The owner and/ or his employees are highly knowledgeable in their particular area of expertise. This added value is not easily duplicated by a mass marketer merchant.

2. THE STORE OFFERS THE BEST SELECTION WITHIN A LIMITED AREA. While the establishment may not have the largest overall selection, in a narrow area of a large category, it does. For example, an exclusive jewelry store may not have the largest selection of watches, but it does offer the most choices of a particular brand (i.e., Rolex). Likewise, a fine men's store may have the

largest selection of Oxxford clothes, a women's apparel shop may feature St. John, and so on.

3. THE STORE PROVIDES A FAST CHECKOUT. Since saving time is an added value, if customers can get out of the store with ease, it's a plus. This is particularly true considering the long checkout lines at some big box stores.

4. THE STORE GIVES CONVENIENT DELIVERY TO THE CUS-TOMER'S HOME OR CAR—WITHOUT A HASSLE. Whether it's a matter of making a delivery all the way to the home or simply the convenience of having a purchase brought to the car, customers value this service.

5. THERE IS AN EASY RETURN POLICY. If it doesn't work, the customer can return the purchase within a reasonable length of time, no questions asked.

6. THE STORE CAN CHARGE A HIGHER PRICE, BUT IT MUST BE REASONABLE. Consumers know that there is a premium to be paid when they shop at a small store. They are willing to pay more for value added, but they will not tolerate being gouged.

7. THE CUSTOMER IS PERSONALLY ACKNOWLEDGED BY THE OWNER AND EMPLOYEES. People feel important when they are recognized by name. This personal touch is usually not available at big box stores. To put it another way, customers are dissatisfied with the impersonal treatment received at many mass merchandise stores.

8. AFTER LEAVING THE STORE, THE CUSTOMER ENJOYS AN ONGOING RELATIONSHIP. Whether it's a phone call, a personal note, or some other form of contact after the sale, customers appreciate gestures that indicate they have a personal relationship with the small business owner or the store's employees.

To succeed as a niche player, it's not necessary to be superior to the mass marketer in all eight of the above areas. But in today's marketplace, it's going to take being superior in at least five of these areas. My recommendation to an entrepreneur who is thinking about being a niche player is to review this list and conclude, "I'm going to make three of these the hallmark of my business."

To elaborate on this list, our research indicates that 18 percent of American consumers say they definitely want to rely on a retail salesperson for assistance. In studies done during the past two years, about one in five people says, "I don't want to shop at Wal-Mart or go into a Kmart or Target, because I want someone to help me."

According to a different ARG study, 32 percent of consumers said they don't want to be rushed or pushed by a salesperson when they shop. Being rushed includes getting a hurry-scurry feeling; as some interviewees put it, "I feel like they want to get me in and out of the store as fast as possible." Others said they simply feel uncomfortable. "There's a mass of people around you." "It's not a relaxed atmosphere." "If I'm trying to decide while somebody else is grabbing that last item off the shelf, I feel pushed." In my opinion, this is the main reason the laid-back neighborhood drugstore has been able to survive.

In another ARG study, 23 percent of people interviewed said they think customer service before and after the sale is all-important. These shoppers say that when they visit a major department store, they value the treatment they receive at the front end. They know upfront they'll have to pay a little more for this special treatment, but they feel it's worth it.

With the right research, you can determine the appropriate niche to pursue in the marketplace. For instance, 11 percent of American consumers say they want to shop for fresh-cut meat. In other words, rather than buy it already packaged, they'd like to watch as the meat is cut in front of them. This percentage doesn't mean they will totally stop supermarket shopping, patronizing only stores with fresh meat. But depending on the population of your market and your particular location, knowing this number can help you calculate whether fresh-cut meat is a viable niche to pursue.

In the same study, when consumers were asked if they wanted to go to a place that sells only fresh vegetables, 28 percent responded they would. Again, this doesn't mean they'd completely give up buying fresh fruit and vegetables at the supermarket. But it does indicate they'd give some of their business to a fresh fruit and vegetable store or even a fruit stand operator. This study also revealed that this particular niche may not be big enough (33 percent or more) to induce the supermarket to alter its presentation of fruit and vegetables.

A CRITICAL DIFFERENCE

A successful enterprise strives for a critical difference that sets it apart from the competition. In each specific industry, the market leader exhibits a distinct difference from its closest competitor, or in some cases from the entire field. Wal-Mart, for instance, is perceived as being warmer and more helpful than Kmart. Southwest Airlines is perceived as the friendliest airline in the sky—even though a competitor tries to claim that trait. As we learned, Southwest's competition thought low price was Southwest's critical difference, but lower prices weren't enough to win away Southwest's customers. We at ARG have noticed that price alone seldom wins. The strategy of simply being the cheapest is not a winning formula, because it does not build customer loyalty and it drives profits lower and lower.

Toys "R" Us is an example of a company that possesses several strengths that give it superiority over its competition. First, everyone, children included, can recognize a Toys "R" Us store from down the street, and it's likely you'll find it near the area's strongest major mall. Second, its stores project a strong selection perception both externally and internally. And three, perhaps the greatest strength of Toys "R" Us is its buying power, which gives it a two-to-four-week jump on its competition. Its buying leverage assures faster delivery than its competition can achieve. Today's children—and they have educated their parents— know that the latest toy is more likely to be found at Toys "R" Us than anywhere else. A child enjoys being the first on the block to have a toy, and choosing Toys "R" Us as the first place shopped will accomplish this.

Toys "R" Us has done such a good job in these three areas that some of its former competition—Children's Palace, Lionel Playworld, etc.— were not perceived as the first store to shop, and have since gone out of business.

For a small toy store to compete against Toys "R" Us, it must find a niche. Perhaps it may specialize in a particular type of merchandise, such as higher-quality, educational, more expensive, or environmental toys. It may employ more attentive salespeople. And it may have better displays of its merchandise and more in-store promotions, say with clowns, magicians, or local sports celebrities. One thing is for certain. A small, local toy store must find a niche—and make sure it has a critical difference. It can't go head to head with Toys "R" Us and win.

For a small niche player competing against established companies that dominate the marketplace, having a critical difference is not merely an option—it's a matter of survival. I believe that one reason so many strip shopping center stores fail is that the architectural covenants of many developers require every storefront to be uniform. With little difference in external appearance—including similar lettering for store names—no one retailer can really stand out. While shopping center owners think such uniformity appeals to shoppers, they do a terrible disservice to their tenants by destroying their tenants' market identity.

A critical difference can be quantified. Our research shows that to compete against a market leader, a niche player must "do his thing" twice as well to be noticed. Let's say, for instance, that you operate an upscale specialty grocery store, and you hope to lure the customers of a neighboring store over to your produce and vegetable department. While, because of square footage constraints, your selection may not be able to compete against the local Publix or Safeway, you can compete in your own little niche. For instance, you might offer twice the freshness, or, during strawberry or melon season, display twice as much product. So here your niche is a combination of seasonal displays mixed with freshness of produce.

However, if the big supermarket receives a rating of 50, and you're doing 70 or 80, that's still not enough to qualify as a critical difference. Again, if you can't do something at least twice as well as the mass marketer does it, you won't be noticed. This method of quantifying a critical difference is applicable to every business.

THE PERSONAL TOUCH

Three winning qualities to place a retailer on the niche player list of eight (characteristics one, seven, and eight—people can get advice, the customer is personally acknowledged, and the relationship is ongoing) are related to the personal touch. In particular, I'm referring to the relationship that exists between the owner of a business and the customer. Our research reveals just how influential these three factors are. We have learned that when the owner is directly involved with a customer, there is an 83 percent chance of repeat business. This number compares to a mere 16 to 38 percent chance of repeat business when a mass marketer's store manager deals with this same customer.

Research surveys have proved customers feel that in a shopping experience there is no greater honor than to be waited on by the owner. It doesn't matter if you're in a fine restaurant, a clothing store, or an automobile dealership—when the owner serves you, no other retail experience can duplicate that special feeling. Think about what it means to you when you walk into a restaurant and are greeted by name by the restaurant owner, who later comes to your table to make a special recommendation of a wine or entree. Or think about a time when the owner of an exclusive men's store comments on the excellent suit selection you made—and then proceeds personally to select for you three ties to complement it. As I said, these personal touches don't happen when you shop at the category killer stores.

When you deal directly with the owner, three things happen that can be matched by no one else. First, the owner is, in fact, the business. When the sign in front says "Giovanni's," and Mr. Giovanni waits on you—or Mr. Goodman, if he bought the business from Mr. Giovanni—he is the owner. No matter what his name is, as the owner, he is Giovanni's personified. So when the owner comes over to say hello to you, it means more than when an employee does it. Something about this special recognition from the owner makes you feel important, more so than when you receive recognition from an employee.

Second, if the owner does something special for you, whether it's only remembering your name, or, say, in a restaurant, buying a round of drinks or comping a dessert, his act reflects a caring attitude on behalf of the entire company. If an employee were to do the same thing, it would be nice—certainly a major plus—but it's not the same as having the owner do it. This goes even further because the owner has the right to do whatever he wants to do. So when the customer would like to negotiate a special deal or requires a special service, the owner has the ability to break all the rules—in fact, he's the ultimate rulebreaker. For instance, if you're shopping for a new car, dealing with a salesperson or a manager is not the same as meeting with the owner. After all, the owner owns the entire dealership's inventory; he has the power and authority to negotiate the best possible deal—he can even lose money on the deal! The same is true when you're working with the general contractor who's custom-building your new home. When you make requests, he can authorize changes that his foreman cannot.

The third thing an owner can do like nobody else is to say thank you. Gratitude expressed by the proprietor conveys that your business was appreciated, because *the company itself is thanking you*. So while a salesperson or a waiter can sincerely say thank you, it's not the same as hearing it from the owner. When it comes from the owner, you think to yourself, "He truly appreciated my patronage, and I'm going to come back and give him more of my business."

One of my favorite stories concerns a client who purchased a family-owned bank. The founder and former owner was a man in his mid-seventies. He served as the bank's chairman, his son was president, and his young grandson was a loan officer. After the acquisition, the bank's business began to drop significantly, particularly business from its big depositors.

It took a while for the mystery to unravel.

When the bank was originally built, the founder's office was located on the second floor. A one-way mirror installed there faced the downstairs lobby, enabling the gentleman to see customers as they walked in and out of the bank. The old man did all his paperwork and telephoning in this office, and whenever he left it, he locked the door, citing "security." As a result, nobody, including his son, knew he had a full view of the first-floor activities. But how else could the chairman always happen to be there to greet big depositors personally when they walked in the front door? Customers loved his warm hellos: "John, I haven't seen you for a while. Boy, it sure is good to see you today. How's the golf game?" Finally, after his father retired, the son discovered the one-way mirror hidden in the office. Only then did he realize how the old man managed miraculously to appear downstairs to greet important customers.

Our study showed that during the period the founder was still active, an incredibly high 90 percent of the bank's customers were loyal to it. Later, when outside managers were brought in to run it, the bank never enjoyed the same level of customer loyalty.

Special treatment from the owner is prized by most people—even other business owners. For instance, the owner of an upscale furniture store recently told me that one of his suppliers gives him royal treatment. "One of my best customers was looking for four hand-painted glass lamp shades, so I called this small manufacturer out in Nebraska who made Victorian lamp shades," he told me.

" 'We only make them four times a year,' the lamp company owner explained, 'and at present, we don't have a single one in our inventory.'

" 'Is there anything you can do for me?' I pleaded. 'This is a very good customer.'

" 'I have one particular customer who I know has extras. I'll ask him to ship four lamp shades directly to your store,' he replied.

"Three days later, four lamp shades arrived, properly packed in a UPS package. My customer was enthralled."

COMPETING AGAINST THE BIG BOYS

In the competitive industrial-scale field are such market leaders as Toledo Scale, Fairbanks Scale, and Cardinal Scale. Although these three companies dominate the industry, by finding a niche, the Thurman Scale Company, based in Columbus, Ohio, has been able to survive and prosper over the years. How does it compete against the big boys? It does so by focusing on a niche in the marketplace that the industry giants are unable—or unwilling—to serve. Thurman's major thrust is the manufacturing of motor vehicle scales built to weigh both on-highway trucks and heavy off-highway trucks that are used primarily in coal mining, copper mining, and dam construction.

"Although one of our customers' trucks may have a book or catalog gross capacity of a hundred tons," explains Millard Cummins, Thurman's former CEO (the company was acquired by Fairbanks in October 1995), "certain end users haul more than dirt or gravel." Some companies load their trucks with slag steel or coal, transporting loads of 180 tons or more. The standard scales manufactured by the industry leaders are not built to accommodate these loads, and consequently are constantly in need of maintenance. This is especially true in coal mining, an industry notorious for equipment breakdowns. By specializing in fulfilling the exacting needs of these users, Thurman scales enjoy a reputation as the standard against which other scales are judged—especially in the Appalachian coal mining region.

"We substantially overbuild our scales, knowing the extremely rough, rugged applications of coal mining," Cummins says. "By custom-engineering and custom-manufacturing our product for these special needs, we fulfill a need that is practically untouched by our competition.

That's because most scale manufacturers are loath to deviate from their standard product line; they prefer to produce a thousand scales at a time rather than a one-of-a-kind that fouls up their engineering and product line. Even when they do custom-make a scale, it's so special for them they have to charge substantially more than our price."

While Thurman's custom-made scales are top of the line in durability, the standard scales made by the three market leaders are substantially less expensive. Because of added steel and individual engineering, a Thurman super-heavy-duty scale may cost $40,000, or, depending on a customer's specific needs, even more than $100,000. According to Cummins, this makes it a tough sale. "When a customer looks at a standard-price-list product," he explains, "and then at ours, it's hard for a purchasing agent to justify the additional cost. This is certainly the case with the purchasing agent who has to convince management it's worth the extra money in the long run, despite the fact that five years down the road, there's a good chance he'll be working somewhere else."

Cummins points out that his scales are sold mainly through a network of more than a hundred distributors, primarily in the East and Midwest. "It costs about one dollar per mile to ship a motor truck scale," he explains, "so the added freight puts us at a disadvantage when we're competing against a regional scale manufacturer, say, somewhere out West in Arizona or California."

In its own region, however, Thurman dominates its niche in its particular market. Its edge can be attributed to producing a highly durable product—and providing superior service. Thurman sales reps routinely accompany their distributors on calls to end users. "By being light on our feet," Cummins emphasizes, "and being willing to go wherever our distributors ask us to go, we are able to custom-make a scale to fit the exact needs of their customer."

During his thirty-five years in the scale business, Cummins claims that there have been two boom times for the company. The first occurred after President Eisenhower signed the bill that created the nation's 40,000-mile interstate highway system. This $77.8 billion road-building program required fifty-to-sixty-foot heavy-duty portable contractor's scales that could be moved from one job site to another. Thurman custom-built a portable scale that, unlike the standard stationary pit scale, could be transported. With these specially built Thurman scales, the government could be assured it was receiving the amount of road construction materials it paid for.

As the era of construction of the interstate highway system came to a close in the mid-1960s, it was business as usual again for Thurman Scale. Then another boom period occurred, caused by the 1973 oil embargo. With the cost of oil skyrocketing, coal was king, and once again, the demand for Thurman scales skyrocketed too.

HOW BIG COMPANIES GET ''NICHED''

For a decade, the American coffee industry has been stuck in a non-growth pattern. In 1985, 50 percent of Americans regularly drank coffee, and in 1995, 50 percent still regularly drank coffee.

The big coffee companies missed the boat because they failed to realize there was an opportunity to grow in their otherwise stagnant market. Instead of undercutting their competition's prices to gain market share, the big boys—Folgers, Nestlé, and Maxwell House—could have done what many of the industry's niche players do. The small companies sell roasted beans to folks who prefer to grind them with cheap, easy-to-use home grinders. With as many as one hundred varieties, ranging in flavor from hazelnut to Swiss mocha almond, the smaller coffee bean specialists won over customers who wanted a fresher cup of coffee than the ground, canned coffee normally displayed on the supermarket shelves could provide. By offering a superior product, the small niche players captured an estimated 20 percent market share of the nation's $4 billion in retail coffee sales.

Maxwell House did attempt to get some of its lost business back. In 1986, the company introduced Maxwell House Private Collection, 100 percent whole Arbacia beans in a thirteen-ounce package, but it was a bomb. Maxwell House's image as run-of-the-mill canned ground coffee was too deeply ingrained in the minds of American consumers. What's more, the company cut corners by roasting premium beans in huge ovens, the same way it roasted cheap beans. The company had a line of eight varieties, entirely too small a sampling for coffee bean lovers who were used to a wide variety of blends and types. And the Maxwell House bags sat in warehouses for as long as six months waiting to be shipped to supermarkets. So much for freshness. The company discontinued the line in 1989.

Meanwhile, the coffee industry's niche players are thriving. Millstone Coffee, Inc., a privately owned company based in Everett, Washington, has sales of $95 million. Its president, Philip Johnson, explains, "Maxwell House didn't understand the market. The whole point is to provide high-quality, extremely fresh coffee, in a setting pleasing to the customer." His firm sells packaged roasted beans in seventy-five varieties.

Another successful niche player is Brothers Gourmet Coffees, a publicly traded company with sales of $146 million. Brothers' original niche was selling coffee to offices. However, Dennis Boyer (who cofounded the company with his brother, Samuel) reveals that they became interested in premium whole bean coffee when they discovered that their customers were unable to differentiate between brands they carried such as Maxwell House and Folgers. Just as it did when the company once peddled its coffee office to office, the company now ships directly from its roasting plants to supermarkets to assure freshness.

Being a niche player can also mean higher profit margins. Brothers' premium whole bean coffee retails for $7.99, compared to $3.69 for a can of Maxwell House's top-of-the-line ground Colombian Supreme.

It should be noted that Folgers, Maxwell House, and Nestlé are well-managed companies. So, you may ask, how did they allow those small niche companies to capture 20 percent market share of the nation's retail coffee sales? Remember, market leaders don't go after business that's less than 33 percent of the total market. And in this case, it wasn't a single coffee company capturing a 20 percent market share—it was several small companies, none of which had even a 5 percent share of the market. Because they give it 100 percent of their time and effort, small players can do exceptional things in their niche. Bigger companies, however, can't devote so much time and effort to a small piece of their total business that they neglect their core business.

WORD-OF-MOUTH

A niche player depends on three things to get people into his store. First, he must have a convenient location so people will find his store. Second, when they do shop his store, he must make sure everybody receives good service. Third, because he doesn't have the resources to advertise like the mass marketer, he must depend on referrals from satisfied customers. In the long run, he will live or die by this word-of-mouth.

Let me illustrate how effective word-of-mouth is: When a person walks into a retail store to make a major purchase such as a TV set, bedroom set, or automobile, if he was referred there by a satisfied customer, our research shows there is an 80 percent chance that the sale will be made.

Something else our research shows is that if a person has a great experience at a store, he will tell six people—and if he has a bad experience, he will tell forty-one. (Incidentally, since our 1981 study, the number of people who will be told of a bad experience has *gone up* from twenty-four.) These numbers reveal something else. There's a ratio of 7:1 working *against* you, which means that for every one angry customer who walks out your door, you must have seven *very* satisfied customers just to offset the negative word-of-mouth created by the angry guy. Without a hefty advertising budget to attract people to your store, it becomes crystal clear why, as a niche player, you must bend over backward to keep your customers satisfied.

With that 7:1 ratio staring you in the face, there isn't much margin for error. If you don't do things right the first time, it's not likely there will be a second time.

We also conducted a business-to-business study, this time on companies doing business with other companies. Here, it was revealed that a ratio of 5:1 applies to spreading the word about a bad experience versus spreading the word about a good experience. As you would expect, unlike friends telling friends, coworkers telling coworkers, and neighbors telling neighbors about a bad buying experience, businesspeople who compete against each other in the same industry aren't as likely to pass the word on what went wrong with XYZ supplier. They do talk to one another, however, at trade association get-togethers. Take, for example, what happened back in the early 1990s when we did a study of a large buying group that had 750 members. We learned that although only 150 of them had had a bad experience with a particular manufacturer, ultimately all members knew to stay away from this company. So, true to the numbers, the ratio was 5:1.

KNOWING YOUR LIMITATIONS

It is a wise niche player who knows his limitations.

Often a niche player who excels in his own little world begins to ooze so much confidence that he believes he can climb Mount Everest. Smitten with his own success, he may decide to expand his base of operations. For the record, I admire self-confidence, and I'm all for expansion— Mattel's Ruth Handler didn't limit her dream in 1958 to one Barbie doll outfit, nor did Willard Marriott stop at one hotel. Business annals are filled with wonderful success stories of entrepreneurs who amassed large fortunes by multiplying their efforts.

But one must not leap *too* hastily. As a niche player, before you're on your way to opening your second operation, you must carefully analyze those strengths to which you attribute your success. A restaurateur, for example, who serves as manager/maître d' of a fine dining establishment may, upon examining his accomplishments, discover that in a second restaurant on the other side of town, his exceptional cooking skills cannot be easily duplicated. Nor, for that matter, can the personal touch he extends when greeting patrons. Hence there is the danger that he may spread himself too thin by dividing his time between two restaurants. For an optometrist or a dentist who makes the decision to branch out through the city, the same is true. Likewise, a haberdasher who built up an exclusive clientele by extending exceptional personal service may discover that the critical difference he had in one shop is not transferrable to a multi-location business. What's more, it takes a totally different set of skills—mainly operational skills—to manage a large business versus a small one.

Then, too, niche players who get carried away with their success sometimes expand into another product category that doesn't complement their niche. For example, a high-end specialty audio store owner who carries a few TV sets as part of his home theater inventory decides to add an entire television lineup to his store. Because of limited space, however, he doesn't have enough selection to represent his new product category, so his expansion is a bust. To make matters worse, this retailer had to reduce his audio assortment to make room for his enlarged television display. So he gets hit with a double whammy! Now neither department has a competitive edge. In addition, he moved into a category where price is more important than it was in his audio business. His advertising also suffers, because his ad budget was split to promote both categories. This results in single ads that display less selection on the audio side of his business—formerly his strong suit!

A manufacturer or wholesaler must use similar caution when contemplating broadening its product line. Before making such a decision, questions must be addressed concerning the compatibility of the new product with the company's existing products. Questions such as: "Do both products have the same channels of distribution?" "Will our sales reps call on the same buyers?" "Will a more expensive (or less expensive) product confuse our existing customers?" "Will expansion into another area hurt our ability to specialize in what we presently do best, and as a result, reduce our current edge?" "Can we afford the necessary promotion and advertising dollars without neglecting our existing product line?" "What impact will the production of a lower price product have on our company image?" The list goes on and on.

For instance, a manufacturer of fine jewelry might try to predict how producing a new line of costume jewelry would alter its present image. Likewise, before deciding to carry beer, a wholesale wine distributor would want to make sure the same retailers and grocery departments that carry its wine would also carry its beer. And, also because of distribution problems, a chair manufacturer that caters to consumers might rethink a decision to make chairs for offices.

A good businessperson must have a keen awareness of his limitations. A small manufacturer of herbal teas, for example, knows that he has little chance of getting his products into large supermarkets; and even if he does, he'll have inferior shelf space. So what does he do? He focuses on distribution to health food stores and specialty food retailers. And he gives them extraordinary service that the big tea companies are unwilling to give to a non-supermarket account. Likewise, a small paper distributor can't compete with the quantity discounts that a big paper company gives to its biggest customers. Instead, he caters to the small printing firm, offering more service than bigger paper companies are willing to provide for small orders. Thus he develops a niche in the marketplace that supports his small but thriving business.

Getting back to the restaurant business again, often there is a temptation for an owner who does a great evening business to listen to customers who say, "I wish you were open at noon. If you were, I'd certainly come here for lunch." After several customers make such comments, he decides he will increase his business by serving lunch. It's a disaster! First, those same customers who say they'd like to eat lunch there do so, but infrequently. Why? They already have other places they frequent for lunch. So, in effect, the restaurateur is battling for customers against an entirely different set of competitors who already have loyal customers for their lunch business. And let's not forget that his overhead is bound to skyrocket, because additional people must be hired and trained to work a lunch shift.

To many, one of the advantages of being a niche player is that in theory, the small entrepreneur is light on his feet; unlike the big corporation, he is not saddled with the baggage of bureaucracy. "Because we're small," a niche player says, "I can turn on a dime. I know exactly who my customers are, and since I'm so close to them, I can quickly respond to their needs."

Still, the niche player must be careful to avoid the mountains of misinformation that surround him. While he is, indeed, close to his customer—and this is particularly true of the small shopkeeper who personally waits on his trade—there is a flip side to this closeness. Your customers may be telling you only what you want to hear. People don't like confrontation, so when criticism is in order, they are likely to refrain from telling you what you really need to hear. And remember, you're also *not* hearing what other customers have to say—the ones who *don't* shop your store.

YOU CAN'T SEE THE FOREST FOR THE TREES

There is still another problem that a niche player faces: He may be so focused that he can't see the forest for the trees. This reminds me of an incident that happened several years ago in Georgia. A retailer in a medium-sized city contacted me with an odd problem. His business had stopped growing during the past five years. "My previous customers are coming back, but I'm not picking up any new ones," he told me. "I'm located in a transient community, and I swear to you, Britt, the people who move to town don't shop me. I can't figure out why, but only the old-timers come to my store."

I visited his store a few days later. John extended some real Southern hospitality; he was kind enough to pick me up at the airport, and he gave me the grand tour of his store as well as the city. After spending a few hours together at a nearby airport hotel, we agreed that my firm would conduct a study for him.

After a survey of the people in the area, our research revealed that 29 percent of the consumers in his marketplace had visited his store—and of the 71 percent who had not, a disproportionate number of them were, indeed, new city residents. This puzzled me. I had never seen a report with such lopsided figures.

I called John, and a date was arranged for me to review my report with him. At the end of our conversation, he apologized for not being able to pick me up at the airport. "No problem," I told him. "I'll rent a car and be at your store by 8:00 a.m. sharp."

John's store was located at the best intersection in the entire city, about fifteen minutes from the airport. On my drive to his store, I was still wondering what could have caused John's business to have such a wide disparity between those who shopped his store and those who did not. With all the traffic that traveled the road past his store, there was no logical reason to support what our survey indicated.

"I'd better concentrate on my driving," I said to myself. I did, but I drove past his store! When I did it a second time, the problem John was experiencing hit me like a ton of bricks.

When John greeted me at his store, I announced, "I know exactly what your problem is, John. The biggest reason people aren't coming to your store is they can't find it."

"What in the world are you talking about?" he exclaimed. "How can anyone not know where I am? We constantly advertise, we have a huge sign, and we're on one of the busiest thoroughfares in the entire state. *Everybody* knows where we are."

"I couldn't find your store myself, John."

"What do you mean? That's impossible. Are you blind?"

"Follow me, John," I said, and headed toward the door. "I want you to see something."

We walked outside, and I said, "Come on over here, John. Walk next to me and let's cross the road and stand on that little island in the middle over there. I want you to see something."

Reluctantly he followed me as we dodged traffic crossing the two lanes to the traffic safety island. "Okay, John, I want you to face the intersection, and out of the corner of your eye, I want you to glance over toward your store and then look back at me."

He followed my instructions, and I asked, "What did you see?"

"I saw my store."

"You just barely saw your store."

"Yeah, but that's what I have the huge sign for," he said, pointing. "Over there."

"Over where?" I asked. "Where's the sign?"

John did a double-take. "Oh, my gosh! The sign isn't there!"

The sign was there, but over the ten years since its installation, a young tree on his property had grown so high that it completely blocked the view. *No one could see the sign for the tree!*

John's face turned beet-red. "I bet you think I'm an idiot, Britt."

"That tree didn't grow up overnight, John," I replied. "It happened so slowly over the years, you didn't notice it, that's all."

That afternoon, John applied to the city for a permit to remove the tree. Within a short time afterward, passersby had a clear view of his sign, and business began to pick up. Within a few years, his sales volume grew from $4.5 million to $7 million.

CONSUMER MIND READER #8

Selling Business Books to Businesspeople

When we conducted a survey to learn the shopping habits of business-people, some interesting information was revealed.

- 52.4 percent of America's businesspeople go to bookstores to look for and buy business-related books. Of those, 51.9 percent like to browse, while 48.1 percent have a specific book in mind that induces them to enter the store.

- 45.6 percent of businesspeople read business-book reviews. Of those, 47.6 percent look for reviews in business magazines, 29 percent read *The Wall Street Journal* book reviews, and 23.5 percent read reviews appearing in either local or national magazines.

- Of businesspeople who read business-book reviews appearing in newspapers, 67.3 percent look for reviews in the newspaper business section, compared to 32.7 percent who look for business-book reviews only in the newspaper's book-review section.

- 60.4 percent of businesspeople stated that an advertisement for a business book influences their buying decision more than a book review does; 35.4 percent stated that a book review is more influential; 4.2 percent were uncertain.

Based on this survey, we conclude that businesspeople are a complex group when it comes to buying business books. We learned several things from this study. First, since nearly half the business-book buyers (48.1 percent) have a specific book in mind before they enter the bookstore, a publisher can't assume that a business book will be bought simply because it's on the shelf. This means the book must be advertised and promoted with significant publicity so that the book buyer will head to the bookstore specifically to purchase it. Second, to our surprise, we learned that a business-book buyer is more influenced by an advertisement than a book review. We thought it would be the other way around, since an advertisement is obviously going to be positive toward the book, while a review by a third party could go either way. Third, more than twice as many businesspeople read their book reviews in the business section of a newspaper instead of the general book-review section that covers all books. This suggests that publishers of business books can achieve better results by sending review copies to a newspaper's business-section book-review editor.

Our study also illustrates that a business book has a much better chance of becoming a best-seller when a publisher executes a multifaceted marketing strategy versus going with a limited publicity campaign that does not include advertising, or a limited advertising campaign that does not include creative publicity.

CHAPTER NINE

THE LONG-TERM STRATEGIST

By viewing the marketplace through the customer's eyes, the long-term strategist sees into his own future. His focus on tomorrow enables him to predict the needs of the customer. Conversely, the short-term strategist who focuses on coping with the present fails to position himself for what will be.

It doesn't take a fortune-teller to foresee the future. It does take a long-term strategist who has studied yesterday's customer and today's customer. Doing that bit of homework enables him to map out where the customer will be tomorrow. Customers rarely make unexplained, giant leaps. In fact, unless the environment around them forces them to, consumers rarely make dramatic changes.

Once he has pinpointed the future needs of the customer, the long-term strategist's goal is simply to work toward fulfilling those needs. His resolve enables him to ignore others who say something is impractical or even impossible; he understands that even so-called experts may be wrong.

And *who are the experts*? Who are these people possessed with such wisdom that we must listen when they caution us about the future? Just a little over a hundred years ago, in 1893, seventy-three prominent Americans were asked to foretell what the nation would be like in 1993. The U.S. Postmaster predicted that the price of a stamp would drop from 2 cents to a penny. A medical authority envisioned people living to the age

of 150. And a prominent sociologist prognosticated a signifi
both crime and divorce.

More recently, the advent of computers was expected to ena
forecast the future. People thought it logical that computers w   ue
used for the largest of institutions and the most technical of problems.
Personal computers and the part they play in everyday life were a total
surprise to these "experts."

Apparently, the issue of who is the expert deserves more examination.
In what area lies the expert's expertise? Do his impeccable credentials allow
him to predict which concept *will* succeed, as well as which will not?

There is indeed an expert—*the only expert in America*—and that is the
consumer. Only the consumer can say what he expects from a product,
how long he is willing to wait for it, and how much he is willing to pay
for it. And the way he tells us is with his dollars.

A DELICATE BALANCING ACT

When times are lean, many managers react by looking for ways to cut
costs. It figures. It's much easier to stop spending money on advertising
or to lay off people than it is to build market share.

Reducing costs is only a temporary fix—and is also a defensive pos-
ture. To stay healthy you must fend off what is sometimes referred to as
"corporate anorexia," a disease that occurs when management gets
hooked on decreasing inventories, closing stores, reducing advertising
budgets, laying off employees, and cutting back on customer services. All
of this concentration and effort on shrinking your business is contrary to
what a healthy company should do. Your objective is to advance, not re-
treat.

In the 1990s, many of America's best-known companies downsized.
One danger of this strategy is that a "survivor's syndrome" begins to
permeate the organization. New ideas and risk-taking dissipate as the
culture of cost-cutting takes precedence over expansion. Rather than try
something new and different, managers avoid uncertainty and spending.

Once the mode of downsizing sets in, management conditions itself to react. In this vicious circle, everyone anticipates what can go wrong; when "What if?" is asked, the worst-case scenario is anticipated.

As the cycle gains momentum, excessive cost-cutting invites a strengthening of the authority of financial and accounting people, who assume the role of merely controlling expenses rather than monitoring and evaluating opportunities that require investments. Top management becomes focused on saving instead of growing. In this "safe" mode, a company still risks something: It risks its ability to grow. In the short run, operating profit may appear to increase, but revenues begin a long decline.

A delicate balancing act is required. While management must carefully monitor expenditures, once the mentality of obsessive cost-cutting takes over, it becomes habit-forming and self-destructive. Slashing costs may have its place on the agenda, but it can take a company only so far. Growth must always be an organization's foremost goal.

A common solution preferred by a shrinking company is to downsize its sales force. Often coupled with this approach is the reduction of customer-service departments, a measure that ultimately requires salespeople to double as customer-service reps. As this occurs, salespeople spend less time in the field seeking new business, and concurrently have less time to service existing customers.

To combat this dilemma, a company must never take its focus off of doing what serves its customer best. Even during times when cost-cutting is mandatory, the customer must never be the one shortchanged. A well-managed company always makes the needs of the customer its number one priority; fulfilling those needs is its reason for existence.

SHORT-TERM PROFITS VS. LONG-TERM GAINS

Publicly owned corporations are frequently afflicted with "quarter-itis," an often terminal disease in the business world. It is a sad fact that somewhere along the way, American business leaders began keeping score of their corporations' progress on a three-month basis. Because it releases quarterly financial reports to the public—which includes everyone, shareholders and competitors alike—management is "graded" on its short-term results, often to the detriment of its long-term goals.

Even worse, publicly traded retail companies are scrutinized for their *monthly* performance. Monthly sales figures are publicly announced, causing the price of their stock to fluctuate as monthly revenues are compared to that month's results for the previous year. In the automobile and truck industry, this year's sales are compared to the previous year's results—for ten-day periods!

When grades are examined by Wall Street, their analysis affects the selling price of the stock. Since a company's owners are its stockholders—to whom management is held accountable—there is a tendency to think short-term so that the traded stock will maintain a favorable price. Unfortunately, this can result in decisions that work against a company's long-term objectives. What's more, it places a publicly owned corporation at a tremendous disadvantage.

Whether they are large or small, well-managed companies think long-term. While this may be common knowledge, what makes it difficult to execute is that it often requires short-term sacrifice. When I point this out to my clients, I attempt to minimize risk by backing up my recommendations with research studies. For example, in 1990, Paul Green approached me to do some research for WG&R, his four-store chain in the Green Bay, Wisconsin, area. At the time, his company was doing about $15 million in sales. When we first met, Paul told me his vision was someday to become the dominant market leader in the Fox Valley trading area.

Based on our research, I advised Paul that for his business to grow as he had described, WG&R would have to invest heavily in a major expansion program that included building larger stores. Following my recommendation, Paul moved his Green Bay store out of its 25,000-square-foot spot into a better-located 47,000-square-foot store.

WG&R did a similar thing with its stores in Manitowoc and Oshkosh, and also built a new warehouse.

It took a lot of courage to do what Paul Green did. After all, he already operated a successful $15 million company that had a 60 percent market share in one of its markets. And according to my initial study on WG&R, the forty-six-year-old retail store's reputation ranked number two out of all the stores in the 470 markets I researched. With a track record like that, a lot of businesspeople wouldn't have wanted to invest in what amounted to reinventing his company. Paul, however, was willing to assume the risk, even though it meant incurring a lot of debt that would, in the short run, cut into his cash flow. Paul Green is a long-term strategist, and this kind of thinking has paid off handsomely for him. By 1995, five years after his expansion program was first initiated, his sales had more than doubled—from $15 million to $32 million.

Still other clients of mine who were willing to incur high upfront expenditures in order to realize long-term profits are Gerry Boschwitz and his father, Rudy. (Incidentally, from 1978 to 1990, the senior Boschwitz served as a Minnesota U.S. senator, and he is running again in November 1996.) In 1992, when I first went to Minneapolis to meet Gerry and Rudy, their company was called Plywood Minnesota.

An interesting name, I thought to myself, especially for a retail operation with twelve stores, ranging in size from 25,000 to 80,000 square feet, that sold mainly kitchen cabinets, carpeting, floor covering, wallpaper, and window treatments.

"Why Plywood Minnesota?" I asked.

"Oh, back in 1963, when the company was founded, we operated out of a warehouse," replied Gerry, "and our main product was prefinished paneling—in particular, unfinished plywood."

After taking a glance around the store, I commented, "But I don't see a whole lot of plywood for sale."

"Oh, plywood's just a minor part of our business today," Gerry explained.

My first research study confirmed what I had suspected all along. The name Plywood Minnesota confused the customer because it identified the company as a retail lumber business. Consequently, because the company's customer was getting older and younger people were not shopping there, retail sales were on the decline. With this knowledge, I recommended that the Boschwitzes not only change the name, but also change the message they'd been sending in their TV commercials. Gerry and his brother, Ken, had been personally appearing in their own commercials for the past ten years, but even Gerry admitted the ads were a little hokey.

"Your television audience thinks the quality of your commercials represents the quality of your product," I told him. "Your image would be enhanced if you would hire a professional production company to make your commercials."

I explained that they were currently projecting the image of a low-end store rather than a company selling a top-of-the-line, name-brand quality product. This image was largely the result of the old ads stressing price only. Little was said about selection and quality.

Today, the Boschwitzes' professionally produced ads always end with the message "More choices, priced right!"

It was a more difficult decision for the company to change its name—indeed, an expensive proposition for any established business to undertake. A name change first requires an expensive ad campaign to inform all existing customers that you're still in business, but under a different name. And then there are the high costs of creating a new logo and converting all exterior and interior signage, stationery, delivery trucks, and so on.

The name change was ingeniously executed by creating a brilliant media blitz that got customers involved. A naming contest was conducted, mainly by radio, using two popular disc jockeys, with the winner receiving a round trip vacation for two to Orlando, Florida. The contest generated hundreds of name suggestions; out of the eight finalists, Plywood Minnesota became Home Valu. The general consensus is that the new name conveys to the consumer that Home Valu sells quality home products at a good price.

ınging an established company's name is never easy in the short

ut over a period of time, it pays off again and again. The Boschwitz family will attest to this: Home Valu is enjoying unprecedented prosperity.

Of course, a company may have a name that doesn't work, but with a good marketing strategy, you can work around it to turn it into a plus. This is what the management of JM Smucker Co. in Orville, Ohio, did with its name. Now, you have to admit, the name "Smucker" sounds like something you'd be called after you stepped out of a New York City taxi and failed to leave a tip! It is not the kind of name you'd like to go through life with. But JM Smucker, the well-known maker of jams and jellies, is a $500 million company that was able to make an asset out of what otherwise would seem a liability. Rather than spending money on changing the name, the company put its money into a national advertising campaign telling the world, "With a name like Smucker's, it has to be good." It worked exceedingly well. Today Smucker's is the leader in its market.

HOW AMERICA'S TOP MANAGERS VIEW THEIR ROLE

In a study conducted during the summer of 1995, approximately five hundred chief executive officers and chief operating officers were interviewed. Among those were some of the most respected business leaders in the United States, including such superstars as General Electric's Jack Welch and the nation's richest individual, Warren Buffet. These five hundred top executives were asked to list in order of importance from one to ten their top priorities in heading their companies. Here's how they responded:

1. Study customer buying habits and changes every six to twelve months.

2. Understand that a unique selling proposition must always be present.

3. Although customer demands may be tough, they are never excessive.

4. Accept responsibility that a downturn in sales is not externally driven but internally driven.

5. Staff and systems can rise to any occasion, but they need time to plan.

6. Sales and marketing are not one and the same.

7. A corporation's reputation is its most valuable asset.

8. Today's goals must reflect tomorrow's objective.

9. Change means opportunity to lead.

10. Leadership is essential, but corporate consensus is a sign of good management.

While this study does not single out a particular individual and reflect his or her views, it dismays me to observe that as a group, these business leaders don't put more emphasis on long-term growth. Only priorities seven and eight give some indication of the importance of long-term thinking. It's interesting that "Understand that a unique selling proposition must always be present" ranks second on this list of priorities, especially in view of another study we did that says 83 percent of all consumers say that all retail stores look alike.

Clearly, there is some discrepancy between what executives practice and what they preach. This is evidenced by corporate America's emphasis on the monthly sales reports and quarterly earning statements of publicly held corporations. This fixation on short-term gains contradicts what the five hundred CEOs and COOs listed as their top priorities.

THE GRAND OPENING

I'm a believer in a new business starting out with a big grand opening. For starters, our research reveals that 94 percent of Americans believe grand opening sales are legitimate. Second, we also learned that the average locally owned retail operation that's been around for thirty years has had only 38 percent of the people in its entire market area shop it. (Mass marketing retailers are not included in this figure.)

We've discovered, however, that an effective grand opening can get 42 percent of an area's consumers to shop a store during its first ninety days in business. Think about this for a moment. If it takes thirty years to get 38 percent of the shoppers to walk in your front door, what if you could short-circuit this thirty-year advantage an established store has, and match or even exceed that number in only ninety days? This doesn't leave you with much of an option. You've got to do it.

Here's still another thing our research told us about what a successful grand opening does during those first ninety days. It creates an image of your company that lasts for seven years. This emphasizes how critical it is to make sure your first impression is a good one—because you're going to have to live with it for the next seven years. In the restaurant industry, the image projected during the first ninety days after opening creates an impact that would have otherwise taken three to five years to accomplish. Of course, this depends on keeping your chef and key people. If they leave you, that's another story.

Talk about thinking long-term—with this information, a retailer has no choice but to invest in a major grand opening to take advantage of this enormous traffic potential. Still, time after time, I hear retailers say, "I didn't put aside a budget for a grand opening," "I want to iron the kinks out before my store is mobbed with customers," or "If our store is good, people will find us anyway." What a missed opportunity!

"You get only one chance to make a strong first impression," I constantly tell my clients who are planning a new store. One person who understands this very well is George Cartledge, Jr., who operates Grand Piano, a successful family-owned company that's headquartered in Roanoke, Virginia, and known throughout the South. Today, Grand Piano has sensational grand openings, but this wasn't always the case. As Cartledge explains, "We used to open a store on Monday, have people register for a drawing during the week, and give prizes away to the winners on Saturday. And that was it."

After George learned about the impact a super grand opening can have on a new store, in 1994, Grand Piano had one for its new 50,000-square-foot store in Johnson City, Tennessee. The event lasted eight weeks. Although I laid out the strategy myself, I must admit it was brilliant. To begin this grand opening, a large direct-mail campaign was conducted, inviting a select group of people to attend a preview, during which time special deals were offered. Recipients could attend "by invitation only" for the first two weeks before the general public was allowed to shop at the store. To keep the sale private, every window in the store was papered up. As you can imagine, it created an air of exclusivity, as well as a certain mystique. This "pre-opening" enabled Grand Piano to do a substantial amount of business before its doors had ever officially opened.

During the next six weeks, three special offers were promoted. For instance, weeks three and four featured the official opening event to the public. Weeks five and six boasted a sale on "late-arriving" stock—of course, it was preplanned for the store to restock its inventory. And the final two weeks was the grand opening countdown—which created a sense of urgency because the sale would soon be over. As I mentioned, the events of the first two weeks were promoted by mail, and those of the last six weeks by a well-coordinated media blitz that included newspaper ads coupled with radio and television commercials. Throughout the grand opening, shoppers registered for a drawing to win a new car.

Of course, a lot of preparation went into making Grand Piano's grand opening a huge success. With four successful grand openings, George understood the importance of having everything in tip-top shape *before* day one. His sales force was fully trained, the store was filled with new merchandise, properly tagged, and lots of colorful signage helped create the excitement that every successful opening must have.

A different client conducted an innovative grand opening by running an unusual contest. A $25,000 winner-take-all competition was offered to the area radio station that could draw the most listeners to attend the store's grand opening through a live radio remote—the station broadcast on site at the store. Compared to the cost of a traditional radio campaign, this was a small amount to pay for the publicity the contest would generate. Five of the area's top radio stations competed, and with half the money going to the winning station's disk jockey, the store received publicity worth many times the $25,000 prize money.

As a footnote, for the next six months *after* the grand opening, the winning station kept broadcasting, "We don't care what the ratings services say, when it came down to the real test—*the grand opening of XYZ store*—we proved that we're the area's number one radio station!" So for six more months, the free publicity blitz continued.

A poorly executed grand opening can have devastating results. As far as I'm concerned, a company that could vie for the dubious honor of having the worst grand opening during the past five years is Ames Department Store. When it took over Zayre, also a discount retailer, it seemed as though a grand opening, to Ames, meant simply changing the sign on the outside of the store. That's because about the only other thing the company did was pull out the Zayre Sunday newspapers inserts and replace them with Ames inserts. There were no radio or television commercials to educate Zayre customers that an acquisition had taken place. And as far as the customers were concerned, Zayre had apparently gone out of business.

Our research showed that during the first ninety days after Ames took over, it lost 60 percent of Zayre's customer base. What a blunder.

In the South, where a lot of the old Zayre's stores were located, there's also a concentration of older consumers, and more than 45 percent of the consumers say that familiarity with a store is very important to them. It's probably a combination of the fact that people are creatures of habit and that they feel comfortable in familiar surroundings, but Ames truly missed the boat with its weak grand opening. And in addition to changing the name of the store externally, the company also laid out the stores with a different format, again confusing the established Zayre's customers. Ames has since gone into bankruptcy. Afterward, its management put the blame on the fact that the company was unable to integrate the computer systems of the two firms, which, in turn, meant they never were able to integrate both companies' distribution and warehousing. In my opinion, however, they had only identified a minor symptom; the main factor was their failure to take into account the value of their existing customers' loyalty.

At the very least, Ames could have had an effective mailing program to win over loyal Zayre customers. Letters could have been sent explaining the switch, with a full-color brochure telling the Ames story, and even offers to provide discounts to Zayre customers making their first Ames purchase. Offers to give these customers an Ames discount card would have also been effective. The main point is that Ames should have had some mailing campaign, especially since our studies show 58 percent of all consumers read new store mailings. Incidentally, this figure is up from a mere 25 percent in the 1970s.

Another interesting observation we made during our grand opening study was that even when a retailer conducts only a re–grand opening, the event can still generate about 50 to 60 percent of what an original grand opening would have realized. So while the re–grand opening, say, after a major remodeling job, may not be as good as the real thing, it's still going to bring a lot of customers to your store. And those retailers who fail to take advantage of such happenings are missing a grand window of opportunity.

BRINGING OUT A NEW PRODUCT

Much like a grand opening, the proper introduction of a new product also presents an excellent window of opportunity. Our research has revealed that when a new product is poorly launched, it necessitates spending nearly 50 percent more in advertising to correct that weakness. For instance, if a company is normally budgeted to spend 6 percent for advertising, after a poor product introduction, a budget of 9 percent will be required for a period of five to ten years to get back on track.

A good example of how this works is the U.S. launchings of Toyota's 1990 Lexus and Nissan's 1990 Infiniti in late 1989. Both launchings introduced to America the first luxury Japanese automobiles by their respective manufacturers. While Toyota was able to market the Lexus effectively by appealing to its targeted audience with eye-catching television commercials, Nissan was unable to do the same with its Infiniti. The company made the horrendous mistake of running, as its first introduction, commercials that were so esoteric they didn't address the customer. When only a small percentage of consumers can afford to purchase a high-priced luxury product, it's essential that that company's marketing message be exactly on target.

The Infiniti dealerships received high marks for their attractive showrooms and professional salespeople, but the company's marketing efforts never succeeded in getting enough potential customers through the doors to see the new cars. Consequently, although the Infiniti is an excellent automobile, the Nissan division has continued to struggle ever since those first 1990 models were brought to American soil. Only with a very attractive (but not very profitable) leasing program has the company been able to put the Infiniti on the road. In terms of actual dollars spent, the company is still paying a stiff penalty for its weak Infiniti introduction back in 1989.

Of course, depending upon the nature of your business, in addition to launching a strong advertising campaign, you might consider conducting customer tours of your factory. Many small manufacturers of nonconsumer products that don't advertise to the general public take advantage of either a new plant opening or an introduction of a new product by inviting their dealers, suppliers, and "friends in general" to attend a big shindig at the company's plant. These affairs offer an excellent opportunity for companies to show off their capable and dedicated staff, the organization's commitment to quality, its high-tech capabilities, and so on. It's also a good way to build strong business-to-business relationships. Their customers meet "real people" in areas such as shipping and handling, bookkeeping and servicing, so when they do need a contact to straighten out a problem, they can talk to somebody whom they know personally—a person with a face.

BRAND NAMES

When it comes to establishing a brand name in the marketplace, there are many variables to consider. One factor, for instance, is how frequently the product is purchased. In the woman's apparel industry, for example, a brand name can become known in as little as six months to a year. On the other hand, if you were to start a furniture manufacturing company that sells a product not purchased on a regular basis, it could take as long as forty years to build up your brand name.

But frequency is not the only factor. Witness supermarket products such as cereal or soup, which can take as long as five to ten years to develop a brand name. That's because those products face so much competition with established brand names.

In a 1994 study we conducted for the Audit Bureau of Circulations, an organization that certifies the circulation figures of publications, we asked two thousand Americans the question "How do you get your information?" Seventy-three percent said television was their number one source, and the other 27 percent said their information sources included either radio, newspapers, magazines, or word-of-mouth.

With this information, our research showed that a manufacturer can build a brand name quickest by advertising on television. Three national TV ads sponsored by a manufacturer will impact consumers to the same degree as forty-one retailers' price and item newspaper ads. So if two manufacturers bring out new products, one with an aggressive national television campaign and the other with a campaign that uses co-op advertising through its retail accounts, the former will make its brand name known thirteen times more quickly.

If your goal is quickly to establish a brand name for your product, it definitely pays to advertise. There's no question that the American consumer's perception of a product's quality is influenced by the message presented in a strong advertising campaign. Take, for example, Hitachi. It is a company with a high-quality product, yet its brand name is not well recognized in the United States. Consequently, few customers walk into a store and announce, "I want to buy a Hitachi TV." Still, Hitachi sells well, because retail salespeople know it's good, so they push it. But then, with a product like a television, a salesperson can demonstrate its quality simply by turning it on and comparing it to other TVs in the store.

A salesperson, however, can't make such a comparison with all products. This is illustrated by what happened several years ago when a large electronics and appliance retailer in the Northeast came to me with a problem. "I can't understand why our washer and dryer business is so weak. We're running about a third of the industry average," he said. It didn't make sense, since the retailer's refrigerator, range, and dishwasher sales were twice the industry average.

Our study showed that while the company had a 78 percent closing rate with refrigerators, it had only an 18 percent closing rate on its laundry products. Upon analyzing the results, we learned that whenever a shopper mentioned his refrigerator was broken down, the store's salespeople were instructed to push its off-brand refrigerators, which had higher markups. Being asked "What do you have in stock today?" was the tip-off that at home there was a refrigerator full of food threatening to spoil. In response to this urgency, the salesperson assured the customer that an off-brand model could be delivered without delay. A washer or dryer purchase, on the other hand, didn't have a similar sense of urgency. Customers felt they could afford to wait several days before running out of clean clothes, while waiting on delivery of a brand-name model.

Additionally, General Electric, Whirlpool, and Maytag were strong brand names in this marketplace. However, we learned that this retailer's salespeople were telling customers, "GE and Maytag are fine, but you really ought to take a look at SpeedQueen." SpeedQueen was a good product, with a stainless-steel tub, but the problem was that customers didn't recognize it as a major brand. And since the customers in that area were very brand-driven, no matter how hard the salespeople pushed Speed-Queen, their closing ratio remained low. Once I pointed this out to the company, their salespeople stopped trying to talk people into buying SpeedQueen. Their closing ratio shot up to 60 percent and their washer and dryer business increased 300 percent. This story illustrates that if the customer has his heart set on a brand-name product, don't fight it—promote it.

Because it takes up to forty years to establish a brand name, long-term commitment is required. In this respect, it's an investment in the future, since, admittedly, the same dollars put into marketing for today could generate more immediate results. But once a brand name is well recognized, it has a definite value. Our research shows that a private-label-brand product such as a computer or microwave oven must be sold for at least 25 percent less than a major-name brand—ideally, 33 to 40 percent less. Studies in 1996 confirm that consumers in general say, "I'm willing to spend more for this brand-name product, because I think it will last longer and perform better."

THE RIGHT IMAGE

If you've been in business for any length of time, your company is projecting an image—good or bad—to the public. To some extent, how you're perceived will have a direct bearing on your long-term success.

Now, there are two schools of thought. The first school thinks, "I'm not going to fuss about my image. Instead, I'll just let my performance speak for itself. Because my company is so good at what it does, people will eventually seek me out. In time, an image will probably evolve, whether I do anything or not."

The second school thinks, "While I'm working diligently at my business, I will also work at creating the image I want. Since a good image is so vital to a business, it's too important to leave to chance."

Obviously, the long-term thinker belongs to the second school of thought. From the time his company is founded, he begins to cultivate a strong image that will present his company in the manner he chooses—he's not willing to risk letting one evolve that *might* or *might not* be right! There is too much at stake!

The biggest and most successful companies in the world spend large sums of money on their images. Major American corporations—General Motors, IBM, General Electric—all have public relations departments and, in addition, hire outside firms for still more consultation. For the same reason that these large corporations are interested in their images, companies of every size should exhibit the same concern.

The little niche player, for example, who operates a small, high-end audio boutique store wants to project an image that tells the customer, "No matter what it takes, I'm going to make sure our product is successfully installed in your home and you're happy with it." To stand behind his rhetoric, the owner must be willing to employ people in his store who are highly knowledgeable about the product. Additionally, these people must be given regular training to stay abreast of the latest changes in technology.

When somebody asks, "When should I start being concerned about my company's image?" I answer, "The time to begin focusing on your image is before you ever open your front door for business." Your image is so important that it must be working for you from the very start. This means the small audio boutique store owner must plan in advance to carry the right product brands prior to his grand opening—and his salespeople must know the state-of-the-art products before they greet the first customer who walks into his store. This is all part of creating the right image. From the very beginning, you must "walk the talk," because first impressions are indeed lasting impressions.

Speaking of impressions, have you wondered what it takes to make a good first impression? Our ongoing research has revealed that most consumers who walk into a retail store notice whether or not your door mat is clean, the salesperson across the room is professionally dressed, your front windows have been washed, your front entrance is neat and organized, your store greeter is smiling, your aisle or walkway is uncluttered, and your front-area merchandise is dust-free.

And now you know why over three fourths of all Americans agree that the primary job of the store manager is to keep the store clean.

Stores that are dirty tell your customer that the store manager and employees don't take pride in where they work—would you want to shop there?

Just how much influence does perception have on shoppers? Our research shows that 60 percent of Americans say they measure a drugstore's selection of merchandise based on how big the store looks from the outside. Another 26 percent measure the store's selection based on its newspaper inserts and circulars, usually found in the Sunday newspaper. They interpret these to mean, "This store must have great selection, because their products on sale won't fit on a single page in the newspaper, so it has to have its own little newspaper." Incredibly, these figures mean that 86 percent of a drugstore's selection image is not based on *selection* at all—but on *perception*! In other words, the image of what consumers perceive to be the selection of inventory is nearly four times more influential than the actual inventory itself—which they have not seen.

Many more such examples confirm that a customer's perception of a company is based on image, not reality. For instance, our research shows that at one time, 70 percent of Americans said they measured customer service in a discount store based on how fast they're checked out. Of course, there is a lot more to servicing a customer than what happens at the checkout counter. And when it comes to advertising, here too perception has a striking influence on people. For example, in the retail furniture industry, if you promote a sale through a large newspaper ad that fails to feature a leather sofa, a startling 86 percent of the people we researched voiced the opinion that the store isn't having a sale on leather sofas. Yet, 69 percent of the same people will think that other sofas are on sale, even if the ad doesn't feature any sofas at all.

Someone once said, "Perception is everything." Of course, this doesn't mean you should try to fool the consumer by portraying something you are not. On the contrary, you should strive to have people perceive you for what you are—and if you're out to project a strong winning image, you have a responsibility to live up to it. Otherwise, you will lose credibility and be viewed as a fraud—this is the last image you want.

Ultimately, the best image a company can project is one of integrity. In a research project we conducted regarding retailers, customers judged a company's integrity on the following:

1. THE CREDIBILITY OF A STORE'S ADVERTISING. A store must deliver what it advertises. For example, if an ad offers a particular product at a special price, the merchandise must be available to be purchased.

2. THE IMAGE OF THE SALESPERSON. Customers form opinions about a store based on how they feel about a salesperson. A salesperson's appearance and manner of speaking can be as important as what he says.

3. THE SPEED AND ACCURACY OF THE CHECKOUT PROCESS. In addition to how quickly a customer gets out of the store, the attitude and service given by the checkout person influence his feeling about the store's integrity. It is important to the customer to be charged the exact amount that appears on the price tag. And in a mass marketer's store, customers are concerned about being properly scanned so they don't pay more than once for a product.

4. LIVING UP TO THE DELIVERY AGREEMENT. If the product is delivered, it must be defect-free, arrive on time, be properly installed, and so on.

5. THE COMPANY'S RESPONSE TO ANY PROBLEM THAT OC-
CURS AFTER THE SALE. The company must continue to treat the
customer with courtesy after the sale. Service is an ongoing process that doesn't cease when the cash register rings.

Integrity is a critical issue, because down deep in the heart of every
customer is the question "Does this company deserve my money?" If
you're perceived as lacking integrity, the customer thinks, "This company
isn't worthy of my business." This was evidenced when a particular retailer was cited by the New York attorney general's office for deceptive
advertising. After being hammered in a front-page story for just two days
and being featured as top story on the evening news, the company lost
40 percent of its customer base. Imagine that—loyalty that took twenty-
five years to build was lost in a matter of only two days!

HAVING A CONTINGENCY PLAN

When a long-term strategy is put together to guide a company over
a period of years, if there is one thing to expect, it's the unexpected. In
today's fast-changing marketplace, no long-term plan can be set in stone.

Again, I emphasize the importance of having Plans B, C, and even D
ready to go in anticipation of your competition's reactions, especially
when executing a predatory marketing strategy. But then it's not only
the competition you must contend with; a multitude of external factors
may warrant altering a long-term strategy. Everything from changes in
the economy to changes in the government's federal policies on foreign
affairs can be a reason to make adjustments. In fact, there are so many
unpredictable variables that contingencies must be factored into every
long-term plan. This means a plan must include "This is what we will
do if Problem X occurs," and "Here is what to do if we face Problem
Y," and so on. Making the decisions up front keeps you from having to
implement hurried, radical change along the way.

With this in mind, a long-term plan must include mileposts along the way that allow management to measure its progress. Not only do mileposts permit a company to evaluate what's going on, but in the case of a publicly owned corporation, it allows investors to understand that while there are some roadblocks, the company is moving in the right direction. This way, when quarterly earnings are down, panic doesn't set in. Don't forget, Wall Street doesn't like surprises. The investment community feels comfortable with a management team that has anticipated problems and has a plan in place to fix them.

CUTTING YOUR LOSSES

Everybody knows you should never throw good money after bad. In theory, it makes sense, but in the real world, it's hard to practice. For example, you buy a $20 stock, which drops two points the following week. There's a reason it dropped, but if you don't know why it fell 10 percent, you should cut your losses and sell before it goes down any further. Personally, I prefer to bite the bullet with a known loss.

There is such a thing, however, as knowing when it's time to get out of a "plan within your plan." All too often, when it has become obvious that something isn't working, management waits too long before admitting it's a bomb. An example of this is the ad campaign "Looking for Herb" that Burger King conducted a few years ago. Even though initial responses showed the campaign to be a loser right off the bat, weeks went by before it was finally cut.

When your customers aren't buying into an idea—no matter how much you like it—you've got to listen to what they're telling you. The single biggest rationale used by otherwise reasonable executives who don't want to accept what their customers are saying is the lame excuse "Well, the customers just haven't figured it out yet. But as soon as they do, this will take off like gangbusters!"

Of course, some companies wait too long before "getting out." Still, when there's a steady flow of red ink, it's better to get out late than not at all.

Note that Anheuser-Busch, the $10.3 billion St. Louis brewer, finally got out of a series of money-losing businesses when it made three major decisions in 1995 and early 1996 to rid itself of some unprofitable units. First, back in the summer of 1995, the company decided its $1.5 billion Campbell Taggart, Inc., bakery unit would be spun off to shareholders. Second, that fall it sold its money-losing baseball team, the St. Louis Cardinals. Third, in February 1996, company chairman August A. Busch III announced Anheuser was shutting down its Eagle Snacks, Inc., unit, thereby taking a hit with a $206 million write-off. The snack unit had operated in the red since Anheuser started it back in 1979. Busch stated that the company would rededicate itself to two core businesses: the super-competitive beer market and its Sea World and Busch Gardens theme parks.

A lesson to be learned from Anheuser's woes is that even a marketing powerhouse can have troubles when it enters a field outside its area of expertise. Back in 1979 when it started Eagle, and in 1982, when it paid $560 million for Campbell, the company had believed the synergies would be mind-boggling. It had made good sense at the time. After all, the company was already in the yeast business, a key ingredient of beer, and with its distribution and marketing muscle, selling salty snacks seemed a sure thing. While its drivers made their regular stops delivering beer to supermarkets and bars, why not have them drop off Eagle snacks, too?

As it turned out, while beer and snacks might go together while watching a football game or boxing match on TV, they aren't a good mix when it comes to distribution. Each fits in a different place in the supermarkets and convenience stores; what's more, they are purchased by different managers. So much for synergy.

Meanwhile, PepsiCo's Frito-Lay unit was not about to sit back and let Eagle take away market share. Frito-Lay decided to subsidize its potato chips and other snack products with the money made from its dominant position in corn chips. This led to slashing of prices, which put the squeeze on its smaller competitors, including Eagle. One distributor summed up the feeling at Anheuser when he commented, "It's no use chasing a bunny that Pepsi will never let me catch." PepsiCo's aggressive marketing strategy worked. Its market share jumped from 40 percent to 50 percent while Anheuser's never rose above 6 percent.

Eagle continued to lose money, and in 1995, its last year in business, with sales of $400 million, the unit had suffered its last loss, dropping another $25 million. This is when the decision was made once and for all to cut its losses. Now Anheuser management can focus on its long-term marketing strategy, which includes making its flagship Budweiser a global brand.

It is the long-term strategist who counts his losses early in the game and gets out quickly. He is better equipped to pull the plug on a short-term setback, because there is a long-term plan in place that keeps him on course. With his plan, he has direction. By remaining focused on a specific objective, he recognizes what may be throwing him off course, then does what's necessary to get back on track.

The short-term thinker, however, doesn't see the big picture—how could he, when he doesn't have a vision of the future? Consequently, he is not aware of what could be causing a negative effect on his business. And while cutting your losses is a good lesson to learn, it is also important to recognize the value of sticking to your initial game plan—even when red ink is flowing.

This is particularly true when a new venture is started. Depending on the particular business, certain short-term, and even long-term, losses should be anticipated and built into the plan. The executive of a new magazine, for example, anticipates several years of losses before the number of subscribers covers the publication's high start-up cost. And drug companies can take as many as eight to ten years to get a new product approved by the FDA; meanwhile, millions of dollars are spent in research, development, and other costs before a profit is realized. When long-term costs are built into your business plan, you won't be as likely to get cold feet when you incur those costs—because you know it's all part of your master plan.

INTERNAL POLITICS

A key element in implementing a successful long-term strategy is to communicate it throughout the organization so everyone knows what's going on. Everyone must have a clear understanding of where the company is headed; otherwise, people in middle- and executive-level positions will have varying perceptions on how to get there.

Typically, managers within the organization have their own agenda. When profit margins are falling, a marketing vice president may want to increase advertising and promotional expenses, while a finance officer focuses on how to cut expenditures, and at the same time a merchandising executive wants to put all the remaining inventory on sale at 50 percent off to make room for next season's goods.

It takes strong leadership to let everyone in the organization know the long-term objectives of the company, so all can see how the short-term activities they propose fit into the overall plan. Unclear communication of company goals can result in everyone pulling in different directions.

In the absence of a long-term strategy, you are put into a defensive position. If you are always reacting to what the competition does, it's very difficult to build an infrastructure within your organization. Without one, even short-term goals are hard to implement. No wonder everyone promotes his own agenda—there is no other agenda.

To overcome internal politics, a CEO must exhibit strong leadership. He must rally everyone to support the company's long-term agenda—all must pull together in the same direction. Once there is consensus on what the strategy will be, those who continue to dissent must ultimately be let go.

WHAT YOU SHOULD KNOW ABOUT THE LONG-TERM STRATEGIST

1. Short-term strategists may produce sales but never a strong corporate image.

2. Customer loyalty takes time to build and involves multiple purchases.

3. A corporate culture is essential for success—it is set by example over time.

4. Long-term planning involves a proactive strategy, which means leadership.

5. For long-term strategists, market changes are anticipated and contingency plans are in place because they welcome change, recognizing it as an opportunity to pull further ahead.

6. Long-term strategists never allow themselves to remain on the defensive.

7. A company with a long view has the greatest chance of success. A company with a strong market identity has a three-times-better chance to succeed.

CONSUMER MIND READER #9

America's Top Ten Family Vacation Activities

We conducted a national research study for this book to find out what Americans do when they take weeklong vacations. We surveyed one thousand families, all with children, and they rated the activities they most enjoy during their family vacations:

Activity	Percentage who engage in activity
1. Taking a break from work	60%
2. Visiting with your children	57
3. Just having the family together	57
4. Eating out as a family	56
5. Visiting with your spouse	48
6. Visiting with other adult family members and friends	43
7. Going to a movie one night	40
8. Going to the beach	36
9. Going to historical places (i.e., Mount Vernon, Fort Sumter)	35
10. Going to amusement parks	35

At the top of the list for the past twenty years, simply being away from work is a welcome relief, Americans continue to say. This indicates that most people are working hard while enduring job-related stress. The other listed activities are mainly family-oriented. The study suggests that most Americans feel they are not spending enough time with their families during the year, so rather than Mom and Pop getting away from the kids, they prefer to spend this time with them. This study provides useful information for the travel industry—which is already benefiting from a total family strategy. For instance, Las Vegas is booming since it became more family-oriented. And Branson, Missouri, home to Silver Dollar City, is another locale that features live family entertainment. Branson is a top tourist attraction because it definitely caters to families. Likewise, the cruise industry is no longer promoting a "love boat" theme, but now markets itself to attract families. Note, too, that America's number one tourist attraction, Disney World, epitomizes the ideal family vacation.

Interestingly, simply being with family and friends for a visit or dinner can be considered a treat for the average American on vacation. Other special vacation treats include being with one's family while going out to dinner, taking in a movie for a night, going to the beach, or visiting a historic place or an amusement park.

This also explains the popularity of four-day holiday weekends where Americans can enjoy many of these preferred vacation activities. A politically related issue surfaces from this research—federal funding for the U.S. Park Service. Protecting America's history is important to these families because of the vacation value of these historic places.

CHAPTER TEN

CUSTOMERS FOR LIFE

It's been said that the easiest thing in the world is to sell somebody something—the hard part is to keep a customer for life.

Joe Girard is hailed as "the world's greatest salesman" according to *The Guinness Book of World Records*. I like the way this super car salesman puts it when he talks to his customer.

"Bill, I hope you get a lemon."

"A lemon?" the customer asks.

"Yeah, I hope the car you just bought is a lemon."

"Why would you want me to buy a lemon?"

"Because then you'll have to bring it back to me, and when you do, I'll give you so much service I'm going to own you for life."

Selling more than thirteen thousand cars for a Detroit Chevrolet dealership earned Joe a place in the *Guinness Book* twelve years running—a record that may never be beat. Much of Joe's success resulted from his understanding of how to extend incredible service to his customers so they keep coming back. A highly successful real estate broker once told me, "Kill your customers with service. Service, service, service. Give them so much service they'll feel guilty even *thinking* about doing business with someone else." How well Joe Girard knows this.

In years past, to generate more business, emphasis was always put on the selling effort. The thinking was: The more sales that are closed, the more company revenues are increased. Today, leading marketing organizations recognize that sales and service are one and the same—the two words are always used together, never one without the other. Taking care of the customer is the name of the game.

When one first begins a sales career, there's a big price to pay. With few exceptions, the novice stockbroker, real estate agent, and insurance agent must invest much time and hard work making cold calls. The law of large numbers begins to work for the new salesperson who calls on enough prospects, and in time, he builds a clientele. After a sizable block of business is on the books, by giving tender loving care to those clients, the salesperson will free himself from reliance on cold calls, because many of his new sales will be repeat business and referrals from satisfied customers.

After two to three years, an estimated 80 percent of his future sales may come from his existing customer base. If, however, a salesperson fails to service his customers properly, he is doomed to pound the pavement year after year. Making cold calls may be tolerable for a short while in order to build a solid sales career, but it's not something anyone would want to do over an entire career.

As the rookie salesperson knows, it's a struggle to start a new business and get it off the ground. Building clientele requires hard work and long hours. And like the salesperson who begins to reap the harvest of planted seeds, a successful entrepreneur builds on satisfied customers' coming back and referring friends.

Here too, the first sale is just the beginning. Once you earn a customer's trust, future purchases increase in size. When you have a large enough customer base, momentum takes over and the business thrives.

SERVICE IS NOT A DEPARTMENT

Our research shows that fewer than 16 percent of Americans claim they have ever had a problem with a piece of furniture they've purchased. In other words, 84 percent of all furniture buyers have never in their lives had to call a retail store with a problem. This remarkable statistic attests to a meaningful phenomenon that spans enterprises in every field. *The manager who thinks that servicing customers centers around the company's service department is likely to wind up with a lot of dissatisfied customers.* That's because a large majority of customers will never have a single contact with the service department.

Depending upon the product, chances are most customers will never have a problem that warrants a visit or a call to the service department. With vacuum sweepers, for instance, the March 1996 *Consumer Reports* stated that one in five cleaners bought since 1990 has broken. When readers were asked about repairs to installed dishwashers bought new between 1988 and 1994, the five best-performing dishwashers—Magic Chef, Whirlpool, Hotpoint, General Electric, and In-Sink-Erator—all had a repair history of less than 10 percent. *Consumer Reports* did a similar repair history survey on washers for the same period. The top-performing washers—Kitchen Aid, Whirlpool, Hotpoint, Sears, and Maytag—scored best. Those washing machines made by these companies that were purchased new between 1988 and 1994 (without a service contract or extended warranty) and needed repairs averaged less than 12 percent.

In the automobile industry, where sales and service are practically synonymous, the number of problems for new purchases decreases every year. According to a J. D. Power study, on the average, GM customers reported 1.18 defects per vehicle, Chrysler customers 1.28 defects per vehicle, and Ford customers 1.13 per vehicle. These numbers compare to Toyota customers reporting a 0.77 defect average, Honda 0.79 per vehicle, and Nissan 0.83 per vehicle. The study was based on responses from more than forty thousand owners of 1996-model-year vehicles in the first ninety days of ownership. When you consider that an average car can have approximately thirty thousand parts, these are remarkably few defects.

Of course, since automobiles require a lot of maintenance, even when there are no problems, cars must be routinely serviced through visits to the service department. But with many other products, it's conceivable that a customer would never have any contact with a company's service people.

Understandably, taking care of customers extends far beyond the service department. A marketing-driven company understands how its customers define all the services they expect, including what they seek from their actual shopping experience. Sadly, many owners and managers are unaware of what's going on in the minds of their customers. I have been hired by failed companies after their return from bankruptcy. In most cases, their management hadn't a clue about what went wrong. One retailer said, "The thing that hurt us the most and put us into bankruptcy was our empty shelves. If we'd had more inventory, we could have survived."

Upon doing a study for that client, however, we learned that only 7 percent of his customers had consciously noticed the shelves weren't as full as they used to be.

"Well, then, Britt," the client asked, "what actually caused my sales to go down?"

"According to what your customers said," I explained, "your business turned sour when they walked through your store and missed an excitement that used to be there. It's not the empty shelf but rather that a product was not there to scream, 'Buy me today!' "

When it comes to service, the excitement I referred to can be many things. For instance, if a customer who comes into your clothing store can't find her size, it doesn't matter what nice salespeople you have or how low your prices are. Service goes far beyond the customer's dealings with what used to be called the complaint department. Today, it can mean a salesperson telling a customer, "This item will be on sale in three days. Would you like me to hold it for you so you can save 20 percent?" It could mean telling a customer, "A shipment of inventory is due Friday. If you tell me the size and color you want, I'll be happy to put one aside for you."

On every top-ten list I've seen in the retail industry, store cleanliness is ranked high when customers are asked to state an opinion on the company's service. Still, some retailers don't even associate a clean store with service!

Service is also judged by the hours a store is open. For example, staying open until 10:00 p.m., or on weekends—or especially on Sunday mornings—is defined as a definite service by some shoppers. With the high crime rates in the nation's inner cities today, having a parking lot with adequate lighting is viewed as a service. Some shopping centers offer valet parking to attract customers who fear being mugged in a dark, isolated parking lot.

TIME AND SERVICE

When you think about servicing customers, you should also consider that consumers shop fewer stores today. Because of increasing time constraints, by the year 2000, Americans making a major purchase will probably visit only 1.3 stores. This is not a result of fewer stores and fewer choices; on the contrary, there are more choices than ever. What's changing is the customer. Today a retailer who advertises a product but then doesn't have it in stock catches more flak than he did five to ten years ago. A consumer today considers that a retailer who runs out of inventory has committed a personal affront. "Look, I read your ad and I came to your store. I gave you my time and now you've abused it."

What this tells us is that today's customer wants to get in and out of that store as fast as possible. He values his time and he expects you to respect it. When it comes to buying furniture, for instance, he *expects* to spend about twenty-three minutes in a store looking at furniture. And although this is his ideal perception of time spent, he will tolerate spending as much as forty-five minutes in a store when actually making a purchase. Our research also reveals that it takes at least 50 percent longer to sell to multiple decision-makers. So if it takes forty-five minutes to sell a single buyer, you can add on another twenty-two and a half minutes when you're selling a couple. A furniture retailer who knows this can employ enough knowledgeable salespeople to provide quick answers to customers.

Retailers who devise more ways to respect the customer's time are providing definite services. For instance, a store could reduce the wait for a salesperson, provide clear signage to direct the customer, have a more natural traffic pattern, and so on. This brand of service is just as important as fast checkout or a prompt delivery truck.

We conducted a study that quantified the importance of a customer's time as it relates to the quality of service in today's marketplace. The question was asked: "Can you easily get away from work to handle a personal problem at home?" This survey was conducted to find out if the average American can go home to meet a delivery person or service person such as a plumber or carpet installer. In 1985, in various areas of the country, nearly 73 percent of working Americans said they were able to go home. Five years later, in 1990, nearly 65 percent said they could. But in 1994, only 38 percent answered affirmatively. The numbers are changing more dramatically as time goes on. At present, the average American claims to have 30 percent less time to shop than just two years ago. Today, a customer who is made to wait while meeting a service person during his lunch hour could be jeopardizing his job.

THROUGH THE CUSTOMER'S EYES

One of my clients, Ivan Steinberg, head of Steinberg's, a chain of successful electronics and appliance stores in Cincinnati, understands the multiple meanings of service very well.

When I first did a study for Steinberg's, Ivan wanted us to find out why his stores were not getting the same amount of repeat business as in the past. Ivan's father had founded the store in 1921, and for years, it sold crystal sets and battery radios. Ivan entered the business in 1950, and shortly thereafter, the store began carrying televisions. Today, with nineteen stores, it is the market leader in the Cincinnati area. However, when Ivan first contacted me, business was beginning to slip. Concerned, he asked me to find out what his customers and other stores' customers thought about Steinberg's.

I delivered the information our research confirmed concerning how Steinberg's service department was viewed. The company was using outside service agencies, which took three to four days to service customers. Ivan had been so close to his business he wasn't aware that the competition was providing superior service. Based on my recommendations, Steinberg's found ways to shorten the time to make service calls, and so business picked up. Then Ivan asked, "With our improved service, Britt, we're starting to get a lot of repeat business from our customers. But what can we do to perform even better?"

"Our study also revealed that your stores look stale," I replied.

"Stale? But they look fine to me," he answered.

"That's because you see them every day and are used to them. Now, if you really want to generate repeat business, here's what I suggest." Then I explained what was needed to redo the physical appearance of his stores.

Following my advice, Steinberg's began a campaign to either remodel or close every store in the chain. It made a huge difference in his business. Then Ivan asked, "What else do you advise?"

I told him, "I think there's a lot you can do with the appearance of your salespeople."

With this recommendation, Steinberg's inaugurated a dress code for its sales force. Today, when you walk into Steinberg's, customers have no problem identifying the salespeople. Every male salesperson wears a dark blue blazer, gray pants, a tie, and a solid blue or white shirt. "They look like they just came out of Harvard," Ivan says proudly. "Now when you see the appearance of our store and our sales force, it's quite impressive. There's really a difference between us and our competition.

"We finally looked through the customer's eyes," Ivan continues, "and we asked, 'Where would you buy? Would you buy from our store or from the competition?' " While Steinberg's always had the reputation for having the lowest price, price by itself is not enough today.

Ivan Steinberg is a fast learner. He recognizes what I tell every client: "Today's biggest challenge with a customer-driven company is that competitors will sometimes add a new and improved service—or customers simply change. This means that the excellent service you provided yesterday may not meet your customers' needs today."

A recent survey we conducted shows that the American consumer measures service in a retail store by the following ten standards, in order of priority:

1. THE EMPLOYEE SHOWS THAT HE OR SHE WANTS TO BE AT WORK. Customers can sense how your people feel about their jobs. Employees who are well treated reflect that in their performance.

2. A SALESPERSON IS AVAILABLE TO OFFER GENUINE SUGGESTIONS. Customers don't want a salesperson to "bother" them, but they do welcome good advice.

3. THE STORE IS CLEAN.

4. STORE SIGNAGE MAKES THE STORE EASY TO SHOP. People don't want to waste time looking for merchandise. Don't confuse them with poor signage.

5. THE SALESPERSON IS KNOWLEDGEABLE AND ALSO KNOWS THE STORE'S POLICIES AND PROCEDURES. In addition to product knowledge, the salesperson should know what the store can and can't do for customers.

6. THE STORE'S RETURN POLICY MAKES THE CUSTOMER FEEL THE RETAILER WANTS TO SATISFY HIM OR HER.

7. THE STORE GUARANTEE HAS NO EXCEPTIONS. Customers don't want to feel a guarantee has fine print that takes away what is provided in the big print.

8. THE STORE HAS WIDE AISLES. This makes it easy and fast to shop the store.

9. THE SALESPERSON IS A WELL-DRESSED PROFESSIONAL.

10. THE STORE HAS A THIRTY-DAY COMPLETE SATISFACTION GUARANTEE. Customers don't really expect you to give them their money back on a product if they have waited an unreasonable length of time to express their dissatisfaction. But they do expect you to provide a broad guarantee for a thirty-day period.

We conducted another study that focused on how companies measure another company's service (i.e., a manufacturer that buys machinery from another manufacturer, a retailer that buys merchandise from a wholesaler, etc.). This study did not involve a consumer product, and, as a result, a different set of criteria is used. The following reasons for satisfaction are in order of priority:

1. THE ORDERS ARE SHIPPED COMPLETE AND IN FULL. When business owners order goods from a manufacturer or supplier, they place great importance on having the complete order shipped on time and in full. They don't want goods coming in piecemeal.

2. THE COMPANY HONORS ITS COMMITMENTS. If a company says it will do something, it follows through. For instance, if the company has agreed to rush an item or provide X amount of advertising dollars, it fulfills that promise.

3. THE COMPANY'S REPS PROMPTLY RETURN CALLS WHEN NOTIFIED OF A PROBLEM. A sales rep must be more than the initial salesperson. He must be available later when something goes wrong. The rep is expected to handle the problem.

4. GOODS ARE DELIVERED ON TIME AND IN GOOD SHAPE. Today's companies won't tolerate late shipments. If it's supposed to be delivered on Monday, it had better arrive on Monday—Tuesday is too late. With more companies running on just-in-time

delivery schedules, they will not tolerate late deliveries—or, worse, damaged goods.

5. SENIOR MANAGEMENT IS EXPECTED TO MAKE REGULAR VISITS TO A CUSTOMER'S HEADQUARTERS. Today's business customers want the company's top decision-makers to visit them at their plant sites. They want senior management to have firsthand exposure to their problems. Although this priority is listed as fifth, it's being expressed more today than in the past. Our studies indicate that 70 percent of managers say they have difficulty getting the top-ranking executives with whom they do business to visit them.

In still another survey we did regarding department stores for a particular client, we learned that there were 147 ways customers measure customer service. Listed here are the first fifteen ways, in order of priority:

1. The store is clean.

2. The displays are impressive.

3. Brand names are properly used and visible.

4. Within eight seconds, the customer is made comfortable.

5. Excellent sale event presentation is matched by low sales prices.

6. The salesperson's professionalism is reflected in his or her attire.

7. Store management communicates, "We are the best," and the customer can feel it.

8. The store gives customers extraordinary treatment through the total retail experience with no breakdown.

9. The customer hears "thank you" and feels it is sincere.

10. The customer's knowledge is respected during an exchange and sharing of information.

11. Customers are asked personal questions—and feel the staff are involved with what they want.

12. Customers see staff as empathetic—as putting themselves in their shoes.

13. The retail experience involves a relationship, not just selling merchandise.

14. The salesperson makes quality suggestions, not phony ones.

15. The salesperson assists the customer to buy quality.

The list of our customer's needs is continually changing, because the customer is continually changing. Speaking of changing, at one time, having a baby-changing table in the men's room wasn't even on the top-hundred list. Today, it's in the top twenty-five.

THE VALUE OF A CUSTOMER

The long-term strategist recognizes that the true value of a customer goes far beyond the initial sale. He realizes that treating the customer with tender loving care at the first sale preserves the possibility of many more orders to follow. He also understands the exorbitant cost involved in making the initial sale.

A Lincoln-Mercury dealer once told me that he calculated that his dealership spent an average of $100 on advertising and promotion per showroom prospect. "Our average closing rate is 25 percent," he told me, "which means our cost per customer is $400. Add this $400 to our other overhead, and you can see how expensive it is to lose a customer because we failed to service him."

Every company can devise a similar formula to determine the "acquisition cost" to make an initial sale. A successful stockbroker told me that during his first two years in sales, he made a hundred cold calls a day, and at the end of each week, he averaged two new clients. When he calculated the cost in both time and money to make five-hundred cold calls, he realized how expensive it was to obtain clients. "The initial order of a new client averaged two hundred shares," he explained, "but the size of a client's orders dramatically increases with the service I provide. Knowing the hard work it takes to get that first sale, and realizing what repeat business can mean, I know I can't afford to lose clients by failing to service them. It's bad enough that there's a certain amount of natural attrition because of clients dying, going bankrupt, having their son-in-law go into the business, and so on. So once I open an account, I'm fanatic about making sure it stays on the books."

While I was discussing acquisition cost with an electronics manufacturer that makes a particular fiber wire used in the computer industry, he told me that his company had practically no advertising budget. "Our business is so specialized there are only about fifty computer companies that can use our product," he explained. "Our advertising consists only of the handful of ads we place in trade magazines. So our acquisition cost is what we spend per year to have two salespeople on the road, calling on our thirty-five customers, and trying to win the business of the other fifteen who don't buy from us." By calculating the total annual expenses for the two salespersons traveling the country, he was able to determine what each sale cost his company.

While no company wants to lose a customer, with a customer base of only thirty-five, a manufacturer cannot afford to lose a single account. Acquisition cost aside, only a finite number of companies are potential buyers. With only so many out there to pitch, if you lose one because of poor servicing, that ex-account can mean market share lost forever.

Something else you should evaluate when analyzing the high cost of getting new business is the comparative worth of a lifetime customer. Let's start by looking at a service that everyone is familiar with—cable television. I went to Bill Bresnan, a legend in the industry, to ask if there was a way to place a lifetime value on a cable customer. Today, Bill serves as CEO of Bresnan Communications, a privately held cable company that serves 180 communities and has recently expanded its operations to Chile and Poland. Bill was formerly president of Teleprompter and chairman and CEO of Group W Cable. I figured if anyone knew the value of a cable customer, Bill did.

"Let's say a couple with cable TV has two children," Bill said, "and we've done a great job at keeping them happy. Since we have a 60 percent penetration rate, let's assume that one of the kids would have become a customer anyhow. But knowing how satisfied his parents were with our service, the second kid also signs up. And let's assume that this couple has two close friends, and again keeping our high penetration rate in mind, we get just one of them because of rave reviews. We'll assume the family friend signed up after a year, and twelve years later, one of the children signed up after leaving home. Based on a twenty-year period, at our average customer monthly rate of $28 and factoring in 3 percent inflation, the couple, their friend, and the grown child would generate a total revenue of $23,000 in cable fees."

Now let's do the same thing with a bigger-ticket item. Take a car dealership, for example. A thirty-year-old man who buys a $25,000 automobile can potentially buy twenty more cars during his lifetime. With inflation factored in, he's potentially a $1 million customer. And this is only the cars he buys for himself. If he's treated right, his wife is likely to be a customer, too. And don't forget the cars he may buy for his children—and their repeat orders when they buy their own cars.

Look what can happen when a car buyer gets stuck with a lemon and the dealer gives him poor service. This unhappy customer is going to bend the ear of seven times as many people as a happy customer. Now consider a car dealer's high acquisition cost in advertising dollars just to get a prospect to walk into his showroom to take a demonstration ride. When a customer voices a complaint, forget about who's right and who's wrong—you can't afford a dissatisfied customer.

Let's take it to another level, on an even bigger-ticket item than an automobile. Let's talk about what happens when a medical equipment company sells expensive scanners such as a magnetic resonance imaging (MRI) machine or a computerized axial tomography (CAT) machine to a radiologist. In this highly competitive field, half a dozen companies like General Electric, Siemans, Phillips, and Picker are fighting tooth and nail to install a machine. Imagine the damage a few dissatisfied radiologists could do. For instance, the Radiology Society of North America holds an annual convention attended by approximately five thousand members. An MRI manufacturer could lose millions of dollars of business during one such three-day weekend.

CUSTOMER LOYALTY

What determines how much a long-term customer is potentially worth is whether you have earned his loyalty. This loyalty is so important that it should be factored in when evaluating the true net worth of a company.

Customer loyalty can be quantified. A Dunkin' Donuts franchise, for example, sells at a premium as compared to other fast-food franchises because a prospective franchisee knows the name recognition drives customers to his stores. He knows that putting a Dunkin' Donuts sign in front of his store will automatically ring up sales on his cash register, because millions of people are loyal Dunkin' Donuts customers. If you have any doubts, try to remember the last time you were traveling out of town and stopped at a local doughnut shop for a cup of coffee. For good reason, Donna's Donuts doesn't generate the same traffic as a nationally recognized brand-name franchise.

In the world of franchising, a franchisee who represents a well-established franchisor has a valuable asset. Whether it's Century 21, H&R Block, or Servicemaster, the name recognition brings customers in the front door. Investing in the franchise of a national organization with a large customer following is costly, but consider that you're actually buying a large customer base.

To determine just how valuable a name is, let's look at the most recognizable brand name in the world—Coca-Cola. The company's roots go back to May 8, 1886. Coca-Cola's modest debut came about when John S. Pemberton, an Atlanta pharmacist and inventor, stirred caramel-colored syrup in a brass kettle. Soon thereafter, it was sold at the soda fountain in the city's largest pharmacy, Jacobs'. Following Pemberton's death in 1891, the real marketing success of Coca-Cola began, when Asa G. Chandler purchased the formula and all rights—for $2,300.

Interestingly, the Coca-Cola formula was never patented. Chandler, a long-term marketing strategist, understood that a patent would protect the formula from use by others for a period of only seventeen years; then, according to patent law, the formula would become public domain. To this day, the formula is not protected by patent law, which means it can be used by anyone who can figure out how to duplicate it. Certainly, for the past several decades, scientists could have broken down the formula in a laboratory and produced a carbonated beverage that would taste like "the real thing." Had this been done—and the law would permit it— that beverage would have little value. What makes the world's most popular soft drink so popular is not the ingredients inside the bottle, but the name on the bottle. No name in the world has as much value. Hundreds of millions of people—possibly even more than a billion—around the globe are loyal Coca-Cola drinkers.

The loyalty customers feel to Coca-Cola is a result not of a unique product, but, instead, of an incredible marketing strategy. You may be shaking your head, saying, "Okay, so Coca-Cola became one of the world's most successful products based on brand loyalty. But what does this have to do with my company?" My answer is, "Plenty, because it illustrates the influence and power customer loyalty has when it is maximized."

While enormous numbers of people are loyal to Coca-Cola, our research reveals that customer loyalty in general has been on the decline. In 1960, it was as high as 50 percent, but by 1970, it dropped to 33 percent, and in 1990, 25 percent. By 1996, it dipped to just 12 percent. One could postulate that people today are less loyal because they have more choices than ever before. But consumers tell us they prefer to be loyal to a company, and when they are not, it's because they haven't found a company that stands out. Consumers are under the impression that many companies they deal with really don't want their business. What's sad is how few companies actually offer a fulfilled shopping experience to the customer who walks in their front door. The same applies to a service business when customers are not being made to feel they're really important.

The message here is that a business can't afford to have customers buy once, then lose them. Our customer loyalty study told us that when 1960 shoppers were asked where they would go for a particular product category, half the people said they would consider only one store. This means that a 1960 retailer had to advertise for only half his customers, compared to today's retailer, who has to advertise for a whopping 86 percent of his customers. These numbers reveal that it takes many more advertising dollars nowadays to get the same results retailers got back in 1960. A store back then could have an advertising budget of 1 or 2 percent; now retailers struggle to keep their advertising budgets below 10 percent.

There are five good things that a retailer can expect from a loyal customer:

1. YOUR STORE IS THE FIRST STORE SHOPPED.

2. THERE IS A HIGHER INTENTION TO BUY ON THE FIRST VISIT.

3. THE CUSTOMER IS MORE LIKELY TO BE RECEPTIVE TO SUGGESTIONS (which create add-on sales).

4. THE CUSTOMER WILL TELL HIS FRIENDS WHERE HE SHOPS. Since a consumer hears only 25 percent as many great shopping experiences compared to ten years ago, today's customer tends to talk more about that good experience than earlier customers did. Remember that there is at least an 80 percent chance that a *referred* customer will buy on his first visit.

5. WHEN SOMETHING GOES WRONG, THERE IS MORE TOLER-
ANCE. Interestingly, a loyal customer is more forgiving and will
give you a second chance when you goof up.

Customers feel loyal to trendmakers, because they give credit to a
company that stands for something. I think this loyalty arises from the
fact that consumers respect a trendmaker for taking risks. A market leader
who stands out above the rest of the pack attracts loyal customers.

An example of what happens when you don't distinguish yourself
from others in your category is illustrated by a 1993 study we conducted
for the mattress industry. We discovered that more than half the people
who purchased a mattress at a bedding specialty store two years later did
not even remember the store! Remember now, this is a purchase that
they seldom make—perhaps once every six or seven years. Because the
store did nothing out of the ordinary to service them, there's nothing to
remember about being in that particular store. As a consequence, when
they prepare to buy their next mattress, they think, "I'll see who has the
best price or who's carrying Sealy." Or if they're looking for a specialty
store, they choose one almost at random: "I'll see who's open and who's
the closest."

THE PARTNERSHIP

In an ideal relationship with a customer, a partnership evolves. No
longer is one party considered the seller and the other the buyer—both
parties are on the same team. In these situations, it's sometimes difficult
to distinguish the salesperson from the customer.

Such unusual relationships sometimes exist between two companies
that have done business together for years and have prospered as a result.
Ideally, each depends on the other in a mutually advantageous relationship.

Dana Corporation is known for building partnerships with its customers. With $7.6 billion in sales, this Toledo-based company is the largest

independent automotive components manufacturer in North America. Dana's impressive list of customers includes Chrysler, General Motors, Mack Trucks, and Jeep. To build long-term relationships with its customers, Dana takes considerable risks to please them. This is illustrated by a story of how Dana serves one of its customers, Ford Motor Company's Kentucky Truck Plant in Louisville. About a mile down the road, Dana's Spicer Universal Joint Division built a regional assembly facility (RAF), a small plant with about fifty employees devoted to making driveshafts and universal joints only for its single customer, Ford. Built originally as a just-in-time facility to ensure prompt and reliable delivery, the building required a calculated risk on Dana's part, since, at the time, Rockwell Standard was also supplying the same parts to Ford. "We believed that as long as we had a competitive price and could give them 100 percent just-in-time delivery, we'd be hard to beat," Southwood J. Morcott, Dana's CEO, explains. It worked. Dana is now Ford's sole supplier of these parts.

Dana's RAF in Louisville exemplifies the kind of efficiency that is attainable when two companies work as a team. There is no paperwork exchanged between the two companies—no orders, no invoices, no checks. All transactions are made by computer. For example, if, by four in the afternoon, X number of units are requested by Kentucky Truck, Dana will make them and have the units on the docks by seven in the morning. And thanks to the computer system, each driveshaft and component is numbered sequentially according to Ford's assembly schedule. "We don't send a bill," Morcott says. "We just have to know how many trucks went out of their plant, and this tells us the number of parts we made for them. Every time a truck clears the line, a billing mechanism is triggered, and we're paid by a wire transfer from their account into ours. The float is less than twenty-four hours."

In another rare partnership, Dana agreed to build two plants to provide chassis for just-in-time delivery to Mack Trucks assembly plants in Winnsboro, South Carolina, and Macungie, Pennsylvania. The relationship began rather formally through a massive document drawn up by both sides. The harmony between the two companies today is evidenced by their progression to the "evergreen contract" Mack has since presented to Dana. The agreement continues indefinitely unless one side wants to get out, which it can do by giving a three-year advance notice to the other company.

GREAT SERVICE STARTS AT THE TOP

Exceptional service starts at the top. The CEO has to believe in it, and he must insist on its execution by every employee. In general, organizations with strong corporate cultures are the most likely to be customer-driven. When IBM began back in 1914, Thomas J. Watson, Sr., began instilling his personal values in the new company. He decreed that three principles would determine all decisions made by management: (1) The individual must be respected. (2) The customer must be given the best possible service. (3) Excellence and superior performance must be pursued. All three of these wonderful bedrock principles focusing on doing what's right for the customer have guided IBM for more than eighty years.

When everyone understands that the customer truly comes first, it becomes "the way to do business." Even when there is a thirty-day complete guarantee, and a dissatisfied customer wants a refund six weeks after a purchase, in a truly customer-driven company, an employee can rectify the situation without having to ask permission from a supervisor. When the written guarantee states that the company is not liable, the company's unwritten commitment to service takes precedent.

I particularly like IBM's first doctrine, respect for the individual. This relates directly to outstanding customer service, because how customers are treated is a matter of respect that has to start from deep within the organization. The CEO has to respect his senior management team, who, in turn, treat their subordinates with regard, and so on down the line throughout the organization. An example of how this works may be a CEO returning all telephone calls, or not keeping anyone waiting for an appointment, or listening to his people, and so on. These and dozens of other little things send a message to his people that he respects them—regardless of title. The CEO who starts this chain reaction leads by example. As my father used to say, "I'd rather see a sermon than hear one."

You don't have to head a multibillion-dollar international corporation before you can issue a decree listing your own bedrock principles. Respecting employees, vendors, and customers has nothing to do with being big or small. Neither does putting a code of ethics in writing. That's right—put what you believe in writing. And better still, publish it in your newsletters and in the literature you mail to your customers, and display it on the walls of your offices and reception room. Don't keep it a secret. Announce it to the world. And once you do, make sure you live by it.

Of course, you must first announce it within the company to your own people. The Ritz-Carlton, one of the world's premier luxury hotel groups, with thirty-two properties in operation, is a prime example. As far as company president Horst Schulze is concerned, you can't start too soon to communicate what you stand for to your people. "During orientation, we ask each newly hired employee to join us in our mission to be the best in hotel service," Schulze says. "Right from the beginning, we define our soul, our vision, and our commitment."

Schulze, who is actively involved in the opening of each new Ritz-Carlton hotel, personally conducts each first-day employee orientation. "Although we serve, we are not servants," he tells employees. "We are ladies and gentlemen serving ladies and gentlemen." This line, along with a list of the twenty basics of servicing hotel guests, is printed on a small laminated card carried by Ritz-Carlton employees. Schulze strives to instill a sense of pride in those who hear his message.

When they are treated like ladies and gentlemen, employees feel good about themselves, and this feeling carries over to the customer.

NEVER PREJUDGE A CUSTOMER

Perhaps every salesperson has a story about a sorry-looking prospect who looks like he doesn't have two dimes to rub together. My favorite happened at a Cadillac dealership in Columbia, South Carolina. One day a man in dirty overalls walked onto the car lot.

The dealership's top salesman approached him and introduced himself.

"It's a real pleasure to make your acquaintance," the salesman said warmly and shook the man's hand. After a few minutes of chat, the salesman asked, "What line of work are you in?"

"I've been farming all my life on a farm just outside of town."

"Really?" the salesman replied. "You know, when I was a kid, I always enjoyed visiting my grandparents' farm."

"That so?" said the farmer. "You know, I've been wanting to own a Cadillac all my life."

"Well, sir, we do have the best selection in the area."

"Yep, I know that," the farmer said. He eyed a Seville, and walked around it a few times. "I believe I want this one."

"That's definitely a beaut," the salesman said.

"I like that one over there, too," the farmer said.

"What do you mean?" the salesman asked.

"Come to think of it, I want two like this one, and two like that one."

When the salesman realized the farmer was serious about buying four, he looked at the farmer in a state of shock. The farmer wanted one car for himself, another for his wife, and two more for his sons. Later he explained that he had just sold his farm for $16 million to a shopping center developer.

"I like your style," he said with a toothy smile. "You know, I visited two other dealerships this morning, and you're the first person who bothered to come up and talk to me."

When I talked to the salesman, he asked, "Britt, do you know what I learned from this experience?"

"No," I said. "Tell me."

"From now on I'm always going to ask somebody if he wants to buy two Cadillacs!"

Need I say more about prejudging a customer?

ADDING INSULT TO INJURY

If you want a sure way to alienate your customers, send them a nice little notice reminding them they haven't used their charge card lately, and be sure to say that if they come in with this certificate, you'll give them a whopping 5 percent off.

The customer will read your note and think, "How can you offer me so little? Don't expect me to drive across town for just a few percent off. That's no special deal at all!" With discounts galore at department stores, today's customer wants a minimum of 15 percent off. Anything less is insulting.

To add insult to the injury, invite your customers to a private sale where you don't have something exclusively for them—something not available to the general public. "Don't try to trick me," they'll respond. "How can you say I'm your preferred customer when what you are offering me can be bought by anyone, anywhere?"

One of the worst things a retailer can do is announce a big sale, but offer relatively few items at big discounts. If you want to enrage customers, advertise a big clearance sale without having adequate marked-down inventory. Or instead of having your regular merchandise on sale, bring in goods that aren't the quality of what you normally sell. When this happens, customers fume. "They didn't even change their prices! They're pulling a scam, trying to make me think I'm getting a better deal." Today's consumers are infuriated when they think a store has wasted their time with misleading advertising.

When a customer has a complaint, one thing is certain—you don't want to do anything to antagonize him further. With this in mind, here are three suggestions for how *not* to handle customer service complaints:

1. TAKING A LONG TIME TO ANSWER THE TELEPHONE. A sure way to agitate a customer is to allow your phone to ring ten or more times. This is certain to make people want to rip their phone out of the wall. When it goes beyond three to five rings, the customer thinks, "How dare they call this customer service when there's no response?"

2. OVERUSE OF AUTOMATED VOICE TELEPHONE SYSTEM WITHIN THE COMPANY. A caller's agitation will double when he has to go through a long session of button-pushing from one voice mail to another to another to another.

3. A LACK OF EMPATHY IN THE SERVICE PERSON'S ACTIONS OR VOICE. Admittedly, it takes a very special person to show empathy at the end of the day after dozens of irate customers have called with complaints—but make sure that that special person is the one interacting with your customers.

We conducted another survey on what today's consumers expect when they register a complaint via the telephone. They wanted:

1. PROMPT ACKNOWLEDGMENT. When a complaint is made, the customer wants quick feedback that his problem is being looked into. If a complaint card is sent in, a company must respond the same day—within hours after receiving it. An estimated 75 percent of consumers perceive a prompt response as a necessity of great customer service.

2. UNDERSTANDING OF THE CUSTOMER'S VIEW. The customer wants to know that the person on the other end of the receiver has empathy. This empathy is exhibited by how the complaint is repeated back to the customer, and then addressed. For ex-

ample, you might say to a customer, "Well, that certainly is not right. No wonder you were upset!" It's not enough to simply say, "Thank you for telling us about your problem."

3. IMMEDIATE ACTION TO RESOLVE THE PROBLEM. Because time is such an important factor, today's customer wants immediate answers and is much less tolerant of getting "the runaround" or "the bureaucratic shuffle."

Back in 1983, when TV advertising by dentists was relatively new, a Charleston dentist asked my advice. "I need a commercial that has wide appeal," he explained, "but I want to be careful not to infuriate my colleagues who haven't yet bought into the idea that we should even be advertising." His practice, which included three other dentists, needed new patients in order to succeed, but the present TV ads were generating only twenty new patients a month.

Following my advice, the firm ran a conservative ad that showed some befores and afters of cosmetic dentistry, and the tag line recommended that the viewer contact his or her own dentist. "If you don't have a dentist," the commercial subtly added, "call the Dental Group."

After one month of running the new commercial, the dentist called me. "The ad bombed," he said.

I thought the ad was good and was disappointed to hear it did so poorly. "I thought that ad would generate a great response," I told him.

"Oh, the response was terrific," he said. "We are indeed getting lots of calls, but we're still getting only about twenty new patients a month."

He explained that nearly 130 inquiries came in during the month. Then it dawned on me. The problem could be something that the person who answered his phone was doing. The dentist decided to stand nearby while the receptionist talked to callers to see if there was anything she could say differently that might help. He discovered that she had absolutely no empathy in her tone of voice when talking to callers. The problem wasn't a weak commercial but instead this particular receptionist's inability to sympathize with the plight of the people who called in. Once he replaced her with someone who did express empathy, his new patient rate shot up to over a hundred per month.

Ever since, I've advised many of my clients periodically to call their company's main number and, under the guise of a customer, see what kind of reception they receive. "See how long the phone rings," I suggest. "You know how frustrating it is to call an airline, trying to get a 'real' person to talk to you. Is your company treating your customers this same way? How long does it take to get through to the right person to schedule a service call or straighten out an invoice?" Many top executives who take the time to check it out personally confess later, "I had no idea our customers were treated so poorly."

I'm sure no businessperson would intentionally offend a customer, as in the case of the dentist's telephone receptionist, but it happens all too often in the world of business. As a million-miles-a-year traveler, I see it firsthand on the road. One of my pet peeves is the way the car rental agencies try to stick it to their customers when they say, "You'll have to initial the places on the form if you *don't* want the insurance."

Like the vast majority of business travelers, I use a credit card. The car rental agencies know that when they receive a major credit card such as American Express, MasterCard, or Visa, the customer is covered for most of the insurance the car rental agency is trying to sell. Yet they still try to get you for an extra $8 to $12 a day (rates vary from city to city). More than once I've asked, "Why are you trying to sell me that insurance when you know I'm using my American Express card and don't need it?"

"I'm only doing what I'm told."

When a manager offers the insurance, I say, "Don't you think that's dishonest? Why should anyone be influenced to buy something you know he doesn't need?"

"I'm sorry, but it's company policy for us to have the form initialed, sir."

Of course, company policy doesn't make something right, so when I hear that, it makes me all the more angry.

Speaking of traveling, I recently boarded a plane at La Guardia Airport. Five minutes before the flight was scheduled to depart, we heard an announcement. "Perhaps you have noticed, ladies and gentlemen—our air-conditioning system is not working. I am sorry to inform you there will be a few minutes' delay."

An hour passed before the next announcement. "Ladies and gentlemen, we're sorry but it will take an estimated twenty minutes before we will depart. Thank you for your understanding and patience." Another long, hot hour passed before the air came on and the plane actually departed.

What bothered me so much, and, I am sure, the other passengers, was that the plane's temperature was in the high nineties, and everyone was feeling miserable. Six crew people stood near the cockpit and kibitzed, taking turns running back and forth to the air-conditioned terminal; meanwhile the hundred or so passengers baked in the hot, crowded airplane. I have since been told by engineers that within a few minutes of looking at the air-conditioning system, the airline service people should have been able to estimate the required time to do the repairs. Then the passengers could have been allowed to move to the terminal, where they could walk about, cool off, and be far more comfortable. But to do so meant that the six crew members would be required to assist everyone in exiting and then reentering—a lot of extra work for them. So, rather than inconvenience themselves, the crew elected to inconvenience one hundred passengers. And airlines wonder why there's so little customer loyalty!

EIGHT TOP CHARACTERISTICS OF AMERICA'S HIGHEST-RATED RETAIL SALESPEOPLE

In a survey we conducted about what traits consumers prefer in retail salespeople, the following is their order of preference:

1. GREETS ME WITH A SMILE. Nothing replaces a warm greeting to immediately gain a customer's trust.

2. MAKES ME FEEL AT EASE. It's important to establish a certain comfort level, in particular when a big-ticket item is being shopped.

3. (tie) EXHIBITS PROFESSIONALISM. Today's consumer wants a knowledgeable salesperson who is well informed about the product. (This attribute is viewed as a time-saver for today's time-conscious customer.)

4. (tie) ANSWERS QUESTIONS BEYOND THIS PURCHASE. A customer expects a salesperson to have knowledge about the product, and even additional knowledge about related products not sold in this store. For example, if a car audio system is being purchased, the salesperson should be able to converse intelligently about car security systems.

5. KNOWS STORE POLICIES. A salesperson must know everything from the company's return policy to how deliveries are handled.

6. QUALIFIES THE CUSTOMER. A salesperson must be a good listener. Before he attempts to sell a product, he should ask questions to find out what product or service would best fill the customer's needs.

7. MAKES ME FEEL THAT THE SALE WON'T STOP AT THE END OF THE SALES PRESENTATION. A customer should be made to feel

comfortable about calling the salesperson *after* the sale. The sales-person who projects a warm feeling achieves this.

8. MAKES ME FEEL MY BUYING DECISION WAS BASED ON HIS INPUT. The customer wants to digest what the salesperson says, and, without feeling pressured, make his own buying decision.

THE T.O. SPECIALIST

In retailing, the T.O. Specialist is the guy to whom a salesperson "turns over" a tough customer. In years past, this was the salesperson who was able to make the hard-to-close sale. From a customer's viewpoint, however, you didn't want to be turned over to this salesman for fear he'd sell you something you didn't want.

As recently as 1994, our surveys showed that only 33 percent of all customers considered it a positive experience to have the T.O. Specialist brought in. By early 1996, however, the number flip-flopped—and 68 percent of all consumers thought it was a positive experience.

What changed their opinions? The T.O. Specialist has new status today. This salesperson can be viewed as the expert within the particular category he works in—the guy who is most knowledgeable.

For the record, the American consumer still dislikes being turned over to a strong closer. But today's T.O. Specialist is viewed differently. Now he's the guy who can tell you what you need to know—so you can get in and out of the store in a jiffy.

WARM FEELINGS

"Thank you" means a lot when it comes from the owner of a business. And although it's not quite the same when a representative of a big com-pany expresses appreciation, it's still quite nice. You should never un-derestimate it.

It's such an easy thing to send a thank-you note to a customer. When you do, make sure it's handwritten. While a lot of people are under impression that this technique is overworked, our research shows that only 10.5 percent of all Americans have ever received such a letter. Our surveys show that in excess of 90 percent of the people who do receive one are very appreciative. I highly recommend that you make this standard procedure. It gets such terrific results and costs so little.

Also remember that you don't have to be a small company to know your customer by name. With effort, everyone can do this.

It gives hotel guests a warm feeling to be addressed by name by the operator when they call the front desk. I love to hear the operators at top hotels say, "May I help you, Mr. Beemer?" Sure, I realize a computer gives them my name, but I still appreciate the fact that the hotel management cares enough to make the effort.

It's true that when you travel first class, most hotels, airlines, and car rental services will give you VIP treatment. But shouldn't all employees of every company treat every customer as if they really care about him—and truly appreciate his business?

JUMPING THROUGH HOOPS

Customers want to experience something extraordinary today, so it's not enough for a company to do only what's expected. In today's marketplace, that doesn't earn any points.

Just how well The Ritz-Carlton Hotel Company understands this is demonstrated by the actions of its people. To encourage employees to go that extra mile for hotel guests, each staff member is empowered to use his or her own best judgment to handle customer complaints. Every employee is authorized to resolve a guest complaint, and can spend up to $2,000 per incident—not per year or per employee—to do so! This means that if a customer isn't satisfied with a meal, an employee can immediately act to take it off his bill. A front desk clerk can use her discretion to put a customer in a penthouse suite at the rate of a single room.

Hotel president Horst Schulze explains, "The $2,000 authorization for guest problem-solving is not about money. Instead, the emphasis is on cultivating a corporate environment that encourages employees to make decisions and speak up." With permission to think on their feet, Ritz-Carlton employees are constantly looking for ways to keep customers happy. It doesn't necessarily take something expensive to win customer loyalty; more often, it's a constant series of little attentions.

For instance, as a woman checked in at one Ritz-Carlton hotel, the bellman heard her say, "I'm embarrassed to pull up in my filthy car." He immediately had her car washed. Another bellman sent a pitcher of orange juice to the room of a guest suffering from a cold. On another occasion, a couple going to a costume party asked where they could purchase coconuts and a grass skirt; the concierge scoured San Francisco until he found them.

The Ritz-Carlton management understands that building relationships with people is what its business is truly about. To help accomplish this, the company's Repeat Guest Program identifies a guest's preferences, and on the next stay, sees to it that those preferences are accommodated. Employing an extensive computer database costing approximately $700,000 per year, the hotel chain tracks the likes and dislikes of more than 500,000 repeat guests. For example, a particular businessperson does not care for alcoholic beverages, so the hotel makes sure the wet bar in his room contains only soft drinks, juices, and his favorite brand of bottled water. And if a guest in Palm Beach wants soft-scrambled eggs on a slightly burned English muffin and three newspapers delivered each morning, this is duly noted and becomes part of the program—whether his next stay is in Sydney or Kansas City.

"Whether they are expressed or unexpressed," Schulze says, "we want to fulfill the wishes of our guests." When a customer-driven person like Horst Schulze heads a company, leadership and enthusiasm permeate the entire organization.

Those who are close to Horst Schulze describe his desire to serve customers as an obsession. Is such an obsession innate or is it a trait which one acquires through training and experience? I asked this question of a friend of mine, Peter Connolly—senior vice president of worldwide communication for the Polo Ralph Lauren Corporation, an international $3.8 billion fashion company. Peter claims to have learned the value of exceptional customer service many years ago as an adolescent. It was the result of an incident that happened back in the 1960s. Peter's father, Peter Connolly, Sr., a devout football fan, became upset after hearing an announcement that the New York Giants games would be blacked out in the Long Island area for the upcoming season. "After that, the only way we could get reception," my friend explained, "was for my brother or me to climb up on the roof to manually turn the antenna so it faced Connecticut, where the game was being telecast. When one of us nearly fell off the roof, my father decided to purchase an expensive antenna with remote control from P. C. Richard.

"Shortly after he bought it, Long Island got hit by the tail end of a hurricane, and it knocked down our antenna. It was clearly an act of God, and certainly P. C. Richard was not responsible. But after my father frantically called the store, a serviceperson came to our house and replaced the antenna in time for Sunday's game. Back then, the several hundred dollars that the antenna cost was a lot of money to my father. He kept waiting for a bill, and finally called to inquire about the cost of the second antenna. To his amazed delight, there was no charge for the service.

"My father was so thankful he eventually bought every television set, air-conditioning unit, washing machine, dryer, microwave, refrigerator, and everything else that's sold at P. C. Richard. And to the day he died in 1995, he told that antenna story, whenever the subject of appliances, television, or even football came up. He was a P. C. Richard customer for life."

CONSUMER MIND READER #10

What Shoppers Dislike Most About Shopping

Two studies of female and male shoppers defined their shopping dislikes. The following top ten items show, in order, what bothers each gender most:

Men's Top Ten Shopping Dislikes

1. Long lines at cash register
2. Rude salespeople
3. Price scans differently from that marked on item
4. No prices on items
5. Pushy salespeople
6. Couldn't find advertised item in stock
7. Can't take things back if not satisfied
8. Dirty rest rooms
9. No one in store to help
10. Unorganized store

Women's Top Ten Shopping Dislikes

1. Long lines at cash register
2. Dirty rest rooms
3. Rude salespeople
4. Pushy salespeople
5. Couldn't find advertised item in stock
6. No prices on items
7. Price scans differently from that marked on item

8. No one in store to help

9. Can't take things back if not satisfied

10. Dirty stores

What is most interesting about these studies we conducted for this book is the differences between genders. While both sexes dislike long lines at cash registers, men are more apt actually to complain about them, along with anything else that wastes time during their shopping experience. Among their top ten peeves, men include an unorganized store—a complaint women don't list at all. Why do men voice this complaint? Because it means time wasted locating an item in a store.

A related survey revealed that men are more likely to go shopping for a single item than are women. Obviously, a shopper in a large store can easily become frustrated if obstacles keep him from finding what he's looking for. Those frustrations are compounded when the price isn't on the item or there's nobody around to help him. He'll be especially impatient standing in a long checkout line, holding only a single item, yet waiting behind customers whose shopping carts are filled with merchandise.

For women, dirty rest rooms are their number two complaint, while men rank it number ten. Likewise, dirty stores, on the top ten list for women, doesn't even rank among men's top ten complaints. Although some retailers may not view cleanliness as a store service, we have repeatedly seen that customers do—especially women, the primary shoppers in America. Knowing this, every company should make a special effort to cater to these specific needs.

CHAPTER ELEVEN

NOTHING IS CONSTANT BUT CHANGE

This is a book about change. Appropriately, this final chapter focuses on our ever-changing marketplace. If one thing is certain, it is that the marketplace never stagnates; the rapid pace at which it changes makes it constantly challenging.

Some managers shun change as if it were the enemy; others welcome change and view it as opportunity. In reality, change is an ally working on behalf of those who seize it as a valued tool.

It is the whim of the consumer that spawns change in the marketplace. Clearly, a company must adapt to these changing needs in order to survive in today's fiercely competitive marketplace. This is no easy task, as witnessed by the large number of major corporations that, over the years, have fallen by the wayside. *Fortune* magazine's May 15, 1995, cover story reveals that of the original 1955 list of Fortune 500 companies, only 160 remain on the list. A total of 1,318 companies have appeared on the list at least once. Forty years ago, it took only $50 million in annual sales for a company to be listed. On the recent list, Dow Corning ranked 500th with sales of $2.2 billion. According to the Consumer Price Index, the dollar was worth approximately 5.5 times more in 1954. This means a company with annual sales of $275 million in 1994 dollars would have made the original Fortune 500 list.

Another interesting comparison is the size of today's companies. In

1954, the entire group of Fortune 500 companies generated sales of $137 billion, compared to General Motors' 1994 revenues of $154.9 billion. GM is in the number one spot today; it also held the number one position in 1954 when its annual sales totaled $9.8 billion. GM's annual sales in 1954 would have been approximately $54 billion in 1994 dollars. Ninety companies on the present list did not even exist in 1955.

The span of four decades is a relatively short period of time, but when reviewing the enormous changes that have occurred in the marketplace, it might as well be an eternity. With advances in technology continuing, it is certain that the list of Fortune 500 companies in the year 2035 will differ significantly from today's.

FIVE SOURCES OF CHANGE

The marketplace is constantly changing, and that change comes from five sources:

1. CONSUMER-DRIVEN CHANGES. The habits and needs of the American consumer are always changing. These are induced by factors from shifts in personal lifestyles to cultural changes. For instance, with the rise of one-parent households and households where both spouses work nine-to-five jobs, Americans have become more conscious of the value of their limited time. Likewise, the technological revolution has altered how and why the consumer buys products. Every generation has introduced changes into the marketplace. The yuppies in the 1980s, for instance, aspired to enjoy a gracious lifestyle. Generation X members in the 1990s are concerned about their future, and therefore they focus on such issues as retirement and health care for their elderly parents. But who could have predicted the significant rise in tattoo parlors catering to Generation X?

2. LOCAL COMPETITION-DRIVEN CHANGES. The competition in your community has a direct influence on how you fare. A

strong competitor can wage a predatory strategy to take your customers away; if he succeeds, you lose substantial market share. Likewise, a national company may come into your local marketplace offering better prices, more selection, and superior service. Witness the effect of Wal-Mart on thousands of local retailers across the United States. The category killers with their big boxes have proved deadly to many locally owned retailers who, for generations, dominated their own niche in the marketplace. Then too, you can be "niched to death" by a swarm of small niche players.

3. GOVERNMENT-DRIVEN CHANGES. Certain laws can be passed that can wreak havoc in an entire industry overnight. For example, note the demise of the tax shelter industry following a revised tax code by the IRS. Or recall that under the auspices of the 1975 Energy Policy and Conservation Act, the government established Corporate Average Fuel Economy (CAFE), which forced automotive manufacturers to come up with cars with improved fuel efficiency. Needless to say, these mandatory improvements resulted in many sleepless nights in Detroit. Likewise, in December 1975, the Federal Energy Administration was ordered to roll back the price of oil $1 per barrel by the following February. This caused repercussions in nearly all industries, even those far removed from oil. And notice that when the government increases or decreases the prime rate, it affects everyone—homeowners, retailers, manufacturers, virtually any individual or entity with a variable interest loan, as well as would-be borrowers. And certainly, the government has the ability to influence inflation, which, in turn, directly influences consumer spending at every level.

4. GLOBALLY DRIVEN CHANGES. As the world continues to shrink, what goes on in the farthest corner of the globe affects every local marketplace. As the economies in faraway nations

fluctuate, ripples are felt everywhere. Changes in the yen and mark influence the price of goods in the United States. Other countries' labor rules and regulations—or lack thereof—impact America's imports and exports, which, sequentially, influence our employment figures. You could pick up this list where I leave off. As you can see, no nation stands alone.

5. INTERNALLY DRIVEN CHANGES. While you must keep an eye on what's happening across the street and around the globe, be equally aware of what goes on *within* your organization. Sometimes it is not forces without but dissension within that destroys a company. Strong management is essential in today's marketplace. There are enough external forces with which to contend; you must rid your organization of inside conflict. A team effort is what's required: everyone pulling in the same direction.

CHANGE—CAUTIOUSLY

"If it ain't broke, don't fix it" is a cliché, and, as a strong advocate of change, I hesitate to mention it. But, I would be remiss if I didn't. Despite the benefits of executing a new marketing strategy, you still must use caution in replacing one that is doing a good job.

Such a lack of prudence occurred in Florida's lottery system when U.S. Senator Lawton Chiles was elected governor in 1990. Heavily advertised and highly promoted, Florida's lottery department had been hailed as one of the most successful in the United States. In 1991, the newly elected governor decided a change was in order, and he named an educator to head the state's lottery program. To Governor Chiles, it seemed a logical appointment; after all, the lottery's earnings were used to support public schools throughout the Sunshine State.

The new regime introduced an entirely revamped advertising campaign which informed the public that proceeds generated by the state lottery went to the schools. The message: *When you buy a lottery ticket, you support the schools. Even if your ticket loses, you still win, because the money goes to education.* No longer did commercials hype how many millions of dollars had accumulated in this week's jackpot, nor did they spin the dream of how *you* could become an instant multimillionaire. Instead, the ads pointed out that funds raised through the lottery would benefit the cause of educating Florida's youth.

Research that we conducted on state lotteries showed that the number one reason a ticket is bought is the buyer's belief that he has a chance to strike it rich. Of course, the consumer understands that the chances of winning are slim, but nobody buys a ticket with the thought of being a guaranteed loser. Second, we learned that people purchase lottery tickets with disposable income. This means they decide to spend their money on a lottery ticket versus spending it on another product. Consumers are not spending excess dollars in their piggy banks. It's an either-or decision. They go to the store to get a lottery ticket the same way they go to the supermarket to purchase a quart of ice cream. Put another way, people don't buy lottery tickets just to be charitable.

This also means a state lottery is competing for the same disposable dollars that everybody else is going after. Once the ads' emphasis switched from winning to "helping out," the customer's perception of the lottery changed. Without the accent on huge prizes that are worth the risk, the sale of lottery tickets in Florida took a nosedive.

It didn't take long before the Florida State Lottery changed back to the marketing strategy that was a proven success. But valuable momentum was lost during that short period, and even six years later, participation in the Florida lottery has not yet returned to its previous peak.

Whether it is a state lottery or an airline, the lesson is always the same. A marketing strategy must address the question "What does the customer want?" In the case of the lottery, the customer wants to win money, not donate money.

CHANGING CUSTOMERS

From a record high of 350,813 cars sold in 1978, by 1995 Cadillac sales slipped to 180,504. The decline of what was once considered the most prestigious American automobile on the road can be directly traced to the oil embargo of 1973, when soaring fuel prices induced buyers to move to smaller cars. Cadillac continued to make large, heavy boats during a period when driving a big car began to seem callous and unpatriotic.

Founded in the early 1900s, the Cadillac Company became a division of General Motors in 1909. Its longtime motto, "Standard of Excellence," was as familiar as its emblem of a wreath-encircled crest. The earliest models were world leaders in drivetrain development and body design. The cars were arrogant and pretentious—an acceptable statement during an era when America itself was grandiose and ambitious. Following World War II, Cadillacs expressed the nation's optimism, even coming equipped with some of the wartime bombers' aerodynamic design features, including soaring tail fins and pointed front bumpers. A Cadillac parked in your driveway meant far more than transportation. It was a symbol of your success; it meant you owned a piece of the American Dream. The very word "Cadillac" came to mean "the most elite" or "the top of the class." If you are at least fifty, you have probably referred to something as "the Cadillac of television sets" or "the Cadillac of computers."

Age is at the root of General Motors' woes with today's Cadillac. While the average age of the entry-level luxury-car owner—defined as somebody who associates an upscale car with a price starting at about $30,000—is forty-six, at Cadillac, which isn't in the entry-level market, the average buyer's age is sixty-three. While younger upscale buyers are attracted to the sleek lines and sophisticated engineering of European and Japanese luxury cars, Cadillac's traditional customers still crave whitewall tires, vinyl roofs, ornate chrome, and plush interiors. Marketing consultant Susan Jacobs points out that the DeVille is the problem. It represents nearly 60 percent of Cadillac's volume, but it was made even more massive three years ago, thereby scaring away anyone who doesn't belong to AARP.

It's true that today's Cadillacs are better than ever, with automotive rating services giving the car high marks for quality and power. While quality has steadily improved during the past decade or so, that's still not enough for the division to make a turnaround. Its dwindling customer base means Cadillac is losing older customers faster than it is picking up young customers. It's only a matter of time before those devoted Cadillac owners will no longer be in the market to purchase new cars. If the division can't switch its marketing strategy to one that appeals to a more youthful customer, it's a bumpy road out there for Cadillac. Until management wins the heart of a younger buyer, the company is destined to continue to lose market share.

A manufacturer whose name has become synonymous with jeans is Levi Strauss & Co., founded sixty years before Cadillac. Cashing in on today's trend toward casual dress in the workplace, Levi's leads the apparel industry in its promotion of casual clothing designed to be worn at the office.

Some say it was luck, while others credit Levi's for the current casual-dress trend. Unquestionably, by catching the wave early and proselytizing aggressively, the company has helped create momentum. As a result, 75 percent of all U.S. companies now allow workers to dress casually at least once a week, according to Levi's research, up from only 37 percent in 1992. Levi's interprets this to mean that five million individuals have twenty million additional uses per week for casual clothing. This translates into an additional eleven million articles of clothing for Levi's to sell every year. While Levi's did not create casual business wear, it has identified the trend and maximized the trend, and is clearly profiting during this window of opportunity.

In late 1992, when Levi's commissioned its study to document the trend toward casual office wear, its findings were included in a newsletter mailed to 65,000 human resource managers. Between 1993 and 1996,

Levi's has visited or advised more than 22,000 U.S. corporations, such as IBM, Nynex, and Aetna Life & Casualty, on the benefits of casual attire in the office. In addition to conducting seminars, Levi's has mailed brochures and videos to human resource managers across the nation espousing the positive effect dress-down clothes can have on morale and productivity.

When trends first indicated the apparel consumer was changing, Levi's was off and running. Therefore, at a time when the apparel industry in general is struggling, Levi's is getting a healthy share of the increase in the casual wear segment.

AN EVER-CHANGING MARKETPLACE

A classic example of a changing marketplace is what happened to Hallmark in the 1990s. Known for its high-quality greeting cards, the Kansas City–based company primarily marketed its product via company-owned and franchised stores located in strip shopping centers and mall centers. For years, Hallmark has been the dominant brand name in its category.

Severe time constraints are being placed on Hallmark's prototype consumer, today's busy American woman. The change in her buying habits is cutting into the strong market share Hallmark once commanded. When she has only one card to buy, a working mother simply doesn't have the time to make a Hallmark outlet her destination store. Instead, she'll pick one up as she breezes through the local drugstore or supermarket for other, more major purchases. No longer is she willing to make a special effort to stop at a Hallmark store at the other end of the strip shopping center or mall. Although she may be willing to go out of her way for several boxes of Christmas or Hanukkah cards, today's woman is reluctant to make a special trip for a single card marking an occasion such as a birthday or wedding.

Another change has occurred that works against Hallmark. Supermarkets, drugstores, and discount stores have expanded into bigger stores, and in doing so, have enhanced their greeting card areas. In addition, American Greetings and Gibson Cards have improved their marketing efforts; today, these rivals provide superior store displays and presentations to the retailers who merchandise their cards.

While Hallmark is still perceived as selling the number one card in America, the company must recognize that its distribution strategy is failing. A specialty card store strategy is not appropriate in today's marketplace, not when the consumer is unwilling to make it his or her prime destination.

In the 1950s and 1960s when consumers had few choices, they couldn't be as selective. But today's consumers no longer choose where they go or what they buy based on a single purpose. Hallmark has become a victim of this change in the marketplace.

While in this instance I singled out only Hallmark, how the consumer views any retailer is based on several factors. For instance, *convenience:* Whether it's a supermarket, drugstore, or bank, a convenient location doesn't guarantee customers will flock to you, because in today's marketplace, a competitor could be across the street or two blocks away.

For many years, the local drugstore thrived because of its convenient location. This alone was enough to win a significant piece of the market share battle. But with the advent of the deep-discount super drugstore, convenience of location alone was no longer sufficient for survival. So in the 1980s, drugstores with convenient locations had to begin discounting their goods, and, for a while, this seemed to work. But then, as the marketplace grew, what was a convenient location was no longer considered so convenient. With new subdivisions and the building of new homes even past the suburbs, the existing drugstores lost their edge because they did not seem as convenient to get to as they once were.

An example of a discount store that lived in a 1950s,'60s, and '70s mindset is Woolworth. For far too many years, the company stuck to its poor locations downtown and in strip shopping centers and shunned big stores. As the twenty-first century approaches, the company now faces hard times, a result of clinging to a marketing strategy that would have been perfect for the year 1975!

Remember too, the consumer's perception is constantly changing. For instance, in the 1960s, a 12,000-square-foot store was considered a superstore for many retail categories. In the 1970s, the consumer's perception of a superstore was 24,000 square feet, and in the 1980s, it doubled again to 48,000 square feet. In the 1990s, the perception of what constitutes a superstore leveled off at 60,000 square feet. This change of perception might not seem important from a consumer's viewpoint, but if you built a small superstore thirty, twenty, or even ten years ago and haven't put on an addition, you have probably already noticed: You have a serious problem.

And look at what is happening in the advertising industry. With a thirty-second television spot during the 1996 Super Bowl going for $1.2 million, and the same thirty-second spot on *Seinfeld* going for $400,000, sponsors have good reason to seek new sources of advertising. Seeking guarantees of big exposure, big corporations are starting to put their names on stadiums across America. In Denver, for instance, it is costing Pepsi-Cola $50 million—paid over a twenty-year period—for the right to have its name on the professional sports arena known as Pepsi Center. In San Francisco, Candlestick Park has been renamed 3Com Park—for $4 million, payable over a four-year period. In St. Louis, there's Trans World Dome; in Vancouver, GM Place; and in Toronto, Air Canada Center. This trend has even reached the college campuses; in Columbus, Ohio, the Ohio State University's new sports arena has been christened Value Center Arena. Why the sports craze? Because for just a million or so a year, marketers are reaching tens of thousands of consumers at every sports event and concert, week in and week out. Compared to thirty-second spots during Super Bowls or sitcoms, it's a good deal for a stadium sponsor. And if the hometown team makes it to a championship, national television exposure is thrown in at no additional charge.

One of the fastest-changing industries, personal computers, has enjoyed an annual growth rate of around 25 percent for the last several years. Corporate America went on a spending spree in the mid-1990s, upgrading its computer capacity to keep pace with technological advances. Consequently, the computer industry enjoyed an unprecedented boom. It seems, however, that computer technology is growing at a faster pace than actual demand for it. Even though superior personal computers are being built, many companies are unwilling to spend the additional money to update. Evidently, the days are over when corporate America bought new equipment first and searched around for applications later.

It doesn't matter whether it's greeting cards or personal computers, change is constant in the marketplace.

TREETOP OBSERVATIONS

As a market researcher, I have a treetop view of the terrain below. This gives me a different perspective on the marketplace. From my vantage point, I see behavioral changes in the men and women who manage companies. While much of the change is positive, the following ten changes should serve as warning signs:

1. LESS PRETESTING OF NEW PRODUCTS. Companies are conducting fewer tests before introducing a new product. This results not only in bringing out fewer new products, but also in a higher failure rate for newly introduced products.

2. LESS CREATIVE MARKETING. There is an abundance of recycled approaches. Evidently, many companies are unwilling to launch an innovative campaign. Their managers would rather follow than lead.

3. A DISPROPORTIONATE AMOUNT OF DOWNSIZING. In the name of improving the bottom line, companies are reducing their workforces and cutting down on expenses. Unfortunately, this

does not generate new sales; in fact, the uncertainty actually *depresses* sales.

4. A TREND TOWARD MORE FRANCHISING. The small, independent businessperson tends to invest in a franchise, suggesting that he is unable to create a viable business plan on his own.

5. IMPROPER USE OF THE LATEST MARKETING CLASSIFICATIONS. An increasing number of businesspeople are *using* the latest buzz words, such as Generation X, Tweeners, and Baby Boomers, to define the marketplace, but, in fact, they don't actually know who these people are, nor do they understand how to cater to them.

6. MISINTERPRETATION OF RESEARCH AND OPINION SURVEYS. Too many businesspeople hear a few opinions and think those accurately represent the feelings of the masses.

7. FAILURE TO IDENTIFY AND EFFECTIVELY LEVERAGE ASSETS. Many businesspeople lack the ability to look at their bottom line and evaluate their assets in order to leverage them.

8. BEING OUT OF TOUCH WITH FRONTLINE EMPLOYEES AND CUSTOMERS. Many top-ranking executives are removed from the customer and employees who deal with the customer. As their companies matured structurally, management gradually lost touch with the marketplace.

9. NOT COMMUNICATING WITH THE CUSTOMER. Decision-makers within the company have not put themselves in a position to receive customer feedback about their product and the service they give.

10. BELIEVING IN QUICK FIXES. Even though a problem might have taken five to ten years to develop, many businesspeople are under the impression that the right action could correct it immediately.

THE ULTIMATE WINNER

Throughout this book, a constant theme prevails—the premise that every marketing strategy ultimately fails. To the uninformed, this may seem a pessimistic view. To the informed, however, it implies change, which, in the world of business, equals constant improvement.

Our system is based not on the failure but on the success of new and improved marketing strategies. Likewise, the success of any marketing strategy raises the bar for other competitors, requiring companies to perform at even higher levels in order to survive. In this sense, our free enterprise system is based on the survival of the strongest. In the long run, only the best companies are able to operate profitably—those that seek out improved ways to attract more customers by providing better value.

In our highly competition-driven marketplace, improvement in product and customer service is essential, and when this happens, the consumer wins. In recent years, we've seen new products from VCRs and camcorders to computers and fax machines—each of which has not only improved in quality since being introduced to the marketplace, but also dropped significantly in price. Services too are continually improving; witness on a local level the same-day delivery of a new refrigerator or mattress, or at the national and international level next-day delivery of packages.

These changes require new and improved marketing strategies, ones that constantly raise the ante for the competition, necessitating that every company do better—and better. A company's survival depends on meeting the demands of this self-adjusting system. In a continuous, unrelenting cycle, and in spite of certain casualties along the way, the system works wonderfully. With this constant improvement, the consumer ultimately wins. And so do those companies that persist in meeting their customers' needs.

Certainly, meeting the needs of customers is integral to our free enterprise system. This steady theme is accompanied by the need to capture market share by staying ahead of the competition—which requires constant change on the part of the company. This staying ahead is today's most difficult challenge.

Hundreds of numbers appear throughout this book—far too many to recite by memory. But if you can log only one number into your memory, it should be the 1.3 stores per major purchase that the American consumer will shop in the year 2000. Coupled with the fact that there will undoubtedly be more stores with more choices than ever, this alarming number substantiates that if you are not the first store shopped, your prospects are severely limited. Not only is this 1.3 number a warning for America's retailers, it is also a strong signal for every manufacturer, distributor, and service company. All customers are demanding more, and if you don't give them what they want, it is certain that your competition will.

This 1.3 number has still another message. It reveals that in order to get more business, you must take customers away from your competition. This requires a predatory marketing strategy that demands you to be stronger in those areas where your competition is strongest. Remember, too, that as you become stronger, so will your competition.

A PERSONAL NOTE FROM THE AUTHOR

I grew up in Bedford, Iowa, a farming community with a population under two thousand, where my father owned a locker plant. At age seven, I began a newspaper route for the *Omaha World Herald*, walking about five miles every morning before school to make my deliveries.

In retrospect, I was different from other kids. Instead of reading the comic strips, I enjoyed reading the news section and, in particular, the editorial page. Politics fascinated me, and at age fourteen, I ran a campaign for a gentleman running for clerk of court against an incumbent who had been unopposed the previous election. I suppose even my candidate didn't take the election too seriously. He appointed me to be his campaign manager because my services were free! Although we started out as the underdog, we won the election, and for the next fifteen years, I was hooked on politics.

I met Bill Scherle, a wonderful man who was planning to run for Congress in 1966. This was not a good time for Republicans—Goldwater had taken a severe beating in his bid for the presidency in 1964, and the Arizona U.S. senator had taken a lot of Republican congressmen with him. In the Republican primary, Scherle was running against R. John Swanson, the unofficial party candidate and a strong favorite to win the nomination. To complicate matters, the Democrats were able to move the primary in Iowa from June to September, hoping to cause turmoil among the winning Republican candidates in November. Mr. Scherle named me to serve as his chairman in Taylor County, where I lived. Imagine asking a fifteen-year-old kid to run a political campaign for his county! Scherle was from the other end of the district, while his opponent, Swanson, lived in nearby Red Oak. Most thought Swanson would carry Taylor County by nine hundred votes. The race came down to the wire, and by a narrow margin of six hundred votes, Scherle won. As it turned out, in my home county he lost by only 176 votes. It was Taylor County that pushed him over the top. I was a local hero of sorts. In November, Scherle won a seat in Congress by a landslide. After that boost to my self-confidence, for the next eight years, I worked off and on for Congressman Scherle while finishing my schooling. After high school, I did undergraduate work at Georgetown and then at Northwest Missouri State, where I got my degree, then I enrolled at Indiana State to complete a master's degree.

After college, I managed or consulted campaigns for congressmen and senators, and between elections, I helped conduct campaign schools. Among one school's attendees were Indiana's Dan Quayle and Idaho's Steve Symms, both running for first terms in Congress. As you know, Quayle went on to become Vice President and Symms became a prominent U.S. senator. In all, I managed or consulted sixteen senatorial and congressional campaigns, winning fourteen of them.

My work in the political arena involved reading polls that clearly defined what my candidates' constituents wanted. Back in the 1970s, we did surveys to identify issues that both our candidates and the public felt strongly about—then we focused on those issues in the candidates' speeches and advertising. Today, however, many political chameleons poll public opinion only to change their philosophies to match what voters want. It's this lack of conviction, I believe, that has caused the American public to become estranged from our political process.

After the 1978 elections, I began to take stock of my future when my father asked me, "Son, when are you going to get a real job?" During this period, after the Nixon debacle with Watergate, the Federal Elections

Commission tied the hands of campaigners with regulations and paper-work, turning my end of the business into a nightmare. In short, the bureaucrats took the fun out of my work. I wanted to be in a field where all the marbles didn't depend on a single day which came around every two and four years—election day.

Interestingly, there is a definite correlation between the research sur-veys I prepared for my early political clients and what I do today for my present retailer clients. A voter makes a decision to either vote or not vote for a candidate. Likewise, a consumer also sees things in black and white when deciding which products to buy and from whom.

In 1971, I made my first visit to Charleston, South Carolina. I was enchanted with the Charleston area. It only took being there a day for me to decide where I'd make my home after leaving the Washington scene. Seven years later, after the 1978 campaigns ended, I moved to Charleston and formed ARG, which is headquartered there to this day. Little did I know that a few years later, I'd be traveling in excess of a million frequent flier miles a year visiting clients in all fifty states from Florida to Alaska. So much for spending time in Charleston.

Spending as much time on airplanes as I do, I had very good fortune in June 1988 on a Friday-night flight to Charleston. I happened to be seated next to a particularly beautiful and charming woman—Jan Cook—who was en route to Charleston to visit her brother. Jan and I started to date, and one year later, we were married. While ARG is still headquar-tered in Charleston, we decided to reside in her hometown, Orlando, to be near her parents. And since I don't spend more than a week or two a year in Charleston, I can live anywhere! As I explained in Chapter 1, the research that I do for my clients must reveal answers that are actionable. To achieve this, I meet with clients at *their* place of business—which today means traveling to every state in the union.

As CEO of a full-service consumer behavior research firm, I'm in-volved in all phases of survey research—questionnaire design, sample con-struction, data analysis, and especially interpretation. I review all research and prepare each client's strategic marketing plan.

In addition to specific research projects, ARG offers an extensive program of client support services, such as store management seminars, advertising director conferences, and merchandising/buyer conferences. Our unique annual CEO conferences keep clients updated on developments in their specific industry.

The only purpose of our research is to provide decision-makers with information that yields solutions to important marketing issues. When it comes to having "customers for life," we take immense pride in the 90 percent ongoing relationship that we have enjoyed with our research clients over the last ten years. This ongoing commitment demonstrates the value our clients place on the specialized information we provide. Market leaders know they must do what's necessary to maintain their leadership position.

I personally visit clients to provide the ongoing consultation on our marketing recommendations. The real test is how the research is used to produce change—positive sales results and increased profit for our client.

NOTES

CHAPTER TWO: Everything You Need to Know About Trends

Page

31 "Category killers have brightened an otherwise dreary retailing scene in the 1990s": Gretchen Morgenson, "Too Much of a Good Thing?" *Forbes*, June 3, 1996, p. 115.

32 ". . . unpretentious lifestyle": Robert Lenzner and Stephen Johnson, "A Few Yards of Denim and Five Copper Rivets," *Forbes*, February 26, 1996, p. 82.

33 "Until the 1970s, products were made to appeal . . .": Joseph Pereira, "Toy Business Focuses More on Marketing and Less on New Ideas," *Wall Street Journal*, February 29, 1996, p. 1.

34 ". . . on the eve of Yom Kippur": Robert L. Shook, *Honda: An American Success Story* (New York: Prentice-Hall, 1990), p. 2.

40 ". . . Herb Peterson, a franchisee in Santa Barbara . . .": Carrie Shook, *Franchising: The Business Strategy That Changed the World* (New York: Prentice-Hall, 1993), p. 150.

CHAPTER THREE: Implementing a Market Strategy

56 "... better positioned to fight off ... competition ...": Zina Moukheiber, "He Who Laughs Last," *Forbes*, January 1, 1996, p. 42.

56 "Snapple's three hundred distributors ...": Moukheiber, p. 42.

57 "... by combining overlapping operations ...": Elyse Tanouye, Steven Lipin, and Stephen D. Moore, "In Huge Drug Merger, Sandoz and Ciba-Geigy Plan to Join Forces," *Wall Street Journal*, March 7, 1996, p. 1.

58 "... coordinated by computers and communications technologies": Bernard Wysocki, Jr., "Improved Distribution, Not Better Production, Is Key Goal in Mergers," *Wall Street Journal*, August 29, 1996, p. 1.

58 " 'So what did I do? I decided to become a consultant ... ' ": Robert L. Shook, *The Greatest Sales Stories Ever Told* (New York: McGraw-Hill, 1995), p. 19.

CHAPTER FOUR: The Numbers Business *Is* a People Business

84 "... single him out from the other men and women": R. J. Shook, *The Winner's Circle II* (New York: New York Institute of Finance, 1995), p. 70.

84 " 'I love being on the floor ... ' ": R. J. Shook, p. 79.

85 " 'A man will do well in commerce ... ' ": R. J. Shook, p. 79.

85 " 'We don't care what charity they give it to ... ' ": R. J. Shook, p. 81.

CHAPTER FIVE: The Vision

104 " ' ... is to get kids and their parents away from the television set and video games ... ' ": Mary Kay Ash, *Mary Kay: You Can Have It All* (Rocklin, Calif.: Prima Publishing, 1995), p. 116.

105 " 'Everything out there was polyester' ": Ash, p. 211.

CHAPTER SIX: Never Underestimate the Competition

136 ". . . slice and dice large amounts of information . . .": Fred R. Bleakley, "To Make More Loans, Banks Use Computers to Identify Candidates," *Wall Street Journal*, March 15, 1996, p. 1.

CHAPTER EIGHT: The Niche Player

189 "100 percent whole Arbacia beans in a thirteen-ounce package . . .": Zina Moukheiber, "Oversleeping," *Forbes*, June 5, 1995, p. 78.

190 " 'The whole point is to provide high quality, extremely fresh coffee . . . ' ": Moukheiber, p. 78.

CHAPTER NINE: The Long-term Strategist

221 ". . . its $1.5 billion Campbell Taggert, Inc., bakery unit . . .": Richard A. Melcher with Greg Burns, "How Eagle Became Extinct," *Business Week*, March 4, 1996, p. 68.

221 " ' . . . chasing a bunny that Pepsi will never let me . . . ' ": Melcher, p. 68.

CHAPTER TEN: Customers for Life

227 " ' . . . I hope you get a lemon' ": Robert L. Shook, *Ten Greatest Salespersons* (New York: Harper & Row, 1978), p. 21.

229 ". . . one in five cleaners bought since 1990 . . .": "Ratings: Vacuum Cleaners and Recommendations," *Consumer Reports*, March 1996, p. 31.

229 ". . . on the average, GM customers reported . . .": Gabriella Stern, "Toyota Vehicles Log Fewest Defects," *Wall Street Journal*, May 5, 1996, p. 5.

241 ". . . stirred caramel-colored syrup in a brass kettle": Anne Hoy, *Coca-Cola: The First Hundred Years* (Atlanta, Ga.: Coca-Cola Company, 1986), p. 11.

244 "... a just-in-time facility to ensure prompt and reliable delivery ...": Robert L. Shook, *Turnaround: The New Ford Motor Company* (New York: Prentice-Hall, 1990), p. 102.

244 "... just-in-time delivery to Mack Trucks assembly plants ...": Ralph Kisiel, "Mack, Dana Shared Risk, Reward," *Automotive News*, December 25, 1995.

CHAPTER ELEVEN: Nothing Is Constant but Change

260 "... 1,318 companies have appeared on the list at least once": Carol J. Loomis, "Forty Years of the 500," *Fortune*, May 15, 1996, p. 182.

265 "From a record high of 350,813 cars sold in 1978 ...": Gabriella Stern, "As Old Cadillac Buyers Age, the GM Division Fights to Halt Slippage," *Wall Street Journal*, August 24, 1995, p. 1.

265 "... by 1995 Cadillac sales slipped to 180,504": Alex Taylor III, "Speed! Power! Status!" *Fortune*, June 10, 1996, p. 52.

265 "Marketing consultant Susan Jacobs points out ...": Taylor, p. 52

266 "... by catching the wave early and proselytizing aggressively ...": Linda Himelstein and Nancy Walser, "Levi's vs. the Dress Code," *Business Week*, April 1, 1996, p. 58.

267 "... Levi's has visited or advised more than 22,000 ...": Himelstein and Walser, p. 57.

269 "... thirty-second spot on *Seinfeld* ...": Mark Lewyn, "See a Game, Shop for a Car, Surf the Net," *Business Week*, January 29, 1996, p. 53.

INDEX